Barefootin'

[Bare*f*ootin']

Life Lessons from

the Road to Freedom

UNITA BLACKWELL

with JoAnne Prichard Morris

CROWN PUBLISHERS

NEW YORK

Library of Congress Cataloging-in-Publication Data
Blackwell, Unita, 1933–
Barefootin' : lessons from the road to freedom / Unita Blackwell;
with JoAnne Prichard Morris.—1st ed.
1. Blackwell, Unita, 1933– 2. African American women civil rights workers—
Mississippi—Biography. 3. Civil rights workers—Mississippi—Biography.
4. African Americans—Suffrage—Mississippi—History—20th century.
5. African Americans—Civil rights—Mississippi—History—20th century.
6. Civil rights movements—Mississippi—History—20th century.
7. Mississippi—Race relations. 8. Women mayors—Mississippi—Mayersville—
Biography. 9. Mayors—Mississippi—Mayersville—Biography.
10. Mayersville (Miss.)—Biography. I. Title: Barefootin'.
II. Morris, JoAnne Prichard. III. Title.
F350.N4B58 2006
323'.092—dc22   2005034953

ISBN 13: 978-0-609-61060-2
ISBN 10: 0-609-61060-0

Printed in the United States of America

Design by Leonard Henderson

10 9 8 7 6 5 4 3 2 1

First Edition

To the memory
of my mother,
who taught me
I could make it,
gave me the courage to try,
and with her
mother wit
showed me the way.

Contents

Preface   ix

Part I *Startin' Off* (1933–1964)   1

  1   You Have the Power Within   3

  2   You Can Make It   9

  3   Let Nature Guide You   26

  4   Look Out for Snakes   31

  5   Put Your Trust in God   40

  6   You Can Make a Difference   46

Part II *Breakin' Free* (1964–1968)   63

  7   Be Ready to Step Out   65

  8   God Helps Those Who Help Themselves   72

  9   Find Strength in Togetherness   78

10   Hold On, and Pray   93

11   Dare to Challenge   103

12   Things May Get Worse Before They Get Better   123

13   Focus on What Matters Most   133

14   Risk Your Heart for What Is Right   146

15   Be Willing to Take Bold Action (and Cry Some, Too)   157

16   Carry On   166

Part III *Movin' On* (1968–2005)   175

17   You Don't Always Have to Fight to Win   177

18   Open Your Eyes to Other Worlds, Other Ways   192

19   Think Big *and* Small   208

20   Tolerance Is Trust   220

21   You Need Roots *and* Wings   230

22   Do All You Can Then Step Aside   241

23   Just a Little Step Will Do   248

Acknowledgments   257

Preface

Take off your shoes and pat your feet,
We're doing a dance that can't be beat!

"**B**AREFOOTIN'" IS A SONG WE used to hear in the juke houses and on the radio. It is about dancing. Dancing for love. Dancing through your troubles. Dancing away the blues. Dancing with hope for the future. Barefootin' is about feeling happy and feeling free.

Barefootin' is a way of life for me, an approach to living—my philosophy of life, you might say. To me barefootin' means facing life as it comes, feeling your way along, figuring out things as you go, finding out who you are—searching, stumbling, dancing, learning. Barefootin' means taking risks, being creative, getting the most out of life, giving yourself to the journey and to the world around you. Barefootin' is about stepping out and moving forward; following a new path even though you don't know where it will lead you; tearing down roadblocks, cutting new roads, and never forgetting where you started.

And where I started was poor, black, and barefooted in a loving, churchgoing family in the Mississippi Delta of the 1930s and '40s and '50s. The experiences of those years of *actual* barefootin' form the basis for the way of approaching life that I call "barefootin'."

I stayed barefooted most of the time when I was coming up. I didn't have but one pair of shoes, and they were hand-me-downs, so I didn't have much choice in the matter. But I probably would have gone barefooted even if I'd had a closet full of shoes. Sinking my bare feet down deep into that fine-as-dust, sandy Delta soil (before it got too hot) just felt good. I played barefooted, and I worked barefooted.

When I was barefooted, I was always aware of where I was. It was just me, out there with the elements. I could feel the dewy cool clover and the squishy mud at the edge of a bayou. Barefooted, I could run faster, climb higher, and dance longer. I was happy and free.

I might stub my toe or step on broken glass when I was barefooted. Or a snake could come sliding across my path. So I had to keep my eyes wide open and watch where I stepped. I had to keep walking when my feet said stop. I was exploring my world, listening to everybody and taking in everything, discovering the good, the mean, and the in-between. I was really discovering myself and finding a way to live.

When I got grown, the civil rights movement came along and changed my life completely. I started barefootin' down the road to freedom, searching and learning. There's no way I could have imagined the things I've done or the places I've been since then. Every new experience taught me new life lessons, and I'd use what I learned to barefoot to the next thing and to another level of freedom and understanding. I've barefooted through the hard-packed dirt of poverty and hate to the green grass of freedom, from the sweet security of family and home to unknown lands on the other side of the world. I've moved from tolerating to fighting to making peace, from just getting by to helping others. From a life of futility, I've barefooted to a life of purpose and fulfillment. This book is the story of my journey and the lessons of life I've learned.

My mother always told me, "Baby, you ain't supposed to tell your neighbor your business." So it hasn't been easy to bare my soul and talk about things I've done, or things that have happened to me. Some of my memories are painful, and I had buried them deep inside me and pushed them down whenever they tried to surface. I've learned some lessons barefootin' through this book, too—like not putting up a front to keep people from knowing how vulnerable I am, not sealing my feelings up inside.

Nothing in my background or in my own personal makeup has led me to keep track of details or remember names and dates. In my family birth dates and anniversaries didn't mean much since we couldn't afford to celebrate them, anyway. And then I stumbled into this condition called old age. I've gotten to the place that sometimes when I try to pull names and dates out of my head, my mind just wants to stop and rest. But this old brain never fails me on the big picture. In describing scenes long past that are not in the public record, I've relied on the southern storytelling tradition of recreating conversations from my memory. I've worked hard to get my life down on paper, and this is as true as I can make it.

Anyhow, I hope that readers will find in this book something more than just the particulars of my life story. I hope the lessons I've learned barefootin' may help guide those of you who despair about your own lives, for whatever reasons, and want to find meaning, a new direction, or who worry about the conditions in the world around you and want to make change from the grassroots up. I want people of any race, age, gender, or station in life to know you don't have to accept things the way they are. You can make change happen, and you can make a difference. I want to set others barefootin' down the road to freedom and a life fulfilled.

Part I

Startin' Off

1933–1964

You Have the Power Within

THE NEWS WHIPPED THROUGH Mayersville like a brushfire: "A bunch of niggers are over at the courthouse." And soon a gang of folks had gathered to see what was going on.

There were eight of us standing in a cluster by the side door of the Issaquena County Courthouse—me and my husband, Jeremiah, Mrs. Ripley, the Siases, and three schoolteachers. I probably stood out in the group since I'm close to six feet tall and near about as black as a person can be. People hadn't ever seen anything like this in our little Mississippi Delta town—black folks didn't hang around the courthouse. Hardly any blacks ever had reason to go to the courthouse at all. And nobody was expecting to see us that morning. Most of the time when black people congregated on the street, they were waiting for a ride to the cotton field or on their way to church. Anybody could tell we weren't going to the field that day because we didn't have on our loose ragged work clothes; we weren't all dressed up for church, either. We were dressed plain but neat. We had come to register to vote.

At that time—June of 1964—only twenty thousand black people were registered to vote in the state of Mississippi. And not a single one of those lived in Issaquena County, way down in the toe of the Mississippi Delta, even though two-thirds of the folks in the county were black. Jeremiah and our seven-year-old son, Jerry, and I lived in a falling-down three-room house that had belonged to Jeremiah's grandmother. I was thirty-one years old, stuck in poverty, and trapped by the color of my skin on a rough road to nowhere, doing what Mississippi black people had been doing for generations—working in the cotton fields. I would've been out chopping cotton that day if two young fellows from the Student Nonviolent Coordinating Committee (SNCC)—"Snick" they called it—hadn't come to town the week before, asking for volunteers to register to vote.

We hadn't been at the courthouse very long when Sheriff Darnell came strolling by. He stopped and rolled his eyes at us, like we were children acting up.

"What are y'all doing here?" The sheriff was playing dumb; he knew full well that the civil rights folks had been in town meeting with us.

"We come to register to vote," I said.

"Vote? What you think you gonna get out of that?"

"It's our right as Americans. The Constitution says so." I had already learned a lot from the civil rights guys.

"Them outside agitators in town have got y'all all riled up," he said. "They'll go on back to wherever they come from in a little while, but you niggers gotta live here all the time, you know. If I was you, I'd get myself on back home." He wasn't real gruff. In those days he didn't even have to raise his voice to get black folks to do what he told them to.

But I said, "No, sir, Sheriff Darnell, we ain't leaving. I believe we'll just stay here until we get in to see Mrs. Vandevender."

Mrs. Mary Vandevender was the circuit clerk for the county, and she was the one who'd give the voter registration test to us. I knew about the test. I'd have to fill out a long application, read a section of the state constitution, and "interpret" it in writing. Whether you passed or not was left entirely up to the person giving the test. That was the law in Mississippi, and that's the way black people had been kept from voting for years, if they ever got that far along in the process. The last time any blacks had tried to register in Issaquena County was about 1950—two fellows who had come home from the Army—and they were turned away at the courthouse door.

"Well, can't but one of you go in there at a time," Sheriff Darnell said. "And the rest of y'all, get over there across the street. It's against the law to stand up this close to the courthouse."

We agreed that since Minnie Ripley was the oldest, she ought to be the first to go in. "Mother Rip" was in her seventies and had lived in Mayersville all her life. Everybody, black and white, knew her and respected her. She was a devoted church worker. She wasn't a very big lady, but she had a big presence about her and always a spring in her step, and she pranced right on into the courthouse.

The rest of us crossed the street to stand under a couple of big oak trees, and Sheriff Darnell ambled off. It was still fairly early in the morning, but the summer sun was already bearing down, and even with my straw sun hat on, I was glad to get in the shade. The grass was worn down under the tree, and we hadn't had a sprinkle of rain in over a month, so the dust was thick and got all up in between my toes in those old slides I was wearing. I had no idea what I was in for, and I must have been anxious and tense, but today, at the age of seventy-two, I remember only how clear my mind was and how determined and strong I felt.

As soon as Mrs. Ripley went inside the courthouse and the sheriff left, Preacher McGee came hustling over to us. A wiry, light-brown-skinned fellow, he was what we called a "jackleg" preacher, one who doesn't have a regular church of his own.

"Y'all need to get on away from here," Preacher McGee said. "Don't stir up nothing." He was nervous and talking fast.

We knew that the sheriff—or some other white man—had enlisted him to convince us to leave. You always had black folks like Preacher McGee who did what the white men told them to. Some of them were scared not to. Others just wanted to pick up a dollar or two. I believe Preacher fit both of those categories.

Soon a bunch of white fellows came driving up in their pickup trucks and started circling the courthouse. Guns were hanging on gun racks in the back window for all of us to see. This was the first time I ever saw guns displayed that way. Before the 1960s, white men did not usually ride around town with a rack of guns in their trucks. You might have seen a gun every once in a while when the person was going out hunting deer or rabbits or something. Those men weren't hunting rabbits that day.

The men parked their pickups on the street around the courthouse, hemming us in. There were half a dozen trucks, as I recall.

They hollered at us from inside their trucks: "Niggers, niggers. Go home, niggers." The sheriff came walking by again. By this time he had picked up his pace and was shouting at us: "Y'all go on home. Get on away from here." Preacher McGee kept walking around, twitching and pleading with us, "Come on, y'all, come on. They mad. Come on, come on. Y'all better come on now."

But we did not leave.

The men climbed out of their trucks and walked over to where we were standing. They brought their long hunting guns with them. I'd seen these men around town and knew who they were—farmers, most of them. They stopped right in front of us and stood there glaring. Nobody said a word. Their faces were bright red. I had never before seen that kind of rush of blood in a person's face. In those days a black person wasn't supposed to make eye contact with whites. But I looked right into the eyes of one of those white fellows. And he looked straight at me, and if eyes could have shot me down, they would have done it. Hate mooned out just like a picture.

I didn't know what was going to happen next or what I would do. I didn't have a gun or any other weapon to protect myself. None of us did. SNCC believed in nonviolence, and we were following SNCC. I was frozen with fear.

Pictures were flashing through my mind: the three civil rights workers who had gone missing in Neshoba County just the week before; Medgar Evers, murdered the previous summer, shot in the back while his wife and little children watched; Emmett Till at the bottom of the Tallahatchie River with a cotton gin fan tied around his neck. I had learned about these violent acts soon after they happened, and others like them, and I knew they were true. But they had never seemed real to me until that day. I had never believed or accepted or understood that something like that could actually happen to me. From birth I'd been taught not to hate white people, or anyone, to work hard and treat people right, and to have faith that goodness would win out over evil and hatred. Even the undeniable reality of my own grandfather's horrendous death did not take hold of me until that day, although I had heard the story dozens of times and knew it well.

My granddaddy, Daddy's father, was working on a sugar plantation down in Louisiana, where he'd grown up and where his own mother had been a slave. One day the white man that owned the plantation accused my grandfather of something. I don't know what it was, whether it was trivial or serious, but, whatever it was, my grandfather was not at fault.

"I did not do that, boss."

"Nigger, are you 'sputing me?"

"No, sir, I ain't 'sputing you. I'm just telling you the truth: I didn't do it."

"No nigger of mine will 'spute me."

And the white man shot him. Killed him dead, right there in the cane field.

The horror of that story and everything came together for me the day those white men with guns surrounded me at the courthouse. I could taste and smell reality. These white men—people I saw around town, who sometimes even smiled and spoke to me—were so consumed with hatred for me that one of them might actually kill me just to keep me from registering to vote. If our first small step toward freedom—registering to vote—threatened white folks that much, I knew then that the right to vote must be a powerful thing. And that's the day I realized I was willing to die for the right to vote. I made up my mind: If I ain't got no freedom, I would rather be dead.

All my life I had known something was wrong with the way I lived. If God was good and loved all His people, as I'd been taught, why did white folks have everything and we got nothing? Didn't the white folks have the same God and read the same Bible? It's strange how you can know something or think you know something and then still really not know it. You know deep inside that most white people think you're not as good as they are, and that some of them, like the enraged men at the courthouse, actually hate you. They hate you just because of the color of your skin. There's no other reason. You've obeyed the law; you've worked their land; you've never done one thing to harm them. Yet you face this smoldering hatred every day, in big ways and small, and you don't understand.

We stayed all day, but I never got inside the courthouse. The clerk let in only two people, and then she didn't tell them whether they passed the registration test or not. But what happened outside the courthouse that day was the turning point of my life.

The gaze of that white man was burned into my consciousness. For days those cold eyes glared at me. Over and over I saw their festering violence and felt the hate in them. But why? Why were these white people, who had money and power, consumed with hatred for a bunch of poor, pitiful black folks? Did they have to hate us Nobodies to feel like they were Somebodies? What did they think we could do to hurt them? They couldn't have thought we were going to take their jobs and land. Were they afraid they couldn't function if they weren't in control of us? I was afraid of losing my life. But what were they afraid of? I was beginning to figure out that we were onto something bigger than I had ever dreamed.

People have said we were courageous to stand there in the face of that white rage. Younger blacks and whites from my state and all around the country have asked me, "Where did you get the courage, Unita?"

I don't know whether it was courage I had or not. But if it was courage, then this is what I know about courage: You don't have to think about courage to have it. You don't have to feel courageous to be courageous. You don't sit down and say you're going to be courageous. At the moment of action, you don't see it as a courageous act. Courage is the most hidden thing from your eye or mind until after it's done. There's some inner something that tells you what's right. You know you have to do it to survive as a human being. You have no choice.

Life had brought me to this moment of truth, and everything instilled in me had, without my knowing, commanded: Be strong. Make your life count for something.

You Can Make It

I WAS RAISED UP TO BE STRONG. When I was just a little thing, I'd be walking barefooted with my mother down dusty plantation roads, and I'd get so tired. "Please, please pick me up and carry me." I begged her, but she'd always say, "Come on, baby; you can make it. You can make it, baby." My mother and a world of other kinfolks taught me that I could make it. Learning to "make it"—to work hard and keep going when your body said stop, to do whatever you had to, to survive—was a necessary lesson for black children in the Mississippi Delta to learn.

Black people in the Delta didn't have an easy life in the 1930s and '40s, when I was coming up. And Lula, in Coahoma County, where I was born, is as Delta as it gets. "Way down in Lula, hard living has hit," Charley Patton sang on his 1930 recording of "Dry Well Blues." We had enough hard living for a lot of blues, which is why so many blues singers came from this county—Son House, Muddy Waters, Robert Johnson, John Lee Hooker. And it was nothing new. Nearly four hundred years before blues music came out of the Delta, Hernando de Soto got his first glimpse of the Mississippi River right in this very vicinity, but the mosquitoes and the Indians gave him the blues, and he didn't stick around long. The blues are still around, although today some folks you hear talking about hard living hitting Lula might have just had a bad day at the gambling casino on the river at the edge of town.

Like Mayersville, where I've lived most of my adult life, Lula is a tiny Mississippi River town in that long, narrow strip of flat land known as the Delta, which extends from just below Memphis down to just above Vicksburg. Lula is fifty miles south of Memphis, about as far up into the north Delta as Mayersville is in the south part. When I was coming up, the little community of Lula consisted of a post office, three or four churches, and a handful of stores—grocery stores, dry goods places, and general stores. Most of the six hundred or so people who called Lula home didn't live right in town but on one of the huge cotton plantations that fanned out from town. A typical Delta plantation in the 1930s had around 2,000 acres (Central Park in New York City has 843 acres) and required more than a hundred black share-cropping families to keep it going—and some were two or three times that big. People who've never been to the area might imagine that a Delta plantation was some fancy setting like the antebellum places you see in the movies. In fact, most of the Delta wasn't cleared and planted until the 1880s and '90s, and a Delta plantation (we pro-nounced it "plan-ā-shun") was a fairly unpretentious setup. Even the boss man's "big house" was usually a plain one-story white frame house. Of course, it seemed like a mansion to us, compared to the hovel where we stayed. Black sharecroppers lived in mean little cabins that were scattered throughout the cotton fields, because each family farmed land around where they lived. When you see those paintings of cotton fields and black people picking cotton, the little houses look so pictur-esque and charming, but I don't believe the people who paint those pictures ever lived in one of them!

I was born on March 18, 1933, in a tiny sharecroppers' shack sit-ting right in the middle of a newly plowed cotton field on Mr. Hamil-ton's Place on the edge of Lula. (We usually referred to plantations as "places.") The whole house—my parents' home at the time—was one small room with a little porch tacked onto the front. Like most Delta black people, my parents plowed and chopped and picked cotton for the white man who owned the land and the house they lived in. My grandmother, my mother's mother—I called her Big Mama or just Mama—lived across the field. Big Mama was a midwife, and on the day I was born she concocted a tea from roots she had dug from the woods close by and gave it to my mother to cut the labor pains, and then she delivered me.

My mother—I have always called her Birt, but her real name was Virdia Mae—asked her older brother, my uncle Sonny Boy, to name me. (Years later, visiting Africa, I was so happy when I discovered people there who follow the same practice. I like to think there's a connection, but no one knows.) I guess my daddy didn't mind; he never called me anything but "Daddy's Girl" anyway. Uncle Sonny Boy gave me the name U. Z. I have never known how or why he chose the initials "U. Z." to be my name, but initials as names were not uncommon for African Americans. Anyway, U. Z.—U. Z. Brown—was all the name I had until I was about twelve years old, when I became Unita Zelma, but that's a story for later.

Daddy's name was Willie Brown, and I was his only child. One of my earliest memories is waking up one morning to find out my daddy had left in the night. I was three years old, so Birt didn't tell me everything then, but I could sense that something strange and disturbing was going on. She was acting secretive, talking in whispers to relatives who came by our little shack. The boss man came by the house several times over the next few weeks looking for Daddy. My mother told him she didn't know where he was. I missed my daddy and worried about him until she explained to me that he had gone to Memphis to get a better job because he loved me so much. The real story was a bit more complicated.

At the time this happened, 1936, my daddy and mother and I were staying in the same house where I was born. Birt and Daddy would leave for the cotton fields about six o'clock in the morning. Birt took me with her to the field. That's what all the mothers had to do with their babies and small children until the kids were old enough to work, too. They carried a quilt for the babies to lie on in the grass at the edge of the field so they could keep an eye on them while they worked. Early in the morning when the dew was heavy on the grass, Birt let me ride on top of the long cotton sack that was strapped across her back and stretched more than eight feet behind her to hold the cotton she picked. When the grass dried out or she got tired, she'd tell me to jump down and play with the other little children. I didn't have toys to play with, so I'd draw pictures in the dirt and make roads and dirt houses or wiggle my toes in the sandy Delta soil.

One morning Birt was late getting to the field. I might have been sick or just stubborn, but it took her longer than usual to get me ready. Daddy had gone on ahead. When Mr. Hamilton, the white plantation owner, went by the field and saw my mother wasn't there, he came straight to our house and barged right in the front door, hollering, "Virdia Mae, what are you doing at the house? You supposed to be in the field."

"I'll be there in a minute. I'm getting my baby fixed to go, boss."

"You know better than to lie around this house all day. You better get yourself and that little nigger baby out in that field."

"Yassah, boss. I'm coming on right now," Mother said. And we went straight to the field.

Usually the boss man would talk to the husband about any problems, but Mr. Hamilton had not said a word to my father. When Daddy found out that Mr. Hamilton had spoken to my mother, he was angry and humiliated. In those days, a black man on a plantation had nothing he could call his own except his wife, his children, and his own dignity. He didn't own the land or the house he lived in. Black men struggled for their dignity, and a large part of it was tied up in their responsibility for wives and children. If a man couldn't claim his wife, he didn't have anything: He wasn't a whole man. It seems strange in today's world to think of a man "owning" a woman—and I'm glad of that—but in that time and that place, that's the way it was.

My daddy was a hardworking, proud man who didn't talk much. So when he said something, it was because he felt strong about it. He confronted Mr. Hamilton.

"Virdia Mae is my wife, and nobody can tell her what to do but me. You're not in charge of my wife, Mr. Hamilton. I am."

I don't know exactly what happened next. Of course, Mr. Hamilton was not used to being spoken to that way by a black man. Whether there was violence or the threat of violence, I don't know. I don't remember ever being told the particulars. Sometimes people don't tell all the details, just push them down inside because they are too painful to talk about. This much I do know: Mr. Hamilton was enraged over Daddy's behavior, and my daddy feared for his life. Daddy well knew that his own father had been killed in the sugar cane fields for less than that, and he decided he had to run. Late that night Daddy grabbed up a few belongings and hopped a freight train to Memphis. He never set foot in Mississippi again.

Not long after Daddy left—a month or so—Mother and I rode the bus to Memphis to be with him. He had found a good job at the ice-house, and we all stayed with his mother, my grandmother Mama Lorenza, and my aunt Rosetta, daddy's sister, who had moved to Memphis a few years before. Pretty soon we got our own apartment in the same building, known as "the White Elephant Flats." Birt was a house-wife for the only time in her life and stayed home with me. I wore frilly store-bought dresses.

But a couple of years later, Birt and Daddy split up. She was a big church lady, who went to church every time the doors opened, and she thought my daddy ought to be as enthusiastic about church as she was. He wasn't a carouser or anything like that; he just didn't like to go to church. So she left him. She always remembered the exact day—June 20, 1938. I was five years old, soon old enough to start school. My mother knew I couldn't get much education in the Mississippi Delta; so we went to West Helena, Arkansas, to live with my great-auntie, Aunt Big-A. I didn't have another new store-bought dress until I was twelve. But Daddy was a wonderful father, and after Birt and I moved to Arkansas, I visited him every chance I got.

Birt and I soon rented a little house in West Helena, right next door to Aunt Big-A, and that's where I lived during the school year. But from late spring into the fall of every year, I went back to Lula to stay with Big Mama and my grandfather, Choctaw, and work in the cotton fields to help them get their crop out. Lula, Mississippi, is right across the river from Helena and West Helena, Arkansas. A ferry crossed the river between Lula and Helena, and I could walk down to the ferry and cross over to the other side. So, even though I went to school in West Helena and often visited my daddy in Memphis, Delta plantation ways are implanted way deep down in the person I am.

I had more kinfolks in Lula than anywhere. Big Mama and Choc-taw, my grandfather, were there, and my sister Augusta lived with them. And I had aunts and uncles and cousins. Augusta was four years older than I was, and she started to school in Lula, and so she just stayed on with Big Mama until she finished going to school; then she moved over to West Helena to live with Mother and me. I also had three uncles and aunts and nine first cousins in Lula. There was my daddy's brother, Uncle Tommy, and his wife, Aunt Gal; Uncle Sonny and Aunt Maud; and my mother's baby brother, Uncle Chalmers and Aunt Rosie. Chalmers and Rosie moved in with Big Mama after Choctaw died. They were the only ones with children, but they made up for the others—they had nine. Since Augusta and I were the oldest, we did a lot of babysitting with our nine Lula cousins. They were like my brothers and sisters, and we're close to this day.

Black families were always trying to find a better working and living arrangement or better treatment, and they moved around, from one place to another. (I think this feeling of impermanence is why southern blacks even today often use the word "stay" instead of "live" or "reside," as in "she stays on State Street.") When I was very small, Big Mama's house was not too far from Highway 61. Later on she and Choctaw moved to a house farther back from the road, near the woods. I remember the second house best, but both houses were about the same. To get there from the highway, you walked down a little dirt road through the cotton fields, which came right up to our front yard. The yard itself didn't have a blade of grass. Big Mama had us scrape it with a hoe to get the grass out, and then we'd sweep the dirt clean with a homemade broom, small tree limbs tied together. She said this was to keep the snakes from sneaking through the grass and then coming up into the house through the holes in the floor. The Delta is all flat lowland, which flooded frequently, and the house sat on wooden stilts about three or four feet up off the ground to keep out high water—and snakes.

The house was built from cypress trees that had been cut down, pulled out of the bayou, sawed into rough boards right there on the plantation, and thrown together with cracks of varying sizes in between them. It consisted of two rooms, side by side, plus a front porch, or gallery, across the front of the house, and a little lean-to kitchen tacked onto the back of one of the rooms. The two rooms were combination bedroom, family room, visiting room, dining room, and bathing room. We did everything but cook in those two rooms. There were three old rusty iron double beds—one in the room where Big Mama and Choctaw slept and two in the other room, where everybody else slept. When my cousins and I were little, several of us would sleep crossways on the bed. Bigger children and adults would lie lengthwise, but one head up, the next feet up, and so on, because more people could sleep in one bed that way. When we had others staying there and all the beds were filled, they slept on pallets on the floor. Sometimes we'd have as many as twelve or fourteen people sleeping in those two rooms.

The windows didn't have any screens on them, and in the summer we slept under mosquito bars made of thin gauzy material we called snake rag. We had coal-oil lamps for light. Only one of the rooms had a fireplace, which was the only source of heat for the house in the winter. With the cold wind whipping through those cracks, it took more than a fireplace to keep us warm. Some nights we'd have so many quilts stacked on top of us we could hardly move a muscle all night long, and we were still cold. The fireplace was also where we put the heavy black flatirons we used to press clothes and where we boiled water to take a bath or to scald chickens before we "picked" them.

In the little kitchen was Big Mama's big wood stove. We didn't have running water, and we got our water in buckets from the hand pump outside and brought it inside to cook and wash pots and pans and dishes with. There were not many dishes and utensils to wash, just a few mismatched plates and bowls that the boss's wife or somebody had given us. We brought these out when the preacher came for dinner. We generally ate out of deep tin pans. And we didn't use utensils much. After I got grown, I discovered that "finger food" was fancy party food, but just about everything we ate then was finger food. Now I eat turnip greens with a fork, but somehow they don't seem to taste as good as they did with my fingers.

The gallery—pronounced "gow-ry"—was where everyone spent most of their time when they were at home—shelling peas, talking, just trying to keep cool. Hanging from wire on the front of our gallery were buckets, old molasses buckets with holes punched in the tops, where we kept our butter. There was a broken piece of mirror on a shelf by the front door. (We didn't have one inside.) On one end of the gallery there was a single wire from the floor to the ceiling with two bottles hanging from it; the one at the top was a brown snuff bottle, and way down low was a drink bottle. This was Uncle Sonny Boy's "guitar." I can see him right now, moving the lower bottle up and down and plunking that wire, making music and singing. When Big Mama was not around, he would sing blues, but let her come into view and those blues would turn into church music so fast you hardly knew he was doing it.

I was six years old when I started working in the cotton fields. Every day except Sunday everybody in the house would get up early and get dressed to go to the field. I wore a dress, and it was nearly down to my ankles. There was no such thing as women and girls wearing short dresses then—and certainly not shorts or long pants. We wore our most ragged and patched clothes, which Big Mama had made from old flour sacks—these were soft and light—or from material we called "lowess" cloth, which was a heavier, loosely woven canvaslike material that cotton-picking sacks were made of. And we always wore a big straw sun hat. The sun hat was a necessity—we wouldn't have made it without our sun hat. And nobody wore shoes. I would have felt silly wearing shoes to the cotton field.

We'd eat some of Big Mama's biscuits or flapjacks with molasses and head out walking to the field about six o'clock. Around ten-thirty or eleven in the morning, Big Mama would go back to the house to fix our dinner, which is what we called the meal in the middle of the day. She would make a big cast-iron skillet of cornbread and cook big pots of vegetables from the garden with "drippings"—grease she'd saved from frying salt pork or sausage when we had it. This was our big meal of the day. We'd all go to the house around one o'clock and eat dinner and then head right back out to work until the sun went down. As we used to say, "We worked from can to can't."

In May and June we "chopped" cotton. That's what everybody called it, but we were actually hoeing the weeds and grass out of the cotton so it could grow and get up a good stand. We would go through a big field twice, chopping it clean each time. After that we just went down there every once in a while when we saw a big clump of Johnson grass or dock weed. Or cockleburs—those were the worst. I was amazed to discover recently that "new age" people dig up cocklebur roots and eat them. They're supposed to be very nutritious. I can't remember that we ever ate any, but I think Big Mama made a cocklebur tea with them to get rid of colds and fever.

July and August were "lay by" time. You couldn't do any more to help the cotton then. It just had to have rain at the right time and hot sun to grow and make bolls. The stuff inside the boll would gradually expand and pop the boll open, just like popcorn. When the bolls spread wide open and the cotton fluffed out soft and white, it was ready to be picked. This was usually in September and October. The schools for blacks in Mississippi didn't take in until after the picking had finished, but I went to school in West Helena, which started in late September, so I'd leave before all the cotton was picked.

But before school started, I picked a lot of cotton. By the time I was twelve, I was picking two hundred pounds a day. We had those long cotton sacks strapped across our backs; we used nine-foot sacks. When I first started picking, the cotton plants were taller than I was. I'd walk between two rows, looking in and around the leaves for the wide-open bolls, and pull out the cotton from the boll and throw it into my sack. And fast! My hands would be working like little machines going down through there. Most women and girls picked one row at a time, but I could pick on both sides at once, and when I grew up to be nearly six feet tall, I could even reach over and pick a third row. We called this picking "two rows and a snatch." Somebody else might be picking three rows over, and the two of us would share the snatch row. Each time I had filled up my sack, I'd pull it over to the side of the field, get another sack, and head back out to the field to fill another sack. I might fill three or four sacks in one day if most of the bolls were filled out good.

But these were the days of sharecropping, and I never saw any money. Choctaw was assigned a portion of land for us to work. Everybody in the family got together—Big Mama, Choctaw, my sister and I, some of my cousins, Birt when she didn't have a job in Arkansas. We broke up the ground, planted the cotton, hoed the weeds out, picked the cotton, loaded it on wagons, and Choctaw took it to be ginned and baled. The landowner sold the cotton, and Choctaw was supposed to get half of the proceeds—minus his "furnish." The "furnish" was everything we'd bought on credit throughout the entire year from the plantation commissary, which included staples—flour and sugar, mostly—and maybe clothes and household items. The boss man would settle up with his "hands" at the end of the year. Choctaw and all the other sharecroppers—it was always the man in the house— would be called by the boss man one day not long before Christmas and get the earnings for everybody living in his house. It wouldn't be much, a few hundred dollars for a whole season's work. If it wasn't as much as the sharecropper thought it should be, he really had no recourse. That's why it was called "sharecropping," we used to say— because we made the crop and the Man took the share!

Choctaw gave Big Mama all the money, and she distributed it when and where it was needed throughout the next year. Big Mama kept the money in her "nation sack." I have no idea why she called it a nation sack. It was a money belt made from pieces of old cotton sacks that she sewed pockets in and tied around her waist. She wore her nation sack under her clothes everywhere she went. I think she must have even slept in it, because I never saw that nation sack anywhere except tied on to her. But she could have left it out in the house in full view, because none of us kids would have touched it. We all knew better than to mess with Big Mama's nation sack.

Everybody knew the sweat and pain that went into earning the money in that nation sack. I knew from my earliest consciousness that we had to make a little bit of money go a long way. Nothing was wasted—not food, clothes, flour sacks, any little scrap of cloth, and certainly not money. We were recycling long before recycling was cool. Everything we had was precious. That's just the way we lived, and I didn't know any other way. But that way of life taught me a lot. I learned the value of money, and also that money isn't everything. I learned that if I worked hard and persevered and was frugal and resourceful, I could make it, and that a difficult, uncertain life was not an unhappy life. These lessons sound like clichés, but they're full of real meaning for me. They were my strength and my survival. I doubt if I could've barefooted onto unfamiliar roads if my kinfolks hadn't made sure I learned them.

Coming up, all I knew was kinfolks. They gave me the love that got me started and that's kept me going for all these years.

My mother, Birt, loved me and taught me and tried to protect me till the day she died—June 30, 2005—at the age of ninety-one. She had a zest for life and enjoyed being with people; they gravitated to her. She showed me how to get along with people. She had what we called "mother wit"—common sense, understanding, the wisdom of the ages passed down through the old folks, especially the women. Birt's mother wit was basically a down-to-earth understanding of human nature, which came out in a multitude of sayings. She had a saying for every situation: "If you lie down with a dog, you'll get up with fleas"; "Don't lay it on the cow when the milk goes sour"; "A new broom sweeps clean, but the old one know where the dirt is"; "Every shut eye ain't asleep, and every grinning mouth ain't happy"; and on and on. Often today, one of her sayings pops into my head, helping me understand what to do. You don't forget mother wit like "Wear life like a loose garment," and it comes in mighty handy when you're barefootin', because you never know what kind of situation you're going to run up against. Birt didn't have much education; she never had land or money or fine jewelry. But she had mother wit, and that's what she left to me. It's the most learned and valuable gift I ever received.

I adored my daddy, and I always knew he adored me. Daddy was always patting me—on top of my head, on my shoulders and arms and back—little touches that told me he was happy I was around. And he never once spanked me. He'd just say, "Daddy's girl don't do that." Although he was a man of few words, he had a powerful presence and could communicate his feelings just by the way he stood, and he was very tall, anyway. He could intuitively sense the feelings of others. Many southern blacks during slavery and Jim Crow days learned to read feelings of white people by necessity, but my daddy was born with that ability. I'm lucky because he passed it on to me.

When I went to Memphis to see my daddy, I sometimes stayed with Mama Lorenza and Aunt Rosetta, especially after Daddy remarried. (He had a jealous wife.) I loved visiting them. Mama Lorenza had grown up in Louisiana and spoke with a Louisiana-French accent, which I loved to hear. I remember she said "mahn" for "man," for instance. And she wore long black dresses; I never saw her ankles. I never saw her without an apron on, either. Mama Lorenza cooked delicious spicy Cajun dishes that I didn't get in Mississippi—jambalaya and gumbo. I felt lucky to have such an exotic grandmother and somehow more special because of her. She's the one who told me about my grand-father getting killed in the cane field.

One of the things that bothers me today is that I don't even know my Louisiana granddaddy's name. As far as I know, no one living knows his name. Somehow then it didn't seem important for me to remember it. Many black families in the Deep South haven't kept track of names of their ancestors or important dates either. Part of it is probably that our people didn't know how to write or read, so these things weren't put down in the family Bible and passed on. But I think it's deeper than that. I think it's about us not knowing who we are and not feeling we matter, from the time of slavery on. African Americans had our identities snatched from us when we were taken from Africa—our ancestors couldn't even keep their names. Our white owners and bosses often just called us "girl" or "nigger," so I think over the years many black families never developed the belief that our names and those of our ancestors matter. If we didn't matter, why should our names?

I'll never forget Aunt Rosetta. She never had any children of her own, and she took a special interest in me. Aunt Rosetta was different from the other women in my family, who worked on the plantation or as domestics. Aunt Rosetta had a city job working in a laundry and a regular salary that seemed like a lot of money to me. She was very frugal and saved her money to buy nice things. The first time I ever saw a wristwatch, it was Aunt Rosetta's. I have much of her furniture now in my house. She was a role model for me—of a woman who held a "real" job and worked to lift herself above her limited background.

Aunt Big-A in West Helena never had children either. She was my great-aunt, Big Mama's sister. For a little while my mother and I lived with her in Arkansas, but later we moved into a little house next door. Her real name was Effie Pinkston, but I called her Aunt Big-A because she had a big stomach. For years I thought she was going to have a baby, but I later found out it was a tumor. She didn't have a doctor and eventually died from the tumor. During World War II, when Mother worked at Chicago Mills, a textile plant in West Helena, Aunt Big-A looked after me and encouraged me in my schoolwork, and she tried to persuade me to learn how to play the piano. She was a big church lady and sang in the choir. Aunt Big-A took in washing and ironing, and I helped her. I loved her very much.

When she was not working for white folks, Aunt Big-A was sitting at her sewing machine. She made all my clothes, so I never was a raggedy child even though we never had much money. Of course, I never had more than two or three decent dresses at a time and two pairs of shoes—one pair for Sunday school and one for everyday. The everyday pair was my old Sunday shoes. I went barefooted most of the time anyway unless it was real cold.

Big Mama—her real name was Mamie Holmes—spoke with authority about everything. As the oldest person in the family in Lula, Big Mama was in charge of everybody else. She was the matriarch. (Choctaw was not with her until her later years.) Big Mama's word was law. But she wasn't stern or gruff. Everybody listened to her and respected her. She was much less likely to give me a switching than Birt was. I knew she meant business, and I didn't want to disappoint her. Everybody loved Big Mama, and she always had a lot of friends and family coming by to see her. Other black plantation people came to her for her medical remedies and advice. All the grandchildren went to her for guidance. We'd tell her a lot more about our lives than we'd tell our parents. And she knew how to read—a rare skill for rural blacks of her generation. In her earlier years she had worked as a cook in white houses, and one white woman wanted her to cook special dishes and taught her to follow recipes. That's how she learned to read, by figuring out how to fix the family's meals. She was a fine cook, too, and always cooking.

Choctaw kept her supplied with vegetables to cook. He always had the biggest vegetable garden of anybody around, as big as a commercial farmer's "truck patch" you might see today, and nobody was allowed in this garden without him. I remember one time, when I was little, he took me out to his garden and was pointing out to me which watermelons were ripe and which ones were not. Then he asked me, "Is that one ripe?" When I said I thought it was, he told me to hit it. When I did, he took his fist and hit it at the same time, and the melon busted open big and red. But I thought I had done it. "Sit down and eat it, right here in my patch," he said. "Take your hand and get down in there, baby." I can see that just as clear—my little hand digging out the heart of that melon and the look of joy on Choctaw's face. When I'd eaten all I could, he said, "Go tell your grandmother!" I ran to the house and told her I had picked out a watermelon and asked her if she wanted some of it. She came out there smiling and hollering, "Choctaw, you're going to ruin that gal!" I could see the love on their faces.

My sister Augusta was quieter and not as rambunctious as I was and, like other big sisters, she got tired of me following her around, copying her all the time. Augusta was actually my half sister—she had a different father—but in my family and in many other black families, we didn't talk about "half" or "step." Augusta and I had the same mother and grandmother, so she was my sister, and that was that. For that matter, Choctaw was not my mother's daddy, but he was married to my grandmother, and it never occurred to me that he was my stepgrandfather. Family was family.

My uncles were honorable men. They felt responsible for Augusta and me, especially regarding the opposite sex. They protected us and were always trying to teach us how to behave around boys. And how not to. "You ain't gonna be no slut," my uncle Sonny Boy would say. When Augusta and I learned later in life that a lot of girls had uncles who took advantage of them, we used to talk about how lucky we were to have such wonderful uncles.

I was closer to Aunt Rosie than to my other aunts in Lula. Aunt Rosie was the person who taught me to fix myself up nice. She liked to fix up and go to the little store we used to call "the Chinaman's store," and she liked to take me with her. In those days, a woman didn't go anywhere except church without a man or a child with her. So Aunt Rosie would put on a cotton print dress, pull her hair up all the way around in an "upsweep" with a "bird's nest" of curls on top, and dab on a little lipstick and powder, and off we'd go to the Chinaman's store. We called it "Chinaman's" for the obvious reason, that Chinese people owned and operated it. The only ethnic group other than blacks and whites that I knew in the Mississippi Delta were the Chinese. Chinese had come in the late 1800s to work in the cotton fields, but they didn't like that kind of work and didn't work as hard as the farmers were accustomed to making black people work. Many of them stayed and opened grocery stores.

I loved going to the Chinaman's store. All the black people did. And we loved the Chinese people who ran it. They were always so glad to see us. They would run around and bow and ask if they could help us. They served us; they catered to us. They spoke English, but with a funny little singsong accent that fascinated me. The Chinese remembered all our names—the parents and all the children. They inquired about our family members: "Sarah? Is she all right?" and "The baby? How's the baby?" We didn't get this kind of attention and respect anywhere else. Many years later, when I traveled in China, I remembered how kind the Delta Chinese had been to me and I tried to treat the people in China the same way.

The store itself looked just about like any other little grocery stores in the area. There was a long counter, where the clerks put all the items they had retrieved from the shelves for us. There was no such thing as self-service in any store at that time. The Chinaman's store had flour and sugar and hoop cheese and clothes and hats and nails and tools, seeds in open bins, and cloth cut from big bolts. The Chinese sold vegetables out of a garden in the back. They had a meat market, and the meat was fresh. In the winter you might see a hog hanging from the rafters and whole fresh chickens being plucked and cut up. (Of course there were no U.S.D.A. stickers on meat in those days.) Sandwich meat—bologna and other processed sandwich meat—was cut from a big loaf. We called it "freshness," which seems funny to me now because it was the only meat that wasn't freshly slaughtered. If we had any money, Aunt Rosie and I always liked to get some "freshness" to take back to the family.

They also sold beer at the Chinaman's store, and there was a slot machine at one end of the counter. Occasionally some chatty, nice man in the store—always black, of course, probably somebody off work from a neighboring place—might buy Aunt Rosie a beer, and they'd talk and laugh and drink their beer. Sometimes he'd give me a nickel to play the slot machine. I'd poke the nickel in, and he would pull the handle. I'd stand there transfixed as the colorful pictures of apples and oranges and lemons spun round and round—hoping that three of the same kind would line up and stop and coins would come tumbling out. But I don't recall that it ever happened. When we got back to the house, Rosie's husband, Uncle Chalmers—he was a preacher and a jealous type—would prod me for information about what we'd done. (Uncle Chalmers brings to mind the old saying, "The rooster make more racket than the hen what lay the egg.") But I never told him a thing.

Aunt Rosie asked Big Mama, "Where did that little fast girl get all that sense?"

"Little fast girl"—that's what the grown folks in my family called me most of the time. It wasn't because I moved in a big hurry or because I was a flirt, but because I was curious, always observing everything around me, asking a lot of questions, looking for something different to do, and trying to get into things. When I asked questions they didn't want to answer or when I wanted to do something or go somewhere they didn't think I should, I was their "little fast girl." They thought I was smart and they were proud of me, and I could hear their love, even when they were correcting me: "Come on, little fast girl, before you get yourself in trouble." The world I grew up in was so controlled by the adults in my family, I couldn't imagine getting into much trouble.

That's the way things were then: Adults were in charge, and children were not allowed to do certain things. You were taught to obey adults. It was the women who taught you this, and in my case, the most important teachers were Birt and Big Mama. I wasn't supposed to talk back or act sassy or question their authority. "Don't be impeddy," they'd say to me if I did. (I think that was a combination of "impudent" and "uppity"—black folks always have been creative with the English language!) If the grown-ups were talking to each other and I was in the room, they didn't want me to pipe up and ask questions or express my own opinions. One of them would say, "Go on outside and play, little fast girl. You don't need to be sitting in here looking right up in my mouth." Now, l always had opinions and I had it in me to express myself and to disagree, so this was a hard lesson for me to learn.

Of course, the switching I might get if I didn't do what they said moved the learning process along. "A hard head makes a soft behind" was the prevailing principle of child care. If I disobeyed or misbehaved, Birt would tell me, "U. Z., go get me a switch off the hedge bush." I'd have to go outside, break off a branch from the privet hedge, and hand it to her. She would strip off all the leaves and switch my little legs. And then Birt would be the one crying. "Oh, baby, I don't want to do this. I wouldn't switch you unless I loved you." At the time, I could have done without some of the love I got.

The love of my family, in all its forms, has meant everything to me through the years. It's been my lifeline and my anchor. When I was trying to find my footing, my family was my solid ground. That security helped me develop the self-worth and confidence I'd need later in life to go charging off into things I knew absolutely nothing about. I was lucky, because otherwise I might not have barefooted my way to freedom. Barefootin' can be risky business.

Lula, Mississippi, Memphis, Tennessee, and West Helena, Arkansas— that was my entire universe when I was growing up, a sliver of earth straddling the Mississippi River, about sixty miles long and fifteen miles across at its widest. But that was big enough until I knew any better. I went from one place to the other place, but the roads all seemed to begin and end in Lula at Big Mama's house.

Big Mama would walk with me to the highway so I could catch the Greyhound to Memphis to visit my daddy. Highway 61 was the only paved road around, two narrow lanes shooting through the flat cotton fields in a beeline north to Memphis. Lula didn't have a bus station, and we'd wait on the side of the road for the bus to come. It wouldn't be long till Big Mama got out her big red and white handkerchief and waved it high in the air, and, just like that, the bus would appear. I thought Big Mama was magic. All she had to do was bring out that magical handkerchief to conjure up a bus out of nowhere to come just for me—a skinny, long-legged, little black girl from the cotton field, on my way to the city to see my daddy.

I was always ready to go to each place, and my family was always glad to see me when I got there. I was happy at all three places, but I loved getting back to Lula. I can hear Big Mama now: "Come on, little fast girl, and let's go to the house and get something to eat. We been missing you."

Let Nature Guide You

I WAS BORN AT A TIME when nature was our survival, our enter-tainment, our inspiration, and our guidance, and in the Missis-sippi Delta there was more nature than anything. We knew by the time of the year where we could find the different plants we needed for food or medicine, or just plain beauty, because nature was at peace with itself. Back then you could depend on the seasons: Winter was winter, fall was fall, the summers were summer, and spring was spring. Nowa-days the seasons are all mixed up, but then everything had its season and you could plan your life by the time of the year. We made molasses and picked up pecans in the fall and killed hogs just before Christmas when it was really cold.

And the moon, too, controlled what we did. You would never plant anything when there was a wasting-away moon, because it would not produce. Babies would be born under a full moon, we believed. (I guess we remembered only the ones that actually *were*.) When people were acting strange or kids misbehaved, Big Mama would say, "Let me see what the moon doing." Growing up around Big Mama and Choc-taw, I was always aware of my attachment to the earth and to the cycles of nature. I guess that's why I grew up to be a person who fights for the wilderness and nature. I can still draw inspiration and guidance from the Delta landscape I've been looking at since I was a child.

Even though Big Mama's yard had no grass, there were always flow-ers growing in the yard—sunflowers and four o'clocks and morning glories. In the fall the elderberry bushes with their clusters of dark purple berries and blazing sumac and goldenrod growing along the ditches and fences lit up the view all around. And, of course, there was a chinaberry tree in the side yard. Every Delta plantation shanty had at least one chinaberry tree. I've read that the species was brought over from India in the early 1800s as an ornamental plant for southern gardens. I didn't see too many in white people's yards, but every black home had at least one chinaberry tree, usually planted at the corner of the house. In the summer the leaves opened out wide, umbrella-like, and made a lot of shade, but it's a chinaberry tree in the winter that is most dramatic: straight dark spreading limbs without any leaves and big clusters of those yellow wrinkled berries hanging like baskets high in the trees. The chinaberry tree was an integral part of our life. Kids with worms ate chinaberries to get rid of them. We played with chinaberries and used them to make popguns. Elderberry limbs were hollow, and boys would poke chinaberries inside and push another smaller stick through to send the berries flying. White boys made them, too, and called them "nigger shooters." A chinaberry has a hole in the center, and I used to remove the yellow gooey outsides and string chinaberries on thread to make jewelry.

We ate vegetables and melons all summer long from Choctaw's garden and put vegetables up in jars for the winter, and we always had some to give away to friends or anybody who needed it. These were the Depression years, but black people lived the same, Depression or not. I remember one time a white man and his wife and three or four pitiful-looking little children walked up to our house. We were living up near the highway then, so I couldn't have been more than five or six years old. Big Mama and I were on the gallery. The white man said, "Auntie"—that's what he called my grandmother—"Auntie, you got any leftover food? My wife and I and the children are hungry." It was strange to me—white people begging for food. I can still see that white man's face, his dull drooping eyes: He was so ashamed. I could just feel it. Big Mama went inside and brought out whatever she had and gave it to them. There was a big pile of onions on the porch, and she handed those to him, too, and they were glad to get them. That was the first time I ever saw anybody eat raw onions. It was also the first time I knew that some white people were poor, too. I have never forgotten that. This helped me to understand white people when I was involved in the civil rights movement, that white people also suffer, and they *need* our help as much as we need theirs.

Besides what Choctaw raised in his garden, food grew wild all around our house and in the woods behind the house. We had a peach tree, a pear tree, and some wild plum trees and a pecan tree in the yard. Blackberry and dewberry vines crawled along the sides of the road, and we picked and ate the berries during the summer. The first things to come out in the spring were the wild greens, which grew in the open spaces. The leaves were flat and spread out and had little wirelike strands hanging on them. You would stick a knife under the leaves and cut them off at the root; then all you had to do was trim them and cook them. Another name for wild greens was "shoutin' pussies." You couldn't use that term with the grown folks, but of course they called them that, too.

In addition to the wild plums, dewberries, and blackberries, there were muscadines, which were large green grapes with red insides that grew on vines in the woods. We picked berries in the summertime and sat up at night mashing them through a sieve to get the juice, which was used for making jelly and wine. Big Mama always had wine in the house for Christmas. With the berry meat that was left Big Mama made preserves or a berry pie. Nothing was thrown away. We did the same thing with muscadines. I used to love to climb the trees where the muscadine vines were and pick the big green grapes when they got ripe in the fall. Muscadine wine was the best kind of wine.

The turtles came out of the woods during the spring rainy season. When I saw one, I'd take off behind that turtle and poke a big old stick in his mouth. The turtle would clamp down on it, and I could drag him in. A turtle would not turn loose. When I got him to the house, Big Mama would pump some water and put it in the big iron pot outside; then she'd build a fire and get the water hot and throw the turtle in. She didn't cook him done, just enough so she could get him out and cut off his head and let the blood drain out. Then she pulled off his skin and hollowed out the shell and scraped it good. The meat would turn out so pretty and white, it looked like chicken. She'd cut the meat into pieces and fry it like chicken.

Men would hunt squirrels and rabbits and birds and raccoons and possums, too. With the exception of pork from the hog we killed once a year and maybe a chicken when the preacher was coming, when we ate meat, it was killed in the wild. To tell the truth, I never did eat much meat. I mostly had vegetables and fish. I think that's why I've been so healthy all my life.

Big Mama made turtle soup, too. I didn't know turtle soup was a delicacy served in fancy restaurants until recent years. To me, eating turtles was just our way of life. I didn't know the value of frogs and frog legs, either. The first time I was in an expensive restaurant and someone said, "Wouldn't you like some frog legs?" I thought I was hearing things. When we wanted frog legs back on the place, the men would just walk out into the woods and gig some frogs with sharp pointed sticks. If I had known that frog legs cost so much in restaurants today, I would've gone into the frog business a long time ago!

And, of course, we fished year-round in the lakes and ponds and ditches nearby. One of the biggest lakes I used to go to with my uncles was Moon Lake, on the edge of Lula. This was the very same Moon Lake that inspired Tennessee Williams when he was growing up in nearby Clarksdale, but I didn't know that at the time. I can see why he liked it and wrote about it. It was a wide, cypress-lined old oxbow lake that had once been a part of the Mississippi River—a dreamy sort of place.

Best of all I loved the woods that curved around the house at the edge of the cotton fields. It was a virgin forest of oaks and sweet gums and sassafras, and the trees made a tent over the marshy earth and tangled vines and underbrush. The trees were so thick in some places that they nearly closed out the sun. After a summer rain, it was cool and quiet and humid under there, shadowy and mystical. Big Mama and Choctaw knew all the wild plants and which ones could be used to treat certain illnesses. They took me with them to find and pick certain things, and I learned which plants to use to make tea for measles or a cough or constipation or pain and which plants to grind and mash into poultices for burns and other skin irritations. I'm sorry now that I didn't carry on the practice because I don't remember these things anymore, but I sure wish I did.

It was the big trees that captured my imagination. I cannot count the hours I spent climbing those trees. I would rather have been up in a tree than about anywhere. It's where I first sensed a taste of freedom and adventure. I'd curl my bare toes around the tree trunk and hold on to the limbs and shinny all the way up to the top. I was on my own. And I could see for miles and miles—unbroken rows and rows of cotton and the narrow dusty or muddy roads running through them, shacks just like ours dotted here and there, the occasional big house that white people lived in, the sloughs and bayous that filled up during the rainy season and dried up to nearly nothing in the parching summer sun. Looking west, I could see the road to the ferry and visualize the ferry itself, piled with people and cars chugging across the river to Arkansas. On a clear day I could see up Highway 61 for miles before it disappeared on the horizon, with Memphis just beyond. As far as I knew, this was the way the whole world looked. But sometimes I wondered what lay beyond West Helena and Memphis, and I promised myself I was going to find out if I could.

Big Mama used to say, "Why does U. Z. stay up in those trees all the time?" And Aunt Rosie would say, "She has a high mind."

I'd be up there until nearly dark sometimes. Then I'd hear Big Mama calling: "Little fast girl, are you up in a tree again? It's suppertime. You better get yourself in this house." And I would scramble down just like a squirrel and run barefooted back to reality and the security of home.

Look Out for Snakes

IT WAS A VERY COLD DAY, and a man was walking down the road. He saw a snake, all curled up and frozen stiff. The man felt sorry for the snake, and he picked him up and held him close to his chest to warm up the poor snake. After a little bit the snake did get warm and started to move around a little, and he bit the man. The man was shocked and in pain, and he said to the snake, "How could you do that to me. I picked you up and saved you from freezing to death, and then you bit me!" And the snake said to the man, "Well, mister, you knew I was a snake when you picked me up."

That was a story I heard many times growing up.

The old folks used to say, "Watch the animals for guidance," and I grew up looking out for snakes. Right in the middle of this land where I discovered the beauty of nature, where nature nourished and inspired me, where I could run barefooted down the road and climb trees, I always kept one eye cocked for snakes. We had moccasins and copperheads and rattlesnakes, as well as harmless grass snakes and chicken snakes. I didn't know one snake from another. As far as I was concerned, a snake was a snake, and I was afraid of them all. Fear of snakes didn't keep me holed up in the house. I just didn't want to make one mad at me. So I guess I lived by the snakes' rules. I figured whatever the snake wanted to do he was going to do; so I got out of his way and let him go on about his business. I wasn't about to pick one up.

*   *   *

It was a peculiar environment. I felt so secure and strong and free-spirited with my kinfolks, but at the same time, there was an under-current of fear, and real freedom was measured out by the thimbleful. Whether I was in Mississippi or Arkansas or Tennessee, I spent nearly all my time with other black people in a totally black world. I went to a black church and a black school and sometimes a little black café or juke joint. The only time I ever interacted with white people was when I was working for them or had to go to the store or the post office. But the power of white people was everywhere. They owned our house; they ran our school; they employed us. They paid us what they wanted to, when they wanted to, and so they controlled us in many other ways.

I don't mean that I was consciously terrified all the time. I learned how to "act right" around white people long before I knew that fear was the reason I did it. "Correct" behavior around white people was so ingrained in our way of life that I don't ever remember being taught it. I developed a sixth sense about white people—what they liked and didn't like. It was a matter of survival then. Like all black children of my generation in the rural South, I didn't know any other way. I know now that that conditioning affected the person I am today for better and worse. I am very wary and sensitive to danger, and alert to the feelings of others.

In addition to the institutionalized rules—like drinking only from "colored" water fountains, sitting in "colored" waiting areas in the courthouse and other public places, sitting in the back of the bus—there was an elaborate system of personal contact. I knew as a matter of course, for example, to say, "Yes, ma'am" and "No, ma'am" and to call white adults Mr. and Mrs. Jones, or whatever. I called their white children Mr. John and Miss Sally even if they were younger than I was. I knew not to be too friendly with them even if the white child wanted me to. A white person never referred to a black female as a lady; she was always a "woman" or "girl"; the only ladies were white ladies. Black men were "boys." A white family could have a seventy-five-year-old "houseboy," and their cook might have been a sixty-year-old "girl."

As a black person I always walked on the other side of the street from the whites, just as I was supposed to; and if a white person was walking toward me on the road, I would get over on the grass and let him or her go by. When I went to the store, I stood back and let the white customers get waited on first. And I never looked a white person in the eye—man or woman.

These customs were not based on politeness. They were based on a very simple fact of the southern way of life—the system. A white person was Somebody, and a black person was Nobody. And that was the way it was supposed to stay—for children and adults as well. From my family I learned that I was supposed to respect all my elders, but a little white boy or girl called my black elders by their first name: "Annie Mae, fix me some ice cream." The black lady who did all the cooking and cleaning for a white family could not eat from that family's plates or drink from their glasses. She drank from a mayonnaise jar. She had to enter the back door of the house and sit in the backseat of the car. And, above all, she did not use the family's toilet. Some white families even had a separate toilet in the garage or utility room for their black servants. Otherwise a black worker had to go outside and hide in the bushes—or just "hold it."

Black children were not supposed to drink Coca-Cola. That's one of those rules that I never remember not knowing. I never asked to buy a Coke; I believed that no white person would sell me one, and I would have never questioned a white person. Instead we drank "bellywashers"—RC Cola, Nehi Strawberry, Double Cola, and Big Orange. Some of my Mississippi Delta white friends tell me they never heard of such a rule and they assumed we drank the other kinds because they were bigger and we got more to drink for a nickel. But the belief among all the black people I knew was certain: Coke was only for whites. Why? I never knew. The Coke issue may seem silly in light of other, more horrendous customs of those days, but I think it shows how deeply instilled was our obligation to uphold, enable, and reinforce white supremacy with our every act.

Before I joined the civil rights movement, anytime I was in the presence of a white person, my role was to make sure the white person did exactly as he or she wished, to make life as easy as possible for that person, and, otherwise, to stay out of the way, to become invisible. In *Invisible Man,* Ralph Ellison wrote that blacks in America were invisible to white people—that is, blacks mattered so little to whites that they hardly even saw them. That is a wonderful and truthful book, but I can honestly say that when I was in the white world, I didn't feel invisible at all. I felt all too visible. In West Helena and especially Memphis, I didn't dare go into the big downtown stores and restaurants and hotels because I would be watched closely and followed so that they could make sure I did not steal anything. I couldn't even pause to look in the windows without being asked, "Nigger, what are you doing here? You know you're not allowed in this area. Get back where you belong." Today we complain about police profiling of blacks and other ethnic minorities; back then it was routine. And we were the majority where I lived.

When my relatives and other grown folks were talking among themselves at night, they nearly always told at least one story about someone who had been thrown off the Man's place or threatened by a white boss. Or they would talk about a beating or sometimes even a lynching they'd heard about. I grew up with these stories, as did all Delta plantation blacks. But my people were not beat down or hateful, and they somehow managed to maintain their personal dignity— maybe only because they didn't want their children and grandchildren to lose hope. My family was low in material possessions, but they were high in spirit. They didn't like the way of life they'd been born into, but—except for my daddy and grandfather—they followed the boss's rules, because he was the boss, until they could find a way out. (And all of them eventually did leave the plantation. My cousins are now scattered from the Midwest to New York City.) So like generations of southern blacks before me, I obeyed the unwritten laws of white society. I obeyed my parents and grandparents, too, but that was different: I did that out of respect, and I knew they loved me. Obedience to white people was a custom based on the simple fear of what might happen to me if I incurred their wrath.

The first time I personally experienced this fear and the hatred that created it was in West Helena, when I was eight years old. My mother asked me to go across the tracks to the post office to pick up the mail for Aunt Big-A. West Helena was a typical small southern town where the railroad tracks divided White Town from Colored Town (white people called it "Nigger Town"). We lived in Colored Town, in an area known as the Quarters, where rows and rows of little houses were crammed in close to each other and set up near the narrow, unpaved streets. There weren't any street signs or streetlights or sidewalks. All the houses were alike—unpainted, with two small rooms, one behind the other, and a front porch. These are known as shotgun houses because if you fired a shotgun through the front door, the bullets would go through the door in the next room and out the back door. We lived in a house right next door to Aunt Big-A. I often went to the post office to get her mail.

The post office was in White Town, along with the dry goods stores. I had been there many times before, and on this particular day, as always, I was happy to get outside. I walked down the street, crossed the tracks, went straight to the post office, and got Aunt Big-A's mail. As I was walking home, minding my own business, a white boy about my age came running toward me, looking in my face and hollering, "NIGGER, NIGGER, NIGGER." I just pushed him away as hard as I could, and when I did I scraped his arm with my fingernail. He looked at his arm and saw there was a little blood on him, and he yelled, "You scratched me, you nigger!" He was screaming at me and turning red, he was so angry. He screeched at the top of his lungs, "I'm gonna get my mama and daddy and we're comin' after y'all tonight! And we're gonna kill you."

I ran home as fast as I could. When Birt came home from work, I told her that a little white boy called me a nigger and screamed at me and said his daddy was coming to get us. And she just grabbed me and held me, and I saw the awful terror that came over her face. She held me for a long time. "Don't worry, baby," she told me, "it's going to be all right." And she rocked me and said, "Don't worry, baby. I'll go down with you." And I knew what that meant: They would just as soon come and kill us as not, and she would die trying to protect me. I have never forgotten the look of fear and anguish on my mother's face. It was my first awareness of the powerful, terrible hatred that poisoned us because of the color of our skin. It's painful even now when I think about it. The only comfort she could give me was to "go down" with me.

I never saw the boy again or his parents, but from then on I knew, in the very core of my being, why I had to be very, very careful around white people—even the kids, or maybe especially the kids. When I was a teenager and walked down the street with friends, white boys would drive by in their cars and throw things at us, and we did not do anything back. To defend ourselves would have only incited more harassment or violence. That's the way it was.

I couldn't figure out why things were this way, why white people hated black people and looked down on us. I would ask my mother and grandmother to tell me what was wrong with us. What had we ever done to hurt them? They did the best they could to explain it. My grandmother told me that all white people weren't hateful; she told me about the white lady she had cooked for who taught her to read. But I knew that white people, mean or nice, did not really want to have anything to do with us. "That's just the way white folks is," Birt would say. "White folks don't know anything about you, baby. They just don't know any better." And she told me over and over that God made me black and He loved me and that I was a good person and an honest person, that I had done nothing wrong. "One of these days things ain't gon' be like they always was. Things gon' get better; these white folks have to let up off of us." This was a sad time that put so much sickness into our society.

Everybody in our family worked. That meant we worked for white people. During my school years, besides chopping and picking cotton in the Delta, I helped Aunt Big-A. She and I would go to a white lady's house, pick up the dirty clothes, and take the washing home, and then we would carry it back all washed and pressed. We did all the ironing with flatirons; we used a coal bucket and set the iron on a grate on top, with hot burning coals underneath, and the ashes came out at the bottom. Sometimes we got burned, but we ironed white shirts with those flatirons without getting a single spot on them. I do not know how we did it. When Aunt Big-A went for her money, she didn't know how much she would be paid. The white lady would say, "How much do I owe you, Effie?" and Aunt Big-A would say, "Whatever you thinks it's worth." She would name an amount—a dollar or two—and Aunt Big-A would say, "Yes'm."

Once I was out of school—which was after the eighth grade—I had to work and take care of myself. A person had to get a job even if it did not pay much. I cleaned houses, worked as a babysitter, cooked hamburgers in a café—anything to get hold of a few dollars. I had been working all my life, so this was nothing new.

I was always a little afraid or uneasy when I worked in white people's houses. They would sometimes sit around and talk about black people—that some black man "needs to be shot" and "we need to teach him his place" and so forth. There were two ways I was afraid: I was worried about what would happen if I didn't say anything, and I was scared if I did say something, it would make them mad. Or I wondered if they were just trying me out: Some white people would do things or say things—just picking at you—to see what your response would be. They might say, "They need to be done hung that nigger" to try to get a reaction out of me, but I couldn't show any expression because if I did, they had succeeded. "Don't let nobody see nothing on your face" was advice my mother had passed along to me at an early age. At these times I felt I had nowhere to turn but to hide in myself.

If I questioned my white employer, I probably wouldn't have a job anymore. One time I was keeping someone's baby, and the mother told me she would pay me two dollars, but she paid me only one dollar. I told her that was not what she had promised, and she said, "Nigger, are you questioning me? Get out of here." There was another time later on, when I was in my twenties; I was working for a woman who was a nurse. I cleaned her house and looked after her kids while she was at work. I'd been saving back a little money for a long time, and Jeremiah, my future husband, who was courting me at the time, had given me a few dollars. When I had saved up three hundred dollars, I bought me an old car. It was a blue Oldsmobile slick-back, and it was a good one. The next day I went to work in my car. When the woman I was working for saw it, she said my car looked better than hers. She was infuriated, and she fired me right there on the spot. She told me I didn't need a job. "If you can buy a car like that, that looks better than mine, I don't need you anymore." I tried to explain to her that I had saved my money. "Yeah, I know," she said, "because you've been saving it off of me!"

The relationship between white women and black women was not always bad. I worked for a wonderful woman who really helped me when I was down sick. She visited me often and brought me medicine and food and whatever else I needed. It was not uncommon for a white woman to talk about her problems to her black maid—problems she was having with her husband or parents or children or friends, which she couldn't say to anyone else. She felt safe, I think, that the black woman was not going to tell anybody she knew. The two of them might even develop a close friendship when they were by themselves. But then, if her husband or a neighbor came into the room, the old rules went right back into play.

I think blacks understood white people a lot better than they understood us. Whites deluded themselves into believing that we were happy to get whatever they gave us, and satisfied. It was obvious how pleased they were with themselves. You could see their eyes light up when you thanked them for some old clothes or costume jewelry. And we knew how to play games with their self-delusion, if necessary, to get what we wanted. "Yassuh, boss. I sho do thank ya" was as likely to be said tongue-in-cheek as not. Some black people were real "Uncle Toms," but some were just Tomming for a reason, and there is a difference. Things like these were strategies for survival. As Birt said, "Every shut eye ain't asleep."

Some things were done just for laughs. Fannie Lou Hamer, the great Mississippi freedom fighter that I came to love like family, used to tell about taking in ironing for white ladies. She said she worked only for women who were about her size, and she'd take their laundry home to wash and iron it over the weekend, but first she'd pick out one of the white lady's dresses and wear it to church on Sunday! The white women never dreamed Fannie Lou would do such a thing. And in our totally segregated society at the time, they would never find out, either.

But I was almost always uneasy around white folks until years later. Coming up, when I was dealing with white people, I never knew what they might do. I might make twenty dollars or I might make ten. I might be welcomed with good cheer or be greeted with indifference or be chased away with epithets or worse. It came down to trust. I didn't know whether or when I could trust someone white. Many black people still have a hard time trusting white people. It's like dealing with snakes: Even when your mind tells you the snake is harmless, you have a hard time believing it.

Distrust breeds more distrust. When you can't trust somebody else, you probably won't be as trustworthy yourself. It was a sick system that poisoned everyone. And black people learned to barefoot their way through and around the system, the same way we learned to walk barefooted in the snake-infested land. Well, not quite the same way. We could avoid white folks and try to trick them, like we did snakes. But if necessary we could chop off a snake's head with a hoe. Not so, the system. We had to live with the system. We learned to keep our eyes wide open all the time.

Sometimes I look over my life and think about the hell I went through just trying to survive. I didn't have an easy time, and many others experienced what I did, or worse. I try not to think about it much. I don't want to feel that pain anymore, that scary pain of not knowing.

Today I interact with as many white people as I do black people. I try to base my trust not on the color of someone's skin but on the goodness within, and I usually know who I can trust and who I can't, white or black. We all understand these things better now. But if any people today want to really understand African Americans, they should know how important the issue of trust is and how difficult broken trust is to overcome.

5

Put Your Trust in God

CHURCH WAS THE ONLY PLACE we could go that was not controlled by white people, and it completed our needs in every part of our lives. The church was our anchor. It held us together. It kept us going. At a time when opportunities for entertainment were limited, the church was our main leisure-time activity. That's where we learned cooperation and leadership. Our church was a house of worship, community center, and country club. I cannot imagine my life without the church.

Nearly everybody on the plantation and in West Helena went to church; as a matter of fact, we didn't have anywhere else to go. We got to see all our friends there and catch up on the news. We were always at church, not just on Sundays. There was something going on just about every day. I would either be attending a program or practicing for one; if I wasn't at my own church, I would be at another one. I come from a churchgoing family in a churchgoing area. We were Baptists—Missionary Baptists, the oldest and largest of the black Baptist churches. In Lula we went to Bethlehem Church. In West Helena, we went to First Baptist Church, M.B. The Reverend J. L. Jerks was our pastor, and he baptized me. In Memphis, I went with Aunt Rosetta to her church. I think I went to church more than the preacher did.

The preacher wasn't there every Sunday, because preachers always preached at more than one church—and still do in small rural communities. They had to, I guess, to make any kind of living. At Lula, the preacher didn't come but once a month, but in West Helena Reverend Jerks came on the first and third Sundays. The rest of the time, church members, young and old, organized and carried out the activities of the church.

The Sunday the preacher came was known as "Pastoral Sunday," and it was an all-day happening. Sunday school was held at nine-thirty, and the main service started at eleven o'clock. At around two on Sunday afternoon, we always had a "program"—a special service put on by a group of church members. It might be a deacon's program, the pastor's anniversary, or a children's program, or the choir would have special singing. Then around six o'clock the young people went to "training union." But nothing was ever on time! The official starting time was only a rough approximation of when a service would begin. We'd just as likely start church at eleven-thirty as eleven, and sometimes we ran right on into the two o'clock program.

The two o'clock programs were mostly for entertainment—as much for the people participating in them as for those in the audience—but of course there was always some preaching and plenty of praying, too. No matter which church group was presenting the program, they always did it with dramatic flourish. For example, when we had the Ushers' Program, men and women ushers would come from all the other churches in the area, and they would all march in together at the beginning of the program. One of the deacons with a booming voice announced each church group as they entered: New Jerusalem, Moon Lake, Mt. Moriah, St. Peter's, Strangers' Home, Bethlehem, Mt. Zion. The women ushers wore white dresses and white caps and white gloves. The men ushers wore black suits with a white shirt and white gloves. Parading into the church, they were a wonderful sight to behold.

For regular church services, then as now, the Mothers of the Church—these were the oldest, most respected women who had been very active in the church for a long time—sat up front on one side, the deacons on the other. The preacher and the choir were up at the front, too, of course. The ushers stood along the walls at the side and back of the room until the preacher announced the text of his sermon; then they sat down.

The service always began with the singing of a "Dr. Watts" hymn. A "Dr. Watts" was one of the old hymns—the lining-out or call-and-response songs, dating back to slavery times and sung without any accompaniment. One of the deacons or Mothers of the Church would usually start a song, such as this:

> *Before this time another year,*
> *I may be dead and gone.*

Then the congregation sang the same line, more or less, but very, very slowly with as many different notes as we could possibly squeeze out of each syllable, creating a kind of musical moaning. I've never heard any other singing like it. We followed the same procedure, line by line, through the whole song.

> *I'll let you know before I go*
> *What will become of me.*

Another one of my favorite Dr. Watts hymns:

> *I love the Lord;*
> *He heard my cries*
> *and pitied every groan,*
> *Long as I live, where trouble lies,*
> *I'll hasten to his throne.*

We sang other hymns, too, with a piano accompaniment, like "Amazing Grace" and "Precious Lord."

We had many great singers in my family. Birt sang in the church choir until shortly before she died. Augusta and I used to sing duets. The first duet we sang was at Bethlehem Church when I was four years old; Augusta was eight. I wish I could remember what we sang. My sister continued her singing in church longer than I did as an adult. She was married to a well-known preacher and singer, the Reverend P. L.

Perkins, who preached in a big church in Helena for many years; before that he had been the manager and a singer for the well-known Blind Boys Quartet.

Most of the civil rights songs that I sang in the 1960s were the same ones I sang in church as a child or songs adapted from them, like "Swing Low, Sweet Chariot, Coming For to Carry Me Home" and "We Shall Overcome." The civil rights movement was about the same kinds of things that you learned and sang about in church—freedom, deliverance, how we were going to "get over," and having faith in God and ourselves that we would make it. The movement simply took these spiritual themes and put them to an earthly purpose. From that day through the civil rights movement right up to now, singing has gotten me "over" many times.

At church, just as at home, I was taught that God loves me, that He loves all people, that He loves black people just as much as he loves white people. Preachers and Sunday school teachers said we don't understand why God made people in different colors. He made flowers of many colors, and He gave people's skin different shades, too. We were like God's flowers, they said. God loves all the different colored flowers the same, and he loves the different colored people the same, too. After all, they said, everybody's the same color on the inside; everybody's blood is red. This message uplifted and soothed me as a child. I took it to heart, and I believed it, but I never quite understood why God didn't clarify this point for the white folks.

The church taught me that Jesus took in outcasts—those people society did not accept as being the best people, like the prostitute at the well. I understood that. We were outcasts in a white world. So what we did was pray for God to give us deliverance from the Old Master, and the Old Master was called by name from the pulpit and the floor. Old Master was the boss man and he was white and he had the power and he was in control of what we did. We believed that God would bring us out from under the Master—just as he did the children of Israel. I always took this to mean in this life, not the afterlife.

The church taught us how we were supposed to treat other people. We followed the Ten Commandments, of course: "Honor thy father and mother" and "Thou shalt not steal" and "Thou shalt not kill" and all the rest. There's no commandment about forgiveness; so the preachers always had a stock of Bible verses about forgiveness! For instance, the preacher would say, "If your enemy slaps you on this cheek, then you turn the other cheek." Now, privately, I thought that was ridiculous—I took it literally—but it was not OK to question the preacher, so I kept my mouth shut. But I said to myself, if somebody slaps me, I'm going to slap that person back. Why should I get all the pain for somebody else's mistake?

The main message I got out of church was the Golden Rule: "Do unto others as you would have them do unto you." The church taught me not to hate people because of the color of their skin. When white people did something hurtful to one of us—didn't pay the amount they promised or kicked somebody off the place on false pretenses—the preacher would likely quote Jesus: "They know not what they do." "That don't mean that the white folks is right," he said, "but you treat them right anyway, and God will bless you." I was taught that if I followed the Golden Rule, good would come back to me. And if I wanted to do good in life for myself, I must also want that for other people. And the reverse was true, too: If I set your house on fire and I lived next door to you, mine would burn down, too.

While one group of people was trying to keep us down, the church was saying, "God is going to bring you through." I've puzzled a lot over what the white people were hearing at their churches. I knew they read the same Bible we did. But it seemed to me that their Golden Rule must have said, "Do unto everybody but black people as you would have them do unto you." Anybody knows they didn't want us to treat them the way they treated us! It was white people in white churches who controlled everything: the political process that kept us out, the social structure that kept us out of the way, and the economic system that kept us down. I've tried and tried to figure out how Christian white people justified these things with the teachings of Jesus in the Bible. In our church we learned that belief in God and the lessons in the Bible connect directly to the way you're supposed to live. The church I know is about loving all people and treating them right. The white churches must have taught them that if they just showed up at church and believed in God, that's all that mattered. Did they actually teach that God and Christ cared about white people only? I don't know. This much I do know: Without my church and my faith that God would pull me through, I don't think I could have survived those days or been prepared to face the future. When I was trying to find my way, the church gave me hope and inspiration.

6

You Can Make a Difference

I'M PROUD OF MY RICH DARK COLORING now, but coming up it was a source of hurt and shame for me. In addition to having to deal with the discrimination of white people, I also had to face the snubs of lighter-skinned black people who thought they were better than I was. Sometimes another child would call me "blue-black," and I'd be so hurt, but Birt would hug me and say, "Don't worry, baby. The blacker the berry, the sweeter the juice."

But I didn't fully believe her. We had not yet heard that "black is beautiful." The saying among blacks I knew was, "If you light, you is all right; if you brown, stick around; but if you black, stand way back!" Hair was the same way. People with kinky hair were not considered as desirable as those with softer and straighter hair like white people have. At school the color of your skin was a big issue, and I attended all-black schools with black teachers. Light-skinned students were thought to be smarter by the teachers, most of whom were light-skinned themselves. The lighter children with "good hair" were the ones teachers usually asked to take part in school programs and class activities. I used to say, "Child, she light, bright, and damned near white, so you know the teacher will call on her." The teacher would usually put the darker kids in the back of the room. So it was hard for a dark-skinned child to get ahead in school.

But I looked up to all my teachers as being knowledgeable and important and had several I liked. One took a special interest in me.

Mrs. Franklin was her name. She was thin and light-skinned, a strict disciplinarian but also a very kind person, and she taught me in the sixth grade. She taught me to pronounce words clearly and to have confidence when speaking in front of groups. Although Mother and Aunt Big-A and Big Mama had encouraged me to make speeches in church, this was different. Mrs. Franklin was my teacher, and she had picked me out of the whole class. Every time we had a school assembly—a plenary, we called it—she'd ask me to make the speech for my class. I would go up to the stage and stand straight with my hands clasped in front of me and give my little speech. My speeches always ended with the same words, which Mrs. Franklin had written for me. I can't remember all the words, but I'll never forget the last three: "Smile. Smile. Smile." As I said the first "smile," I turned my head to the left; the second one, to the right; and for the last "smile," I looked straight ahead, smiled, and then bowed as I had been instructed. The other children and the teachers, too, would laugh and clap every time I did it. It was my first experience with entertaining a large group. I loved it.

One afternoon Mrs. Franklin asked me to come to her room after school. When I got there, she had several books out on her desk. I sat down, and she said she had something very important to talk to me about. She told me I was smart and spoke well and I had the ability to make something of myself—to find work beyond the cotton field and do well, accomplish something.

"You can be Somebody," she said, "but U. Z. is no name for a person who wants to make a name for herself. You need a real name, not just initials."

That was fine with me, so we started looking in her books for names that began with U and Z. We chose Zelma for the Z. Finding a name beginning with U was more difficult. Mrs. Franklin had a book about Spanish people, and in that book we found the name Unita. She was so excited.

"Unita—that's it!"

She pronounced every syllable clearly: "Yew-nee-ta." I especially liked the sound of it. I practiced saying it. To make the U sound, I had to pucker my lips like I was about to kiss someone, and then I spread my mouth wide in a smile to say "nee ta." It's almost impossible to say

"Unita" without smiling. I wrote "Unita" in longhand several times with big loopy *U*'s.

I loved my new name—the way it sounded, the way it looked, and the way I felt when I said it. Everything about Unita seemed exotic. And it was mine alone; I had never known anyone else named Unita. To be twelve years old and get a special new name was thrilling. Instantly I felt special inside. I did not know the word "unique" then, but I knew what it felt like.

I reported this event to my mother when I got home. "Birt, I've got a new name! Mrs. Franklin gave me a new name."

"Oh, and what is it?"

"Unita!"

"Uh, huh. That's nice, baby," she said in that slightly disinterested way mothers have that told me I would always be U. Z. to her.

But to almost everyone else, since that day, I've been Unita.

Westside, the school for black children in West Helena, only went to the eighth grade. That's as high as most black children went in those days. To go to high school, you had to be able to provide your own ride or pay someone to take you to Eliza Miller High School in Helena, which went to the tenth grade. It was only five miles away, but we did not have a car or the money to pay for a ride. I was used to walking everywhere, but walking to and from school would have taken at least an hour and a half twice a day. It seems strange now, when young people move around so easily, that I could not get to a school five miles away.

My family was the poorest of the poor. It was 1947. My mother had gotten a good job working at Chicago Mills during World War II, going to work at 5:45 in the evening and getting off at 4:15 in the morning. But when the war was over, the men came back and took the jobs, and Birt went back to work as a domestic, cleaning house for white people as she had done before the war. She also hired out to work in the cotton fields around West Helena in the spring and summer, if she didn't have domestic jobs. I'd been working in the fields in Arkansas every summer since Big Mama moved from Lula, making what little money I could to contribute to our family's income.

I didn't have anyone pushing me to go further in school. My family believed in education, and they made sure I learned to read, write, and do arithmetic, and now I could do those things very well. They knew how much I loved to read—they saw me reading all the time. To them I was an educated person. Although they were wonderful in so many ways, nobody in my family had gone to school very much. They were field laborers, and their lives were all about work, not school. Plantation schools, which were controlled by the cotton season, were out of session more than they were in session. My grandmother, Aunt Big-A, and my mother all learned to read as adults. Considering how little schooling they had had, my finishing the eighth grade was a big achievement, like finishing high school—or maybe even college—today.

We grew up fast in those times. And I was ready to be grown and out on my own. Maybe this was my way of fulfilling Mrs. Franklin's challenge to be Somebody. But, like many teenagers, I was really all mixed up. I wanted to be Somebody but had no idea what to do with myself. I didn't really know what Somebody did. I was fourteen when I completed the eighth grade, and I had a boyfriend, A. D., who was sixteen. He wanted me to marry him, but our families said we were too young to marry, and he moved away to Chicago. I was upset for a while, but not being able to get married didn't bother me as much as wanting more freedom to go and do as I pleased. The truth is: There was nothing for me to do in West Helena. We had a saying, "Times are so hard it makes a monkey eat red pepper, when he only cares for black." So, for the next few years, until I got together with Jeremiah Blackwell, I had to be content with kicking up my heels around West Helena and sometimes in Memphis, too.

I visited my daddy in Memphis fairly often. I usually stayed with Aunt Rosetta, and I picked up little odd jobs while I was there. Since Aunt Rosetta worked in a laundry, she could always find some work for me to do. And in the evening I went down to Beale Street. It was five or six blocks from Wellington Street, where my Memphis family lived, and I'd walk down there with a group of friends or a date. Beale Street was The Place for black folks then, not the tourist area it is now. It was ours. Blacks—and only blacks—crowded onto its sidewalks all day and all night. There were colorful signs and blinking lights. Beale

Street was a happy, lively place, and a little bit sinful. I felt daring and grown-up on Beale Street.

Blues filled the dark little clubs and spilled into the night air. This was the music I had grown up with, but on Beale Street even the blues were "uptown"—somehow fancier than the blues I knew in Mississippi and Arkansas. I loved going down to amateur night at the Palace Theater so I could hear B. B. King, when he first started out. He was thin and handsome, and he would close his eyes and sway while he played his guitar, "Lucille," and all the girls really carried on over him. I see B. B. every now and then when he comes to Mississippi, and we always laugh about the Beale Street days. B. B. can still charm the ladies!

I loved visiting Memphis, but I spent most of the time in Arkansas. I continued living with my mother for a while in West Helena; Augusta was living there, too. We both worked for white people in their houses during the day, and at night Augusta and I went out to the cafés to dance and drink and listen to music and talk. The black café was and still is the pulse of the southern black experience. Sometimes a café might be called a juke joint, a juke house, or a club. But they were all cafés, and they were all pretty much the same. They weren't very big, just one room usually—a hole-in-the-wall somewhere, with home-made tables and mismatched chairs, booths, and probably a counter with stools. There was nothing fancy about them. And they were open day and night. You could get greens and black-eyed peas and neck bones and rib tips and sweet potatoes and sweet iced tea at any time of day. They sold beer, and you could sneak in "hot whiskey"—white lightning—or half pints of "seal whiskey," which was the store-bought kind.

There was always music at a café. Sometimes it would be one person playing a guitar and singing. I remember hearing Houston Stackhouse a good bit. Stackhouse played on KFFA radio in Helena, along with Robert Nighthawk, Tommy Johnson, Sonny Boy Williamson, Pinetop Perkins, Muddy Waters, and a bunch of others. I remember seeing all of them. Helena was a blues center. Other times, on the weekend, there'd be somebody on drums, a piano player, and a saxo-phonist. And there was usually a jukebox, too. I remember the first time I ever saw a jukebox. It was at Miss Berta's café. I was about twelve years old, and my friend Alberta Willhite and I had slipped out of church and walked over to Miss Berta's to dance. Her café had a big side room where people danced. And the day we skipped church, I went into the side room and there it was: the jukebox, rounded on the top, glowing red and yellow and music coming out of it. I saw those big 78-rpm records stacked up, and when I put a nickel in, the record would move out of the stack and drop, the arm would go across, and I could see the needle touch the record. I don't think I'd ever even seen an automatic record player at the time! We had a radio and I'd seen Victrolas, but nobody I knew had a record player, and I was spellbound by this wonder.

We used to listen to big band music on the jukebox—Tommy Dorsey and Glenn Miller and Count Basie—and other mainstream American popular music of the late forties and early fifties—Nat King Cole, Frank Sinatra. (It wasn't like today when jukeboxes in black cafés feature only black musicians—from blues, rhythm and blues, soul, right on up to hip-hop.) And we'd dance—swing dance, jitterbug, or slow drag. Lord, I loved to dance. I still love to dance. When I was raised, Christian girls were not supposed to drink, dance, or smoke. But my mother and grandmother, as religious as they were, danced. They did not ever take a drink, though.

My sister and I liked to drink beer, and we wanted to go out with boys and stay out late. So, after a time, Augusta and I rented an apartment together downtown in Helena, not too far from the Mississippi River, and for a few years, we were party girls, out there enjoying life. But we wouldn't have dared bring our boyfriends back, even to our own place.

Working, partying, and going to church—that was my whole life. No matter how hard I partied on Saturday night, I always went to church on Sunday morning and sang in the choir. I was having fun and working hard, but I was just drifting along. I was just trying to grow up, I guess—still wanting to be Somebody but still not knowing how.

Looking back, I see that I was learning how to be Somebody even though I wasn't moving forward. I was meeting people, making new friends, seeing another side of life, finding out how people lived when they let their hair down. Being out from under the protective cloak of my family telling me what to do gave me a chance to learn things about myself I didn't know, too. But I wasn't pondering my identity; I was living it—standing on my own two feet and enjoying life.

I look at young people today who are scuffling trying to make it and don't know what they are going to do with themselves and what they are going to do with their lives. They are just living from one day to the next. But I have hope for them, because I was a person just like that. I say to them, as Mrs. Franklin said to me, "You can make something of yourself. You can be Somebody."

I met Jeremiah Blackwell when I was in my early twenties. I was sitting in a little café with my sister and some friends, and he came in with another fellow. They came over and talked to us. I thought he was nice looking and great fun, and he was buying the beer! He worked for the U.S. Army Corps of Engineers as a cook on a boat that went up and down the Mississippi River, and that in itself made him different from any other man I had known.

I had never known anyone like Jeremiah. He was very talkative, a man I could talk to about many subjects. He had his own opinions and he was outspoken and he did not care whether anyone agreed with him or not. In fact, he preferred for you not to agree. Jeremiah always loved to argue and cuss, but then he'd laugh. (This would get to be a problem later on.) Working on the riverboats had let him get around and talk to lots of different people, and he seemed to have confidence in himself. He was a very freethinking man. And he was free himself. That's what appealed to me the most about him in the beginning.

He was on the river for about four months of the year, and he would come to West Helena to see me when he wasn't working on the boat. We started going out, staying out late partying, and having fun. He was not the jealous, controlling type, and he was very progressive in his attitude toward women. He believed in a woman's right to be her own person, and he never tried to restrict me from doing whatever I wanted to. He would say, "You are a grown woman. You have a mind, and you are in charge of your own body." This attitude was very unusual among black men—among all men—then and now.

He'd bought an old red and white bread wagon that we drove

around in. It had only two seats, which were up front; behind those seats was open space. When somebody else wanted a ride, Jeremiah would say, "If you want to ride with us, bring your own damn chair." One day, after we had been going out together for a couple of years, we climbed into the bread wagon, took the ferry to Clarksdale, and got married—without any planning whatsoever. A justice of the peace married us at the courthouse. Jeremiah bought a bottle of whiskey, and we came right on back to my apartment in Helena and celebrated. (My sister had married and moved out by then.) Soon we rented a long shotgun house in Helena.

Jeremiah is a light-skinned black man. He has all the features of a white person—his hair, his cheekbones, and the flatness of his body. You look at Jeremiah, and, if you do not know him, you might think he's white. He made sure, however, that everyone knew he was black. Once we went into an appliance store in Helena together, and I was looking at the televisions. Jeremiah was standing over to the side. The salesman walked right by me and went up to Jeremiah and asked if he could help him. Jeremiah knew he had come to him thinking he was white, and he said, no, he was not interested in buying anything. "But my wife is right over there, and she is thinking about buying a television." The man just looked at him and then walked over to me. But, after that, I wasn't thinking about buying anything from him.

Jeremiah grew up in Mayersville. His family, unlike mine, had owned a little land in the Mayersville area, bought after the Civil War. His family had been politically active during Reconstruction. One of his grandfather's brothers was in the state legislature; another was a judge. Over the years they lost most of the land—they couldn't pay the taxes, and white farmers bought the land from the county for the taxes, as often happened to newly freed black people.

Jeremiah never knew his father or his mother. His father was believed to be a white man in the community. Nobody talked about it out in public, but in Mayersville, like all small communities, one person's heavily guarded secrets are usually common knowledge to everybody else. He was a twin, and his mother had given birth to him and his brother in the back of a drugstore in Greenville. Because Jeremiah was a sickly baby, he was brought back to his grandmother, his mother's mother. His own mother never came back home to Mayersville—

maybe out of shame or because Jeremiah's white father told her not to; no one knows why. Jeremiah never knew what happened to his twin brother, but some people said his mother had given him away. Many years later, when I was researching the title to some Blackwell property we wanted to build a house on, I found out that Jeremiah's mother had died in Arkansas and was buried in a potter's field. We found the twin's birth certificate, but we could not locate him, so he was presumed dead.

Stories like the tale of Jeremiah's mother were not uncommon in those days. A black woman had no say-so over her own body. If a white man wanted a black woman, he had her, even if she was married or had a boyfriend. Since Jeremiah was so adamant in his belief in my rights as a person, I can't help but think that his attitude was the result of what had happened to his mother, who did not own her own body. (Today, we have strong black women who are not afraid to stand up to whites, and they don't need a man to help them. A white man—a married man with a couple of daughters—approached one of my good friends. My friend had sons. When he started carrying on about having sex with her, she had the perfect answer: "When you let your daughters date my sons, I'll take you up on your offer." She didn't have any more trouble out of that white man.)

Jeremiah was brought up by his grandmother. Vashti could read and write well, and at one time she had taught school in a little country Rosenwald School[1] out from Mayersville. I knew Miss Vashti. She was soft-spoken and very determined. The first time we went down to Mayersville to see her, she wanted us to help her get her welfare check. She said Mrs. Shipp at the welfare department told her that she no longer qualified to receive a check because Jeremiah was sending her money. Sometimes Jeremiah had sent her a few dollars in the mail— five or ten dollars every now and then—and the welfare department had found out about it. But I did not believe that was enough to keep her from getting her welfare check. I also figured that the only way the wel-

---

1. In 1913, millionaire Julius Rosenwald teamed with Booker T. Washington to fund the construction of more than five thousand schools for blacks in the South.

fare people could know about the money was that someone at the post office was opening her mail. Mayersville is a very small place. The whole system in the South was set up to make sure that blacks did not have money, because money would give us a sense of security and freedom.

So I went down there with Jeremiah to check into things. And I talked directly to Mrs. Shipp. I told her that Miss Vashti did not get any money to speak of from Jeremiah.

"He just can take care of himself," I said.

"Well," she said, "we know that he has been sending her some money."

"Ma'am," I said, "I do not know how you could know that unless someone is opening her mail."

I was polite and nice about it, but I didn't want anybody to take advantage of Jeremiah's old grandmother. I told Mrs. Shipp I thought that opening someone else's mail was a federal offense. White folks in the late 1950s were not used to blacks questioning what they said. I loved to read, and I knew from reading the newspaper that mail tampering was against the law. I said I would go over to the post office and see what was going on.

"We know what we are doing," she said, in a controlled, cold voice.

I walked straight over to the post office and confronted the postmaster. He denied opening the mail, but, I'll tell you this much: Miss Vashti didn't have any more problems out of the welfare department after that.

Miss Vashti was happy about getting her welfare check, and I was pretty pleased, myself, that I'd been successful. I think this was the first time I had ever stood up to a white person to get what rightfully belonged to another black person. Just barefootin' along, I had taken charge of something. And I had made a difference. One black woman had changed the way one thing was done in the Mississippi Delta. If that could happen at that time and place, I knew it was possible for one person to make a difference anywhere, anytime.

My only child, Jeremiah Blackwell Jr., was born July 2, 1957, in the Helena hospital. We called him Jerry. No daddy has ever been prouder of a son than Jeremiah was. My husband put himself in charge of his baby, and he made sure everybody else knew it. I remember when we got home from the hospital, Birt came right over to see about the baby and me, and Jeremiah tied a white hospital mask on her face. She was indignant at the very idea of being told what to do by any man when it came to handling babies. "I know about babies!" she snapped, and she jerked that mask off and threw it on the floor. Jeremiah wouldn't let a diaper stay wet a second before he put a new one on. He boiled water and scalded the diapers and put them through three rinse waters. I'll admit he was very helpful to me, but his constant baby-tending and detailed instructions could be worrisome, especially to my mother and sister, who also wanted to take care of the baby. They were sure glad when he left in the fall to go back to work on the boat.

While he was working on the river that winter, I became very sick. Jerry was six months old. I started hemorrhaging profusely, and Augusta took me to the hospital. I was lucky to be living in Helena, Arkansas, so I could get in a hospital close by. The Helena hospital took in black and white people. In the Mississippi Delta, the only hospital that would have taken a black person was about fifty miles away in the all-black town of Mound Bayou, Mississippi.

My doctor, Dr. Kirkman, said I needed a blood transfusion. I don't think they had blood banks the way they do today, so Augusta somehow got in touch with Jeremiah, and he and a friend of his came immediately to the hospital and gave blood for me. But the doctor and nurses could not seem to get the hemorrhaging to stop. I was very, very sick, and the doctor was afraid I might not make it.

One day my mother was sitting in the room with me. I remember going in and out of awareness, and then I heard her scream, "My child is dying." After that I faintly heard her say, "My child is dead." I didn't hear anything more.

And then I could feel myself moving into this other universe. I was enveloped by the bluest sky I'd ever seen and surrounded by wispy clouds and little fine sparkles of dazzling light shooting out in all directions. I moved like I was being carried on a cloud, and I was transported deeper and deeper into this glorious, light-filled space. It was like a Shekinah Glory—a spectacular light that is the visible presence of God.

I don't know any words strong enough to describe the feelings of tranquillity and peace and joy I experienced. It seemed like a long time that I was swept up in this celestial world. Then, all of a sudden, I was stopped. Something indefinable and unknown, like whatever had moved me onward, was now pulling me back. My spirit wanted to keep on going, but it couldn't. As I struggled to overcome the barrier, I heard a voice coming out of the clouds. The voice was not male or female, and I did not see anyone speaking. I didn't see any image other than the clouds and light all around me.

The voice said, "Not yet. You have work to do."

The words were as clear and firm as any I have ever heard.

When I came to myself and opened my eyes, I was in a dim, murky place. Gradually I began to make out the features of my hospital room—the window with filtered light, the mirror over the lavatory. When I tried to bring one hand to my eyes, I realized that my head—my whole body—was covered in a sheet. I pulled it down and looked around the room. No one else was there. I didn't know how long it had been since I'd heard my mother scream. The door to the hall was closed, and I didn't see any of my personal things around. Where was everyone? What had they done to my room? Was I dead or alive? I had to find out. I kept a little Bible under my pillow, and I turned over on my side a little so I could slide my hand underneath the pillow. As I moved my hand under the cool folds, I felt the stiff, bumpy edge on my little Bible. I pulled it out and put it on my chest.

In a little while, I heard the door open, and I looked to see that it was a nurse. I was lying straight out with the Bible, and she came over to my bed and got down close to my face and looked right into my eyes. I must have blinked or moved my eyes.

"You's alive!" she screamed. "What happened to you?"

I did not speak—I guess I couldn't or maybe I didn't know I could—but I reached down and picked up the little Bible, and I looked at it and held it up for her to see. I think I was trying to tell her that God had brought me back to life. She gazed down at me, and her face was so twisted and wrinkled out of shape I wasn't sure what she might do, but then she ran out of the room screaming, "I've got to get the doctor." I heard her shrieking as she ran down the hall, "Dr. Kirkman! Doctor! Doctor! Doctor!"

Very soon Dr. Kirkman came into my room, and he stood at the foot of my bed, looking at me for a long minute. "Unita?" he said.

I don't know whether I answered him, but I know I gave him a smile. "My God!" he whispered. "My God!"

The doctor called in people from all over the hospital to see me. They surrounded my bed and looked at me in wonder and disbelief. "You are looking at a miracle," he said. He had been the one who checked my vital signs and pronounced me dead. From that time on, Dr. Kirkman called me a miracle. He loved me till the day he died, and he always told others, "This woman knows God."

The message I received was clear and firm: "Not yet. You have work to do." It was not a suggestion or a question, but it wasn't an order, either. It was a simple statement of fact. My life had a purpose—something larger than myself—and I had to discover it. To me it was a summons, a charge to keep.

I didn't go out looking for the work I was supposed to do because I didn't have any idea what I was looking for. But from that day in 1957 on, the voice and the words "Not yet. You have work to do" have been just as plain in my head as they were then. Somehow I believed that if an unexpected voice could bring me back from the dead, something as powerful and unexpected would come along to show me what work I was supposed to do. I was right, but I did not discover my work through a heavenly voice or a brilliant flash of glory. And I didn't find it out right away. My life's work unfolded slowly.

We stayed on in Helena a couple of years more after my illness, keeping on as we had before. I'd pick up whatever work I could, as a domestic and as a short-order cook. Jeremiah was still working on the boat for the Corps of Engineers, and the rest of the time he found odd jobs—cooking at the country club, picking cotton. We'd get out on the weekends and go to the little cafés.

When Miss Vashti died, her house in Mayersville passed to Jeremiah. It was a small shotgun house about like the one we rented in Helena, but we could live in it and not have to pay rent. Mayersville is right on the Mississippi River, too, like Helena, so Jeremiah could just as easily get on the boat to work from there. We both figured we could pick up odd jobs in Mayersville just as well as in Helena. Maybe we wouldn't have to work as hard, and I'd get to spend more time with my little boy. So, a few months after Miss Vashti's death, in 1960, Jeremiah and I loaded up all our belongings in the bread wagon and my slick-back Olds, crossed over to the Mississippi side of the river, and headed down Highway 1, the old River Road, to Mayersville.

It turned out to be harder than I thought to live in Mayersville. Even though I'd grown up in the Mississippi Delta, I didn't understand the people there—the black people—and they didn't understand me. I was not from there. I was an outsider, and I didn't fit the norm there. Everybody there knew each other; they'd grown up together. Many of them were related to each other and had relatives all around them. I wasn't kin to anybody, except to my husband and my child, and I had been used to living in larger towns, Helena and West Helena and Memphis, where people went places—where, to begin with, there were more places to go, little clubs and lots of cafés, even movie theaters. Mayersville was very isolated, with only one small café where blacks could socialize. In Mayersville the women weren't allowed by their husbands to go out much. If they did go out, they went with their husbands.

And another thing: I could drive a car. The women in Mayersville did not drive. Not many black folks even had cars. When I moved to Mayersville, I went anywhere I wanted to, the way I always had, and Jeremiah didn't jump on me and make a fuss about it. He'd say, "You go on; I'll keep the baby." So, I went. I'd go down to the one little café in Mayersville or get in my car and drive forty-five miles up to Greenville. Something was always happening there on Nelson Street, *the* place for Delta blacks to dance and drink and have a good time—a jumping street lined with cafés and clubs, like the Flowing Fountain, that stayed open late and packed people in for live entertainment. The only person who'd go with me was my friend Coreen. She didn't have a husband.

I don't think the men in that little town in those days ever did accept my sense of freedom. They said my husband was crazy because he let me go anywhere I wanted to go. I guess they thought I was a bad influence on their women. The hometown Mayersville ladies were considered nice because they stayed at home and fastened the door.

And I drank beer in public. The other women drank, too, but they were locked up in their houses drinking home brew. Outside of work—which meant working in the fields, except for a few of the women who cooked and cleaned white people's houses—there wasn't much else to do in Mayersville but drink. And I did some drinking in those days. I did too much drinking, in fact. Sometimes I'd have to eat garlic on Sunday morning before I went to church so folks couldn't smell the liquor on my breath. I became about the only black woman drinking and going places that the town had ever seen who wasn't a slut.

When Jeremiah wasn't working as a cook on the boat, we were chopping and picking cotton on the Wilkerson Place. Mr. Wilkerson told Jeremiah and me to take over one big field, because we really worked hard and cleaned his field good, whether we were chopping or picking. I never understood why some people would do all that work chopping the weeds and not make the field look clean and neat. He paid us by the day. We made three dollars a day for chopping cotton, and we picked cotton for two dollars a hundred (pounds). I could pick three hundred pounds of cotton in a day as a grown woman. Six dollars a day—that was good money in 1960.

The only thing I could do in Mayersville, other than go to the field and church and drink a little beer, was to join the Home Demonstration Club. A bunch of us would gather in a little building behind the courthouse, and a refined young black lady would talk to us about cooking and cleaning and decorating our houses. Never mind that we were all living in shacks. She had us making jewelry boxes with fifty cents' worth of cloth, some macaroni, and a cigar box. I stuck the cloth down in the cigar box and glued it to the bottom and sides, and then I began gluing the macaroni on the outside to decorate it. That became very boring right quick.

I was sitting there gluing macaroni on my cigar box, and I got to thinking, "What am I doing buying macaroni to make a jewelry box, when I don't even have macaroni to eat and I don't have any jewelry to go in my jewelry box?" So I got up my macaroni and went home and cooked it. That was my last time at the Home Demonstration Club.

We heard people talking about how you could make a whole lot of money picking tomatoes in Florida, and Jeremiah and I jumped at that chance. Since the tomato-picking months were February through

April, we could go down after Jeremiah got back home from the boat and work for two or three months and then come back in time to work in the cotton fields. We scratched up the money for the trip, and Jeremiah and I and the baby headed out in our old car for Immokalee, Florida, down in the southwestern part of the state. It took us four days to get there, and we slept in the car. You know black people couldn't just drive up to a motel and get a room then, and we couldn't have paid for it anyway, but you could pull off the road and sleep without worrying about being robbed or shot. We were so excited. We were going to be migrant workers and get rich!

When we got down there, things weren't much better than they were at home. We all stayed in one room, and we had to cook in it, too. We paid ten dollars a week for that room. The three of us slept in the same bed, and we cooked over an oil stove. For the first two or three weeks, we didn't eat anything but Irish potatoes because they were so cheap. And now I can cook Irish potatoes every kind of way.

The first day I went out to pick tomatoes, somebody mentioned that there were big black snakes out there in the fields. They said, "Be sure you watch out for snakes, but those snakes won't hurt you."

I said, "I don't fool around with snakes of any kind." I got out of there right then and went straight to a tomato canning factory and got a job peeling tomatoes. I never went back to the tomato fields again. I thought I was going to make a hundred dollars a week like some of the people who had been peeling tomatoes all their lives, but I couldn't peel fast enough. We did survive, though, and I came to like it pretty well down there.

We went down to Florida for two or three picking seasons in a row. Of course, we did not make all that money we were supposed to. Besides the work, there was a lot of partying, and people were having a good time. At the end of picking season in 1964, I told Jeremiah I was not going back to Mayersville. I was tired of Mayersville, and I didn't want to be bothered by folks who didn't understand me and didn't want to go anywhere. But he didn't want to stay in Florida—our expenses were more, he said, and we didn't end up any better off than we were in Mississippi, and we went around and around arguing about what we were going to do. Then one day Jeremiah slipped out and drove back to Mississippi without me—and he took Jerry with him!

That crushed me. Jeremiah knew how to get me home: taking my baby! So I caught a bus and went right on back to Mayersville, where my little boy was.

I was glad to be back with my little boy and Jeremiah, too, after I got over being mad at him for taking Jerry without telling me. Jerry would be six that summer, and he'd start first grade in the fall. So we began to settle back into our old routine.

But I was worried whether I could ever be satisfied living in Mayersville and working in the cotton field. I came home from Florida with a hopeless, helpless feeling about life. All we were doing was trying to survive, like we always had. Getting by, making do was what I'd been doing all my life, but I wanted something more. I felt isolated and lonely and useless. I thought about Mrs. Franklin's confidence in my ability and what I'd learned about myself helping Miss Vashti get her check. The voice I'd heard when I was dying became clearer and louder in my mind. I desperately needed some "work to do" that would relieve the emptiness inside, breathe life into me, and give me hope for the future. I couldn't imagine what it would be, and I had no idea how to get it.

"Lord, help me," I prayed. "I believe I'm cut out for something more than making macaroni jewelry boxes."

My message must have gotten through, because it wasn't long after I got back that my life turned around.

Part II

Breakin' Free

1964–1968

Be Ready to Step Out

Y OU NEVER KNOW WHAT TOMORROW'S going to bring. There's no way to predict what will be coming down the road. So you have to keep one eye cocked and be available and ready to step out when inspiration comes your way. You need to be open to the possibilities. That's the basic logic behind barefootin'. If I had stayed in Florida, I wouldn't have been here when the civil rights workers came to Mayersville in the summer of 1964.

Jeremiah and I had a brand-new television set that we'd bought with our tomato money. Only one or two other black families in town had a TV then. People would come by our house just like they were going to a picture show and sit on our porch and all around outside and peep through the windows and watch whatever was on. I began seeing on television that people from "up north"—college students and civil rights leaders—would be in our state that summer to help black people register to vote.

Civil rights activists had been coming to Mississippi for three or four summers, protesting the treatment of black people, but I had never seen any of them. The first big group came in buses in 1961; they called themselves "Freedom Riders." The white people called them "outside agitators," and the governor had them all arrested and thrown in jail. He put some of them in maximum security at Parchman, the state penitentiary. Other civil rights workers had come in

1962 and 1963—we called them "Freedom Riders," too. They went to the more populated central Delta towns—Greenwood, Indianola, Ruleville, Clarksdale—and to Jackson and Canton, and McComb, in the extreme southwestern part of the state. Mayersville is so isolated, even from other Delta towns, it didn't seem possible that Freedom Riders would ever find us.

In the early sixties, however, like most rural Mississippi black people, I was not involved with the civil rights movement that swirled around our state and region, even though I'd heard about it. It was Martin Luther King Jr. who first brought the message to me. My brother-in-law, Reverend Perkins, told me about him, and then I started reading about him and hearing him on the radio. By the time Martin Luther King Jr. made his "I Have a Dream" speech at the March on Washington in 1963, he was beginning to reach me and others in the black masses—those who were most fearful and dependent on white people. Martin Luther King was a preacher. We believed and respected preachers. And we had never seen a preacher standing up and talking out loud, eye to eye with white people about the injustices we suffered at their hands and why we should do something about it. Growing up, I had heard preachers using the scriptures to calm our fears and give us the strength to endure injustice and hardship and have faith that one day "things gon' get better." But Dr. King used the scriptures to tell us that God didn't want us to be cowards. He taught that the power of God is in us. If you believe in God, King preached, you can stand for right in the face of adversity. Martin Luther King inspired in me the daring to challenge white dominance. But my daring stayed bottled up inside me. I didn't yet know what to do with it.

As soon as we returned from Florida, we began hearing whispers around Mayersville that some Freedom Riders had gone to Henry Sias's house for a secret meeting. Mr. Sias was a black man in his eighties, a retired schoolteacher, who owned a little land that he farmed just south of Mayersville. Farming his own land made Mr. Sias an unusual black man to start with: He didn't have to work for a white man. He belonged to the NAACP—the only NAACP member in the entire county at the time—so the white people considered him a radical. I didn't even know what the NAACP was then. Black people looked up to Mr. Sias because he was an educator and because he didn't kowtow to white people: Mr. Sias even dared to carry a gun. But the black people in Mayersville didn't go down to the Sias house to find out what was going on because they could lose their jobs, their houses, or maybe their lives if their white employer or Klan types found out. But the rumors had aroused my curiosity, and I sure hoped they were true. Not long afterward, Mr. Sias spoke with Jeremiah and told him the civil rights workers were coming but not to let the word out. We knew how to keep a secret. Blacks are a secretive people; for years our people's lives had depended on keeping secrets.

The truth is, I'd never really thought much about voting or about registering to vote. In 1963, only 3 percent of voting-age black people were registered to vote in the entire state. A few brave black veterans of World War II—like Dr. Aaron Henry in Clarksdale, Amzie Moore in Cleveland, C. C. Bryant in McComb, Medgar Evers in Jackson—had quietly begun trying to get voters registered and suggested the possibility of change when they came back to the state after the war. Their efforts appealed primarily to the small black middle class— teachers, the few professional blacks, and small businessmen in the state. But the vast majority of Mississippi black people were just like me—poor and uneducated, and not aware of their activities. About the only time the subject of voting ever came up in my life in the Mississippi Delta was when I heard that somebody's boss made it clear to his workers that he would not allow "his niggers" to vote. This was one of those understood rules in Mississippi: Voting was for white people only. So ignorance and fear kept most of us right where we'd always been. I wasn't even sure, in fact, how voting was supposed to help me, but the more I heard about white people being so against it, the more I started thinking there must be something to this voting.

People who weren't in Mississippi in the 1950s and '60s may find it difficult to believe the frenzy of resistance that white people—officials in state government and private individuals—had worked themselves into after the U.S. Supreme Court ruled in the 1954 *Brown v. Board of Education* decision that segregated public schools were against the law. White farmers, business and professional men, and civic leaders in the state immediately formed the white Citizens' Council to fight school desegregation and maintain white supremacy. Before, they hadn't worried too much about keeping blacks "in their place," relying on that holdover slavery mentality, but when the federal government started "interfering" with their "way of life," the power structure went into high gear.

In 1956 the state formed the Mississippi State Sovereignty Commission "to protect the sovereignty of the state of Mississippi . . . from encroachment thereon by the Federal Government." The commission was essentially a state-supported spy agency charged with discovering and obstructing any person or group, black or white, who were suspected of favoring civil rights for black people. The state legislature tightened voter registration laws, did away with compulsory school attendance, and even ratified a constitutional amendment that allowed the legislature to abolish public schools rather than integrate them. Politicians attached the label "Communist" to anyone or anything that promoted equal rights for black people, and the state's newspapers and radio and television stations served as their mouthpieces. Billboards featuring an enormous photograph of Dr. King with the banner "Martin Luther King at a Communist Training Camp" sprang up across the state, the work of an unnamed white supremacy group. The "training camp" was, in fact, a civil rights seminar at the Highlander Folk School in Monteagle, Tennessee.

In 1955, the year after the *Brown* decision, Emmett Till, a fourteen-year-old black child visiting from Chicago, was murdered not far from where I was born. The white murderers tied a cotton gin fan to him and threw him in the Tallahatchie River, and an all-white jury quickly acquitted them.

In 1961 a white mob brutally beat a group of college students and professors attempting a sit-in to integrate the Woolworth's lunch counter in downtown Jackson. The police stood by and watched.

Violence broke out at Ole Miss in 1962 when the U.S. Court of Appeals for the Fifth Circuit ruled that a black man, James Meredith, had to be allowed to enroll. Two people were killed as hundreds of students battled U.S. marshals who were there to protect Mr. Meredith.

Even in Mayersville, we started hearing more and more about church bombings and murders and the Klan. In the summer of 1963 a gunman murdered Medgar Evers, the Jackson NAACP director, in his own driveway with his wife, Myrlie, and their three children watching. A white man from Greenwood named Byron De La Beckwith was charged with his murder. They tried him twice but there were hung juries both times, and Beckwith went back to Greenwood to live exactly as he had before. (Beckwith was finally convicted in 1994.)

By 1964 the die-hard segregationists had really dug in, and there was a resurgence of the Ku Klux Klan. Resistance softened slightly among a small number of moderate white Mississippians who'd been shocked by the Meredith riot and the Evers assassination. But few white people in Mississippi welcomed the civil rights workers who were coming into the state to carry out a massive voter registration project that summer. SNCC, CORE, and COFO were despicable sounds to the ears of most white people in the Mississippi Delta, identifying the worst of the worst: "outside agitators" from the Student Nonviolent Coordinating Committee, the Congress of Racial Equality, and the Council of Federated Organizations .

The welcome those young civil rights workers did receive was terrifying. Andrew Goodman, James Chaney, and Michael Schwerner were in the first group who came that summer, and others were still in Oxford, Ohio, getting their training. They arrived in Meridian, Mississippi, which was Chaney's hometown, late on June 20. The next afternoon, a sheriff's deputy arrested them forty miles away in Neshoba County, threw them in jail, and released them at ten-thirty that night. They never returned to Meridian. "Missing" was the official proclamation, but we all feared the worst. The worst had occurred, but we wouldn't know that for sure until August 4, when the three bodies were finally discovered, buried under fifteen feet of red clay in the backwoods of Neshoba County. The disappearance of and search for the three young men, the accompanying rumors, and the intense local and national news coverage created the backdrop for "Freedom Summer."

In late June, all the way across the state from Neshoba County, in Mayersville, life was going on pretty much like it always had. The cotton was waist high, and the temperature was in the nineties. The front porch was our only refuge from the heat. So late one Saturday afternoon, I was sitting on my front porch with my friend Coreen. We were drinking homemade beer, laughing and carrying on, and talking about nothing, just trying to keep our spirits up and not think about how hard we worked and how little we had to show for it. If I'd let myself dwell on the fact that I was getting older and going nowhere fast, I would've gone nuts. Anyway, it was Saturday, and I'd had to work only till noon chopping cotton. Coreen and I liked to sit out on the porch and see if anybody we knew was coming into town. Not too many black people had cars, so most people we saw would be walking. My house was on a narrow dirt side road fifty yards or so from Highway 1. The land is flat, and about all you could see in front and around the sides of the house for miles and miles around was cotton, row upon row of young cotton plants that were getting ready to bloom. So we had a good view of anybody walking up the highway.

We were looking down the highway into the haze that always hangs on the Delta horizon, and we saw two people walking way down the road, coming toward town. They were walking so fast, it didn't take them long to get up close enough for us to tell they were young black fellows. We had never seen anybody walk that fast in the summer in the Mississippi Delta.

"Coreen, those guys are walking mighty fast to be from around here. You think they might be some of those Freedom Riders that we been hearing them speak of?"

"Girl, they walking too fast," Coreen said. "That's got to be some of them."

They turned off the highway at my road and came on up toward my house. They were still walking fast. When they got up to my house, they slowed down just a little bit. They looked like they were around eighteen to twenty years old. I was pretty sure I had never seen them around here before.

"Hello," one of them said, in a friendly, polite way.

Then, in a strange accent, the other guy said, "Hel-loo."

I knew for sure then they weren't from around here. Anybody from Mississippi would have said, "How y'all feeling?" or something like that.

So we just said, "Hi," trying to be proper. And they kept right on fast-stepping into town.

"I sure would like to get a chance to meet those fellows," I said.

"Not me. I'm not about to get mixed up with them folks."

"Well, Coreen, I'd just like to hear what they have to say. They might be able to help us."

"They'll get you killed, Unita. You know if white folks around here find out you mixed up with Freedom Riders, you liable to be dead."

"I don't know what difference it would make," I said. "I'm dying anyway."

8

God Helps Those
Who Help Themselves

I DIDN'T HAVE TO WAIT LONG for a chance to meet the two young men who had walked by my house. The next day they came to my church, Moon Lake Missionary Baptist.

As on most every Sunday of my life, I went to Sunday school at nine-thirty. At that time I was teaching a children's class. We didn't have separate rooms for Sunday school; everything happened in the same room, where each class kind of bunched up together in a different section of the room. I had my little group in one corner in the back. During the middle of the lesson, I noticed those same two fellows coming in the front door. Even if I hadn't seen them before, they would have been easy to notice because they weren't dressed up for church. They were wearing blue jeans. This was the first time I had seen people come to church with blue jeans on. But I went right on talking to the kids about how they had to work hard and try to do right and make a good life for themselves. "God helps those that help themselves," I told them. That was my lesson that day. That's what I had been taught all my life, and if I didn't totally believe it, at least I wanted to think it was true.

This was Pastoral Sunday, so our preacher would be there for church. He came once a month from Lake Providence, Louisiana. When Sunday school was over, some people milled around, and others of us got seated to wait for the preacher to get there. I noticed that the two guys were waiting around, too. I kept watching them, and I could tell that one of them was watching me. So after a little bit, trying to be nice and being curious, I walked over and asked them if they wanted to say anything to our church members. Things were real informal, and church members took an active part. They responded that they would. By this time most people were seated.

The first young man to talk said he was from Brooklyn, New York, and his name was Louis Grant. Well, he got up and was talking so proper with his funny accent and throwing his hands around. We never had seen anybody do that. And we didn't understand one word he said. Then the other fellow stood up; he said his name was Bob Wright, and he was from Virginia. When he talked, he said words we could understand. He told us they would like to come back and have a meeting with the whole church congregation about how we could register to vote and how it would help us get a better life. "Just like that lady back there was telling the children," he said, "God helps those who help themselves." I thought, well, it seems like I did get across to somebody here in Sunday school this morning.

While they were talking, one of our church members, Deacon Johnny Barnes, was humming and moaning and singing, "Oh, Lord, um-hmm." He just kept going "Um-hmm, Lord. Um-hmm" straight through their whole talk.

When they finished, Barnes stood up and said, "Well, I have to tell y'all what the sheriff said. The sheriff said we couldn't have these outsiders coming in and talking at our church and riling up the people."

I wondered, now how could Johnny Barnes have talked to the sheriff about this, because the men just asked for the meeting this morning.

"Who said that?" I asked him.

And he said, "Sheriff Darnell did."

Then someone spoke up and told the young men that we'd have to ask the preacher when he got there about having a meeting.

I didn't say anything else. I had a strong suspicion that Barnes hadn't talked to the sheriff; he was just scared. So I slipped out of the church. I wanted to use a telephone, and I had to walk down the street to a little grocery store, because black people didn't have any phones then. The store belonged to the white folks, but a black man named Tony worked there. Tony said, OK, I could use the phone. He didn't have any idea I was fixing to call the sheriff. I got the sheriff on the phone.

"Mr. Darnell?"

He said, "Yes."

"Somebody in my church said you said we couldn't have meetings in our church." I told him that I didn't know that the sheriff was in charge of our church. He got so mad.

"Who told that lie? Who told you that?" He was angry with me. "Whoever told that lie—that's all right—I'm going to sue them and put them in jail for slandering me." Now, this was the first time in my life that I had heard you could put somebody in jail for telling a lie. That was a revelation to me.

"OK, well, I'm going to tell you who said it. Johnny Barnes said it; so you get him." That's what I told him.

And I went on back to church.

By the time I got back, the preacher had come, and we started the regular service. In a little bit, the preacher welcomed the two visitors and invited them to speak to the congregation. The Virginia guy, Bob, did all of the talking this time. I think they had figured out that we couldn't understand Louis. When he brought up the subject of a meeting, Mr. Barnes spoke up again and made his statement about the sheriff. This time I put my hand up and stood and asked if I could say a few words for the benefit of Mr. Barnes and all the other people there.

"I have talked to Sheriff Darnell," I said. Mr. Barnes started up again with his singing and um-hmming.

"And the sheriff told me that everwho said he said we couldn't have meetings in our church was a liar and he was going to put him in jail."

The church got real quiet. Then Mr. Barnes went, "Um-hum, oh, Lord," and there were a few smiles around.

The preacher spoke up and said the freedom workers were having meetings in the church over in Louisiana, and it would be all right to have a meeting here at Moon Lake. So one was set up for one night the following week—I think it was on Wednesday, right after our regular prayer meeting. They asked us to come and bring our friends and neighbors with us to learn how we could register to vote.

About twenty people showed up at Moon Lake Church for the meeting the following week. Bob and Louis explained that they were college students and were part of a large group of students from all across the country who were spending the summer in Mississippi to help black people get registered to vote. They explained how black people had just as much right to vote as white people and that it was written in the United States Constitution. They said if we could vote, we could elect people who would help us have a decent life—a better house, better living conditions, better schools. They said they were there to help us get registered. They explained the process and said they would go with us to the courthouse.

Then Louis asked, "Who will volunteer?"

The church got real quiet for a minute, and nobody moved at first. Then people started cutting their eyes and craning their necks to see what everybody else was doing. I saw people fidgeting and shifting in the pews.

Lord knows I wanted a better life. But I knew we'd be put out of work if we tried to register to vote—that's "the way things was." If we stepped out of our place, the white "boss man" would show us that he was still in control. We needed what little money we made working in the fields, but I had been worrying about money all my life. And I got to thinking about what I had told the Sunday school children: "God helps those that help themselves." I figured the time had come to put those words into practice myself. I was barefootin' into new territory, and I didn't know where the road would lead me, but I knew I'd never get anywhere if I didn't take the first step.

When I started to jump up and volunteer, my husband pulled on my dress and said, "Don't stand up till I stand up." He wasn't trying to restrain me or control me; he wanted to present a united front to the eyes of the other church members. I sat there a minute or two longer waiting for Jeremiah to stand up, and he wasn't getting up, so I just gave him a jigging in his side with my elbow. He got up, and I got up.

I've been standing up ever since.

Jeremiah and I went with the others to the courthouse the following week to register. That was when the white guys with guns surrounded us, and I made up my mind to put my life on the line for freedom. The next day Jeremiah and I went to the field to work, and soon Mr.

Wilkerson drove up in his truck. He called Jeremiah off to the side. He'd heard we'd taken up with those outsider agitators and gone to the courthouse to register to vote. Jeremiah told him that was true.

"Well, I don't want to see you and your wife around my cotton fields anymore."

And that was that. Jeremiah came and got me and we went home. That was the last time I ever worked in a cotton field.

Finding another job was out of the question. There wasn't a white man or woman anywhere around Mayersville who would have hired us or any other black person who tried to register to vote or associated with the civil rights workers. As we said, the Law of the Klan was the Law of the Land. Getting put out of work was just one more thing that made me understand how important the right to vote was. And I was more determined than ever to get it.

I went back to the courthouse the next day and the next until I finally got inside to register. Although I lived just a block away, it was the first time I'd ever been through the doors of the courthouse. I went in the side door to the circuit clerk's office. Mrs. Vandevender, the clerk, came up to the counter. I told her I had come to "redish." ("Redish" was southern blacks' word for "register.") She was totally expressionless. She told me to sit down at a little table, and she gave me a form and said to fill it out. I had never seen the registration form before, so I looked at it and took my time, and she stood there with a blank look, hanging over the banister while I filled it out. I had to give my full name and address and tell who I worked for. On down, it asked what oath I would take—general or minister's oath.

"Mrs. Vandevender, what oath you reckon I should take?" I was polite. I knew that just being there was being aggressive enough to rankle her.

"I can't help you," she said. "You have to do it yourself." Mrs. Vandevender was not angry or impatient, but she wasn't sympathetic either. She didn't hinder or help. We had broken open her world, and she knew she had to do her job, but she didn't want to react. Maybe she didn't know how.

Then she handed me a book with the Mississippi Constitution in it and pointed out a section for me to copy onto a sheet of paper. Then

I was asked to write a "reasonable interpretation" of it. It was section 182, and this is what it says:

> The power to tax corporations and their property shall never be surrendered or abridged by any contract or grant to which the State or any political subdivision thereof may be a party, except that the legislature may grant exemption from taxation in the encouragement of manufactures and other new enterprises of public utility extending for a period of not exceeding 5 years, the time of such exemptions to commence from date of charter, if to a corporation; if to an individual enterprise, then from the commencement of work; but when the legislature grants such exemptions for a period of 5 years or less, it shall be done by general laws, which shall distinctly enumerate the classes of manufactures and other new enterprises of public utility entitled to such exemptions, and shall prescribe the mode and manner in which the right to such exemptions shall be determined.

I've always loved to read, and I'm a good reader, but never had I stumbled into words that were so tangled up. And I didn't know a thing about corporate taxes. But I wrote down something and gave it to Mrs. Vandevender. She told me I could come back in thirty days and find out if I passed. I thanked her and said I would be back. I figured my application would be rejected, but just going in there and facing Mrs. Vandevender eye-to-eye gave me a good feeling. Every step I took gave me more confidence and strength to take the next one.

9

Find Strength in Togetherness

WHEN THE MOVEMENT CAME into my life, it was like a big drenching rain had finally come after a long dry spell. I just ran out in it and soaked it up. Deep inside, I'd been waiting for this all my life. I couldn't get enough of it. I couldn't do enough. I couldn't learn enough. Being a freedom fighter didn't just become part of my life; it *was* my life.

I was the kind of person the Student Nonviolent Coordinating Committee was looking for. SNCC (pronounced snick) came to Mississippi that summer not only to register black voters but to find leaders at the grassroots level who would carry on the work. SNCC was a southern grassroots organization, founded in 1960 by student sit-in protestors in North Carolina. Ella Baker, a leader in the movement since the 1940s and at the time a director of the Southern Christian Leadership Conference (SCLC), was instrumental in guiding the students. She advised the students to form a separate group, rather than become a youth wing of SCLC or another civil rights group. Miss Baker had come to believe that SCLC was too centered on the personal magnetism of Martin Luther King Jr. She thought that activism would be most effective if it came from the oppressed people themselves and that students could best provide the energy and commitment necessary for organizing people at the grassroots level.

A brilliant young New York schoolteacher and SNCC staff member named Bob Moses had brought Ella Baker's concept to Mississippi in

1961. Bob organized local people in Pike County in south Mississippi
and then in the Delta; he'd experienced firsthand the rabid, often violent, white resistance. He also knew how badly Mississippi blacks
needed help, and wanted it. Amzie Moore, the longtime NAACP leader
from Cleveland, Mississippi, convinced Moses that the key to change
in Mississippi was the vote. Building on Moore's advice and his earlier
experiences, Bob Moses organized and directed a massive effort in the
summer of 1964 to recruit college students from across the country,
like Bob Wright and Louis Grant, train them, and send them to Mississippi to educate and organize local blacks to register to vote, and to
develop local grassroots leadership in Mississippi. This was the Mississippi Summer Project of 1964—now known as Freedom Summer—
and it involved SNCC and CORE, the Congress of Racial Equality.
These two groups joined under an umbrella organization known as
COFO, the Council of Federated Organizations, with Bob Moses serving as director. Martin Luther King's Southern Christian Leadership
Conference supported COFO's efforts but did not participate directly.

I came to know and respect Bob Moses that summer. He was and is
the gentlest and quietest of men and not at all the fiery kind of person
you might expect to be in charge of a radical, in-your-face movement.
He was well educated—an intellectual, really—with a Ph.D. in philosophy from Harvard. He was the first person I ever knew with a Ph.D. I
didn't even know then what a Ph.D. was, but I knew it had to be something great if Bob Moses had one.

SNCC had found me, and I was ready and willing to learn everything they had to teach. And what wonderful and wise young teachers
they sent. After Bob Wright and Louis Grant, Muriel Tillinghast was
the next SNCC person I got to know. She was a light-brown-skinned
woman in her twenties who had recently graduated from Howard University. She came to Mayersville very soon after they did. She was a
SNCC project director based in the Greenville office, and unlike the
students she stayed on after the summer. Muriel spent a lot of time in
Mayersville, and she stayed at my house while she was here, sleeping
in my front room. For someone so young and petite, she had a serene
strength about her.

When she told me she was a teacher, I assumed that she was a regular schoolteacher—teaching reading, writing, arithmetic, and such.

But Muriel taught things more rare and precious: She taught me about African American history and black leaders and contributions they had made throughout American history and world history, too. I'd set up gatherings in churches and at my house—a dozen or more crowded in the tiny front room—and Muriel would tell us how we were a people with a history of greatness. When we were children in school, the only black people we had heard about were Booker T. Washington and George Washington Carver, great men who had found a way to accommodate to the white South. Now we were hearing about a different sort of black leader: Frederick Douglass and W. E. B. Du Bois and Harriet Tubman, Ida Wells-Barnett, and Zora Neale Hurston, rebels and intellectuals and artists—and women. Muriel brought terrific books about black history for us to read, and she read us poetry that black poets had written about black struggles and dreams throughout American history, from Phillis Wheatley to Margaret Walker. What Muriel Tillinghast really taught us was to have pride in ourselves because we as black people had potential. Muriel Tillinghast truly gave me the education of my life.

Muriel wore her hair in what we later called an "Afro" or a "natural"—not big and wild but short and neat. Me, I called it "nappy-headed." I had been straightening my hair for years, and all the other black women I knew had been, too. By the time I was seven or eight years old, my mother and grandmother were "warm-combing" my hair to get the kinks out. As far as I knew, there was no such thing as a black woman not straightening her hair. If you saw somebody walking down the street without her hair straightened, you would have said, "Child, you got to do something about your nappy head." I had never seen any grown black woman with unstraightened hair out in public, and I thought Muriel's hair was funny looking. I was embarrassed for her and kept trying to help her look better.

Sunday was coming up soon, and I was supposed to take her to church with me. I said, "Louise down the street can fix your hair for you. I can take you down to see her." And she would say, "OK. I'll do that sometime." Or she would say, "Oh, yes, I've got to wash it." And I thought, well, it looks to me like it's already washed. But she never would go to see Louise to get her hair fixed. When Sunday came, she tied a bandana around her head. Now, that didn't look like church to

me. You didn't wear a bandana to church; you wore that to the field. I
didn't say anything to her about her bandana, but all the women in
church kind of sniggled about it.

When I started in again the next day working on Muriel to get her
hair fixed before the next Sunday, she had a talk with me. She
explained that her hair was part of her identity as a black person. She
was not ashamed because her hair was not as straight as a white person's hair. A person's goodness is not determined by how straight her
hair is, she told me. Black people are different: Our skin color and the
texture of our hair are different from those of white people, but we are
good human beings, and beautiful, too. Of course, Big Mama and Birt
had said these things when I was little, but Muriel was an educated
woman, a college graduate, and she had been out in the world. She was
openly confident of her worth as a black person. She was living out in
public what she believed. And so Muriel's nappy hair became another
of her lessons for me. By the next year, I was wearing my hair in a natural, too.

Over that year I was in a constant state of excitement about learning all these things about my people and myself and what we could do
to make our lives better. Overnight, I went from field hand to full-time
freedom fighter. I began helping Louis and Bob and Muriel set up meetings and talking to friends and neighbors about the need to try to register. "Nothing from nothing leaves nothing," I would tell people. "If you
ain't got nothing now, you can't lose nothing."

Stokely Carmichael was in charge of SNCC activities in the Second
Congressional District, which was the Delta, where I lived. His office
was in Greenwood. He soon heard that there was a woman in Issaquena County who wasn't afraid to stand up and talk to people about
voting and freedom. And he came to Mayersville to talk to me about
becoming a SNCC field representative. That was the first time I met
him. Stokely was electrifying. He had grown up in the West Indies and
spoke with an accent and rhythm I found fascinating, and when he
talked, his dark eyes flashed with excitement. He made me want to
jump up and follow him. Stokely was only twenty-two years old at the
time, but he was already a veteran Mississippi civil rights worker. A
graduate of Howard University, he'd been one of the Freedom Riders
thrown in Parchman in 1961 and had come back the next summer to

organize people in the Delta. Stokely (along with Charlie Cobb and Ivanhoe Donaldson) had come to Issaquena County to see Henry Sias in the spring about civil rights workers coming here.

Stokely was as animated as Bob Moses was reserved. They were two very different men with very different styles but equally powerful in their influence. They were both charismatic in their own ways, but more than that, they were effective. I imagine those of us who worked for voter registration that summer—grassroots people and students, alike—know more about the laws of the land and the ideals of this country than most people walking down the street today know. We were schooled and motivated to learn by two of the best.

Stokely drove me to Ruleville to meet Fannie Lou Hamer, the amazing woman who would become a dear friend for the rest of her life and my mentor as a grassroots organizer and freedom fighter. Mrs. Hamer—she was always "Mrs. Hamer" to me—was in her mid-forties and had been involved for a couple of years with the SNCC people, who had been coming to the central part of the Delta. She lived in Ruleville, in Sunflower County, not ten miles from the home of U.S. senator James Eastland, well known for his segregationist views and votes. One of the earliest rural Delta blacks to join the civil rights movement, Mrs. Hamer had dared to register to vote in the fall of 1962 and was forced to leave the plantation where she and her husband lived and worked. Mrs. Hamer threw herself into the movement and began attending workshops and events outside the state, while doing whatever she could back home to organize. In 1963, when she returned to Mississippi from one of her trips, she was jailed and brutally beaten in Winona.

Mrs. Hamer had polio as a child and walked with a limp. She was a short person, a little plump, and she was so warm she made me feel at home from the first minute I saw her. In Mississippi, if you don't know a person, you probably know someone that person knows, and we soon discovered that she knew my uncle Jesse. He had gotten her the house she was in when she and her husband, Pap, had to leave the plantation.

We sat down, and she started talking about how she had been beat up in the Winona jail the year before—how they dragged her down the hall and then made her lie on her stomach on a cot and had another inmate beat her with a blackjack till her body was hard. And I sat there and listened to her and got madder and madder and madder. And then she said, "Honey, when I got through being beat, I looked at him and said, 'Your lip is quivering,' and that man was so mad he didn't know what to do."

I wanted to cry and I wanted to laugh. Mrs. Hamer could tell you things in pain and then make you fall out laughing. She could make you want to be in this movement even if you didn't want to. But I already knew I wanted to.

She said, "You mad, ain't you?"

And I said, "Yeah, and you ought to be, too."

She said, "We mad all right, but it ain't going solve our problems to sit here and be mad. You got to get mad enough to go out and get people to try to register to vote."

Shortly after that, I went to work with her as a SNCC field representative.

"Girl, we Snickers now," she said.

Soon after I joined the SNCC staff, Mrs. Hamer and I went to Atlanta to learn about what we were supposed to do as field representatives, or organizers. I met the most fantastic people I'd ever known. The civil rights leaders were all there—people who have remained my friends throughout the years: Ella Baker, John Lewis, national SNCC director, and Julian Bond, the communications director. But I was more excited about meeting the student activists from across the country. That was the first time I'd ever been around such a large group of bright, educated young people, both black and white. I was amazed and thrilled over all those students, who were teaching me so much. The two of us—Mrs. Hamer and I—were older than most of the other SNCC staff and volunteers, but they welcomed us. Many of them told Mrs. Hamer and me that we were their teachers. This was the first of many such gatherings.

I felt like I had come into a long-lost family. My new family would become bigger and bigger.

When I became a SNCC organizer, I was just a person who thought I didn't know anything. I didn't even know I was becoming an organizer.

I was paid eleven dollars every two weeks if they had it. And most of the time they didn't have it, so we worked and we ate beans and cheese. I didn't know that you could mix them together till one of the white SNCC women said that's what the Spanish people did. I was learning a new way of life. Our house in Mayersville became a hub for civil rights people, supporters from other states, and local volunteers, who were running in and out, all day and all night. It was known as a freedom house—a place where others working in the movement could come to get directions or information about activities. Civil rights workers always knew that they could come to our house and sit around and talk about the movement and feel a sense of protection and togetherness. They became our extended family, really. Both Jeremiah and Jerry were very much a part of the scene. Visitors played and joked with Jerry, who was seven, and he enjoyed the attention. Jeremiah was consumed by the movement, too, though he wasn't a SNCC worker. He spoke at meetings and kept up with all the activities. He also listened and learned what local whites and blacks were saying. So having a house full of strangers presented no problem for him. Besides, he's a talker, and he loved having lots of interesting people around who'd listen to him.

To have wonderful new friends—black and white, educated, people of means, some of them, who'd been places and done things I'd never even dreamed of—sitting on the floor or in the old broke-down furniture in my front room, talking about our lives and times, gave me a feeling I'd never had before. Nobody had to say that all of us were equal; we could feel it. These were the first moments of my life when I knew that people outside my family respected me for what I knew and what I had to offer. They wanted to know *my* ideas, to get *my* advice about what *they* should do. I was telling them what to do. Even in my own community, as a woman my opinion didn't mean much unless it was in agreement with a man's. I had been beat way down, and the realization that I had something of value to give someone else was a powerful sensation. At the time I didn't even know how to describe it, but it gave me strength.

As a SNCC field representative that summer, I organized my own county and nearby counties—arranged mass meetings and talked to people individually about voter registration. I had to locate preachers who weren't afraid to let us use their churches for meetings, help the SNCC volunteers set up the meetings in those areas and get people there, and speak at the meetings. I had to find sympathetic people who would help out in their own communities—like Annie Laurie Reed, Willie Fleming, Minnie Ripley, and Henry Sias did in Issaquena County. I'd go anywhere to talk to people who had never thought they'd vote or that their lives might ever be any better. Since the student volunteers were from all over the country, they didn't know all our customs and ways, so I was teaching them how to operate here, according to the ways of our people.

For me, it was like growing up all over again. I was learning new ways to act, too. At SNCC training sessions and on my own, I was learning the techniques of nonviolent civil disobedience. For example, if somebody physically attacked me, I was supposed to go limp and roll up into a fetal position and put my hands over my head. And I had to learn verbal restraint. If a white person called me names or said ugly things to me, I was taught never to argue but to stay cool to keep from escalating the argument. When someone else is fishing for a fight and you don't swallow their bait, they don't know what to do next. If they can't get a rise out of you, usually they just get frustrated and leave. I was discovering how to be an activist and grassroots organizer.

In Mississippi most of the grassroots organizers—the real movers of the people—were women: Fannie Lou Hamer, Annie Devine in Canton, and Victoria Gray in Hattiesburg, among others. Those three women got started a little earlier than I did, but I got right in there with them. Although men held most of the titled jobs in movement organizations, very few black men got involved locally. Most black men in the rural areas had more to lose financially than their wives. The husband's income, even though it wasn't much, was usually the mainstay of the family; and on a plantation, the rest of the family's employment depended on the man's. Also, we probably got away with more because white people didn't see black women as being as much of a threat as black men were; they had no idea how important the work of black women was within our own culture. Black women had always kept our churches and families going, even though we weren't preachers or deacons or the head of the house. So it wasn't a big step up for black women to keep the movement moving. It was a freeing

experience for us to get out in front of our own people and be acknowledged by men and women as leaders. (It's no mystery why the women's
movement of the 1970s grew out of the civil rights movement.)

But many black people in the Delta—women as well as men—were
scared to associate with SNCC or COFO people. They were afraid
they'd lose their jobs and homes—just plain afraid, afraid of the unknown. So I had to be very careful in making an approach. Even
though I was black myself and from the Delta, I couldn't barge in
somewhere and make a big pitch. Several of us might go to a café and
sit around talking to the people about anything, just being friendly. We
might buy a beer or two for some of them. If the people weren't comfortable with you, you weren't going to be able to reach them. Anytime
you want to work with people, or get them to work with you, you need
to make a personal connection. We let them ask what we were doing in
town. And then I might say, "You know, where I live, people are going
down to register to vote. It's the law that black people can register and
vote." Then I might tell them there was going to be a meeting at such
and such place, and ask why didn't they go see what it was about. We'd
answer their questions and keep everything low-key. We didn't argue
with anybody; we just acknowledged what they said.

If they were fearful yet really interested, I'd get more involved: "I'm
scared, too, but we've got to stand together. If all of us get together, we
can do it." Then I might offer to give them a ride and go to the courthouse with them. I never tried to paint too rosy a picture, though, and
always let folks know that "it ain't gonna be easy."

I attended regular church services in the other communities in the
surrounding counties. At some point during the service, the preacher
recognized visitors and asked them to stand. When I stood, he'd ask if
I wanted to say anything to the congregation. I'd keep my comments
brief, tell them about a meeting planned, or just let them know that if
they wanted more information or help they could talk to me after
church. We'd try to look as nice as we could when we went to church,
but I never got those SNCC students out of wearing their blue jeans! (I
think that was all they brought.)

I tried to identify the black leaders on the plantations; there was
always someone on each place the other workers looked to for guidance. I'd try to talk to that person. "You the head," I said. "You got to

do it first." Most of the time I wouldn't go onto the plantation to talk; I'd find out where the leader went to church or where he or she liked to go on Saturday night. We were careful. We didn't want to get shot. Annie Laurie, who became one of my grassroots workers and a dear friend, was living on a plantation when she encouraged her neighbors to go down and register to vote. When her boss heard about it, he told her, "Take all your young'uns and get away from here and don't come back." She had no place to go. Willie Fleming, who worked on the same plantation, had just come back from the Army. "After all I've been through for my country," he said. "I'll be damn if I'm going to let them think they can scare me. I'll go with you, Annie Laurie." And he left the plantation, too.

Finding places for Annie Laurie and others to live when they were faced with such situations was one of my projects. The National Council of Churches and civil rights supporters had set up a fund, and we bought a small plot of land and found a little trailer for her. She still lives on the land, and she lived in the same trailer until very recently, when her children bought her a new one. My work took so many different turns, depending on where I was and who I was talking to. My mind was always working to find the right approach, the right thing to do and say. Resourcefulness—creative making-do—is a by-product of growing up poor, so finding solutions to problems seemed to come naturally to me. Without realizing it, I'd been preparing for this job all my life.

A large part of organizing was being open to people and listening and observing to see what was needed. My natural inclination to close observation and an ability to read people had been honed as a means of getting along in a world controlled by whites. I discovered I needed this skill in dealing with black people, too. Besides finding those who were sympathetic and needed help, I had to be able to sense someone who was going to snitch to white folks. I wanted to be sure the person was really with us when I tried to help him, or my efforts would backfire. Like the old folks said, "Don't fatten frogs for snakes!"

My upbringing had taught me another thing, too—how to keep my mouth shut—and this habit was crucial in helping me become an organizer and freedom fighter. When I was talking to people about setting up meetings or working around local concerns, I had to be able to keep things in confidence so I didn't get them in trouble. Secretiveness was essential in creating strategy—identifying areas to go into and who would go, anticipating the problems we might encounter, and deciding how to deal with them. I attended strategy sessions with the SNCC staff and volunteers at least once a week in Greenville, at the SNCC office on Nelson Street, upstairs above a laundry. Every couple of weeks we'd meet with others from our congressional district in Greenwood. We discussed what was going on in particular communities—progress, problems, whether we needed to send someone else in, that sort of thing. Strategy meetings were top secret. Only the participants knew the meeting times.

One of the best things about our strategy meetings was being with people who were going through the same experiences. The issues were still there, but I felt more comfortable and relieved to be able to discuss them openly. I could relax and get out from under the pressures I was dealing with all day long, every day. I needed this. We all needed each other. Fighting for freedom is serious business, and this togetherness was necessary to keep our spirits going and strengthen our commitment. People working together on a common good—that's what the civil rights movement was about. All social movements depend on people moving together.

To create and sustain that feeling of togetherness—group spirit—we had mass meetings at the grassroots level. Mass meetings were our main means of getting our message across to our own people. Not only could we talk to many people at once, but by coming together we all gathered strength from each other. There was a mass meeting in my area nearly every night. We tried to have at least one or two meetings a week in the vicinity of Mayersville. These were usually held either at my church, Moon Lake Baptist, or at Henry Sias's church, down in the "deadening" (an open place where trees had been allowed to die). You have to reach people where they are. Our people were in church. Our churches had always held us together, and they did in those times, too. There wasn't really any other place we could meet. Nobody had a house big enough, and public buildings were not open to us. If it hadn't been for churches, we probably couldn't have had the movement.

We couldn't get into all black churches. Many of them were on plantations, and the preachers were told by the plantation owners or somebody else in the white community to tell us to stay out. Then the preacher would talk to us and say, "Leave this stuff alone. Let the Lord fix it." Or sometimes we'd plan a meeting and some of the blacks would go tell it to their boss, and we'd have to cancel the meeting. The whites would send a black person in to our meetings to find out what we were planning. If we suspected we had a snitch in the crowd, we'd change our message. We always had somebody staying outside the front door to see if anybody was coming to try to interrupt our meeting. We had all kinds of problems like this, but somehow we always managed to find churches where we could have our mass meetings.

Black people in the Deep South felt they were held up by a Higher Power. My goal was to get blacks registered to vote and to understand their rights as American citizens and human beings, but my message was essentially a religious one. When I spoke to a group, I'd say something like this:

> The Lord has sent these young people to help us out of our troubles, just like Moses went and got the children of Israel out of Egypt and took them to the Promised Land. God gave us intelligence and free will, and He wants us to use it. God wants us to have enough food to eat, to live better, and to be able to educate our children. The Bible says, "You have not because you ask not" and "Ask and you shall receive." Now, you know God has never forced anything on anybody, but you have to be willing to do something. If you make one step, God will make two or three steps, but you've got to make the first one. God helps those who help themselves. We have to go deep and ask ourselves, too. Have I done all I can to do what God wants me to, so that I will be at peace with myself?

Struggle and fear and desperation were in the hearts of everybody and on the lips of the people at a mass meeting. Folks would stand up and tell about how Mr. So-and-So had thrown him off his place or was threatening to, how they didn't have money to live on—not enough to eat—and they couldn't get any credit. These meetings were powerful and painful, too. As the organizer, I had the job of motivating people and keeping things moving. I would get up every night and speak, and I'd get other people to go with me and speak to get the congregation started talking. My friend Annie Laurie often went with me and spoke about being thrown off the plantation and not having a place for herself and her nine children to live. Annie Laurie was so into freedom, people listened. She could really tell her story.

Singing was the most powerful part of our mass meetings; we sang and sang and sang—freedom songs, church songs, church songs we made into freedom songs. Singing brought the people in and held us all together. It connected us to a Higher Power, and it lifted our spirits. Singing made us feel the need for freedom and inspired in us the belief that we could have it. Freedom songs provided the emotional link to the message. We'd preach freedom and then we'd sing freedom, and everybody got it. Without the compassion and honesty of freedom songs, I don't believe many people would have connected to the movement.

Singing for some people is an opportunity to express thoughts and feelings; black people sing mostly to satisfy a deep longing on the inside. Whether it's blues or gospel music or freedom songs, we sing to help us feel that things will get better. We sing for inspiration, as we've done for generations. Our love of music, I think, grew out of being used and oppressed. We had no material possessions. All we had that we could hang on to was music. The women in my family had always worked in the church, and they sang. *Black people never had anything but a song.* The songs of African Americans have given this country its truly American musical art. Our singing gave the civil rights movement its heart.

The singing in the movement was out of this world. At mass meetings we'd stand up and sing and pat our hands to get folks loosened up. It usually took a good while for people to get to the meeting, so we'd sing until everybody got there and then we'd sing some more. When I was in charge of the meeting, I'd usually lead out the singing, with something like this:

Do you want your freedom?
Certainly Lord. [response from congregation]
Will you redish to vote?
Certainly, certainly, certainly Lord.

We sometimes made up lyrics to fit our needs. I'd keep starting off whatever hit me. It might be "This little light of mine, I'm gonna let it shine." Or I might sing out,

> *Ain't going to let nobody turn me 'round, turn me 'round,*
> *turn me around*
> *Ain't going to let nobody turn me 'round*
> *I'm gonna keep on a-walking, keep on a-talking, marching*
> *up to freedom land.*

Verse after verse we'd sing: "Ain't going to let segregation turn me 'round"; "Ain't going to let no sheriff turn me 'round"; "Ain't going to let the boss man turn me 'round." Or we might name names—Sheriff So-and-So or Mr. Jones or whoever. Each verse ended with "I'm gonna keep on a-walking, keep on a-talking, marching up to freedom land."

Most of the freedom songs were old gospel songs or spirituals that were adapted to the movement. The old song "Woke up this morning with my mind stayed on Jesus" became "Woke up this morning with my mind stayed on freedom." "Keep Your Eyes on the Prize" was another favorite; it came from "Keep Your Hand on the Plow." We might take a song like "Down by the Riverside" and change it to fit the situation: "Going down to the courthouse / Trying to redish to vote / Trying to redish to vote." We sang "We Shall Overcome," of course; the music was from the old spiritual "No More Auction Block for Me," and the words came from the hymn "I'll Overcome One Day." We had so many wonderful songs—uplifting songs and call-to-action songs. And sorrow songs, which drew us together by reminding us of our fear and pain while also strengthening us to face it together, like this old spiritual:

> *This may be the last time*
> *This may be the last time*

May be the last time we all meet together
May be the last time we all sing together
May be the last time we all shout together
May be the last time we all pray together
May be the last time we all bow together

This may be the last time
May be the last time, I don't know.

A song like "This May Be the Last Time" called for a prayer. We did a lot of praying at those mass meetings. We prayed for guidance, for protection, for strength. We prayed for togetherness. A line in our prayers I heard often—and still hear—conveys the essence of what religious faith meant to the civil rights movement and what the movement meant to its people: "Lord, bind us together so close, one won't fall for another."

That prayer is just as profound today, and it moves me every time I hear it. It's my prayer for all of us, black and white and red and yellow, in this nation and throughout the world. We all do have to stick together and hold one another up. This truth is essential when you're setting out on the road to freedom or initiating a plan for major change in society: You need the strength that comes from togetherness.

10

Hold On, and Pray

THIS WAS A TIME AND PLACE where terror reigned. Civil rights activists were the targets of black-hating white people in Mississippi. If there was anything worse than an outside agitator, it was a homegrown agitator. And that's what I was. I was SNCC, and I was from the Mississippi Delta. Most whites in the Delta found the NAACP loathsome enough, but SNCC and COFO just unhinged them. All white Mississippians were not hateful and violent, but those who were made our lives living hell—and they included not only members of the Klan but also those who made the laws and were supposed to enforce them, from the governor on down. The very people who were supposed to protect us—the sheriff, the police, and local and state officials—were often the ones who terrorized us or looked the other way when someone else did.

During these terrible years of the middle 1960s, black people who got involved with the civil rights movement were likely to be harmed or threatened with harm at any time. We lived in fear. There was always fear. We didn't know if people were coming after us or when they were coming or what they were going to do to us. So we felt terrorized all the time. And we were nonviolent, those of us in SNCC. I never carried a gun. I had never been one to resort to violence, and I still don't.

The KKK was putting out crosses, burning churches, shooting black people, taking people and throwing them in the river. Goodman,

Chaney, and Schwerner in Neshoba County are the most widely known victims of the summer of 1964, but there were others. While looking for the Neshoba County victims that summer, searchers found three other young men, all black, in the Mississippi and Big Black Rivers. Their murderers have never been brought to justice. Acts of antagonism ranged from annoyance to outright brutality and bloodshed. There was always general harassment—threatening telephone calls, people running us off the road—just meanness for the sake of meanness. Some white folks would waylay me on one highway and I'd go to another, but they would be there, too. They'd take the air out of my tires, set nails across the road. They would do juvenile things like that.

But some things they did went beyond that and were truly disgusting and sick. I was driving back from Rolling Fork one afternoon—it's only ten miles—and I had car trouble. I pulled my car onto the shoulder and started walking back to town to get some help. I was just walking along when two white men in a truck drove up and parked on the side of the road and started taunting me, making explicit sexual demands. When I didn't respond the way they thought I should, they growled and snarled like vicious old dogs, hollering out terrible, nasty things about me, right to my face—the cruelest and most vulgar things I've ever heard in my life. It was frightening, yes, but even more sickening. They finally gunned the motor and tore off down the road, hooting and hollering like fools.

I was constantly being arrested. The sheriff and police could be as dangerous as anybody—or more dangerous. The only law enforcement in my county, Issaquena, was the sheriff and his deputies and the state highway patrol. Mayersville didn't have a police force then. In Rolling Fork there was a police department and the Sharkey County sheriff's department. The highway didn't even come through our town, just on the edge of it, but the highway patrol parked near my house, all the time watching my house or patrolling it. When we'd come out, they'd be sitting there waiting on us. I could simply back out of my driveway and get a ticket for something. Maybe my car was parked one inch beyond the grass in my yard. I'd drive down the road, and they'd find something I was doing wrong, silly, stupid things—driving fifty-five in a sixty-mile-an-hour zone, for instance, or driving without my headlights on in the middle of the afternoon. They'd drive up close behind me and try to force me off the road or make me exceed the speed limit.

The Rolling Fork policemen would sit around and wait for civil rights workers to come through there and give us a ticket. The police gave one SNCC volunteer, a nice Jewish kid, so many tickets I think even they finally got tired of it. They would stop us for anything—or nothing—and make us all get out of the car, and they'd search us, tell all of the men to take their hats off. And you better be sure you say, "Yes, sir." I'd take my ticket and have to go to the police station in Rolling Fork to pay it. Some of those white policemen couldn't even write. On several occasions I had to write out my own ticket! During one period I was arrested every day for thirty days straight, but I was locked up in the Rolling Fork jail only a couple of times, each time for a short while and never overnight.

Many years later I learned that when the white editor of the Rolling Fork paper, Hal DeCell, discovered I had been jailed in Rolling Fork, he quietly reported it to Aaron Henry, the longtime NAACP leader, who arranged to have bail posted for me. There were some good white people who supported what I was doing, but they had to be secretive about it, or they too would become a target. Mr. DeCell is no longer living, but I was able to thank him before he died. Mrs. DeCell ran the paper after his death and turned out to be outspoken about equal rights. His son told me that his father's kindness to me during those terrible days is a source of pride for him now.

Bob Fitzpatrick, a white George Washington University law student, came down to work with the NAACP Legal Defense Fund on desegregation matters. He stayed at my house. A couple of white men who saw him in Mayersville always called him "nigger lover," and they'd talk about him "laying around in the niggers' houses." One day Bob was driving behind a school bus to determine whether black children were being allowed to ride the bus with white ones. One of those men saw him and followed him to a little store in Mayersville, threw him down, and kicked and brutally beat him, breaking two of his ribs and knocking him unconscious. Somebody called me, and I rushed over to the store to see about him. He was in bad shape. He was still on the floor, beat up and bleeding, just lying there, barely able to move.

This really shook me up. I couldn't believe that white people would do this to another white person. (As if that wasn't bad enough, the owner of the store where the beating took place was a justice of the peace, and he fined Bob one hundred dollars for driving recklessly behind a school bus.)

Black and white civil rights workers in the Deep South had to be very careful if they were riding together in a car. A white person riding in the car with black people had to crouch down on the floor when a car passed so no one would see him or her, or we would take something to cover the white person. Merely seeing blacks and whites together in any kind of equal situation was enough to send white law enforcement officials and some in the general public into a frenzy, and anything might happen. This truth was demonstrated most tragically by the murder of Viola Liuzzo, a white activist and mother who took part in the Selma-to-Montgomery march. After the march was over, she and a black volunteer were driving on Highway 80 between Selma and Montgomery, when a car full of Klansmen pulled up beside her car and shot and killed her. A group of us—several black women and one white woman—had gone over to march into Montgomery on the last day, and we were on our way home on this same highway, just ahead of her, when she was killed, although we didn't know what happened until the next day. Probably the only reason the white woman riding with us is alive today is that we covered her up every time we slowed down. We knew we had to be prepared, and I had grabbed up an old bed sheet and a quilt before we left.

Civil rights workers in Mississippi were afraid to drink water in some towns, and sometimes we would get sick eating food out somewhere and discover that arsenic was in the food—not enough to kill us, just enough to make us very sick. It was impossible most places to get together socially out in public places or have parties. We had to find some neutral ground. Tougaloo College, a historically black school on the outskirts of Jackson, was home base and a haven for all of the civil rights workers. Greenville was the only town in the Delta where we could get together and not be bothered. Greenville had a number of moderate whites, including Hodding Carter Jr., the editor of the *Delta Democrat Times* newspaper, who won a Pulitzer for a series of editorials attacking the Klan, and four black policemen, unheard of elsewhere in the state at the time.

Greenwood, only fifty miles east, was out of the question. The racial tension was the worst in Greenwood, the hometown of Medgar Evers's known assassin Byron De La Beckwith, who had received a rousing official welcome home at the courthouse after his hung jury. The COFO headquarters was in Greenwood, and when we tried to meet there to plan our voter registration work, the police would cut us off, coming from every direction. They wanted to keep us isolated. A local young black man, Silas McGhee, was shot in the temple as he dozed in his car outside a black café, where COFO workers had gathered. McGhee's shooting was the culmination of a summer-long campaign of harassment, arrests, and violence by the police and angry white citizens against the civil rights workers in general and the McGhee family in particular. Soon after the Civil Rights Act of 1964 went into effect in early July, which outlawed segregation in public places, Silas had dared to sit with white people in a Greenwood movie theater. (Silas McGhee survived the shooting, although the bullet lodged in his throat, requiring emergency surgery and a lengthy stay in University Medical Center in Jackson.)

Nighttime was the worst time. I never slept at night. Jeremiah slept at night, and I stayed up and watched out to see if someone was headed our way with trouble. If I sensed a problem, I'd wake up Jeremiah and get my child and myself of the way. We'd run and hide in the garden behind butter bean arbors so they couldn't see us from the direction they were coming down the road. Night was a fearful time. That's the reason, I guess, that I'm a night person now.

The Klan folks would come through and throw Molotov cocktails into my yard. Molotov cocktails are homemade bombs. My husband had been in the Army, and he knew what they were. They'd put some gasoline in a bottle and push an old rag down in it for a wick. Then they'd light the rag and throw the bottle. One morning when my little boy, Jerry, was out playing in the yard, he saw a Molotov cocktail. He didn't know what it was, of course; it was just something different and it interested him, and so he grabbed it up. When I recognized what it was, I was afraid it might go off. I couldn't tell whether the wick was smoldering, and I didn't want to take any chances. I didn't want to see my child blown up in front of my eyes, and I had to think fast. I knew if somebody was going to be killed, I wanted it to be me and not my child. But I didn't want to scare him, so I just walked over and said,

"Give it to Mama, baby. Just ease it to me." And that little boy just laid the Molotov cocktail in my hand. I ran with it to an open space and threw it down. It did not explode.

Some of the men in Mayersville who supported SNCC activities but weren't affiliated with the group did sometimes carry guns. They served as community protectors, but they never shot to kill anyone. One of them told me outright he couldn't be in a nonviolent movement. "Y'all can be nonviolent," he said, "but I ain't going to let them folks come up here and shoot and not have nothing to shoot back with." For a while there was a bunch of white teenagers who'd drive by our houses and set crosses on fire, throw stuff out—Molotov cocktails, fireworks, whatever disturbing or dangerous thing they could find. Then three or four of our black protectors started walking the streets with guns. They didn't want to shoot the kids, but they did want to scare the hell out of them; so they came up behind their car and made a circle around it. These guys were marksmen: They could shoot the eyelashes off a flying bird! So they shot at the top of the back window and shattered the glass. Those white children got out of town in a hurry, and we never saw them again. As far as I know, the kids never reported the incident.

I had crosses burned in my yard many times by the KKK—or maybe they weren't all members of the Klan, but they acted like them. Sometimes we knew who the people were by their truck; other times they would borrow some old rattletrap truck from a black man to try to throw us off. The crosses were pieces of board tacked together, wrapped in rags, and soaked in oil. A cross had one long pointed end so the men could jump out of the truck, stick it in the ground, light it, and be back in the truck and gone before you knew what was happening. These were not isolated incidents happening every once in a while. If something wasn't happening at my house, it was at somebody else's.

One night in particular stands out. That night I was at home ironing. I was supposed to be at a church meeting, but I stayed home. Jeremiah wasn't there; I think he must have been working on the riverboat. Jerry was asleep, and Coreen was there with me. She had come over to use the telephone. Not but two or three black folks in town had telephones then, and I hadn't had mine long.

I'd been hounding the phone company for years; I finally had to sue them to get my phone. When the telephone man came to my house to bring my telephone, he asked me what color phone I wanted. I said, "What color have you got?" He told me he had black, white, red, and yellow, and I said, "I'll take one of each." So he installed four telephones in our little house. I had a phone on one wall and another phone across the room on a table, another one by the couch, and one by my bed. People used to get a kick out of all my telephones and the numbers I'd written on the wall—SNCC office numbers in Mississippi, Atlanta, and Washington, the FBI, Sargent Shriver, Bobby Kennedy. We called it the "Freedom Wall."

I was glad to let my friends use my phone. After Coreen did her telephone business, she stayed to visit with me while I finished my ironing. We were in the front room talking when all of a sudden we heard a shot, and then I saw a blaze through my window. "Hit the floor," I hollered. Then the truck pulled off: tack-a-lacka-tack-a-lack. I had heard that truck before: It belonged to a black fellow. But I knew it wasn't a black guy who set the cross.

SNCC had a system of people we were to call if something happened to someone in the community. The first thing I was supposed to do when they came along and put a cross in my yard was to call Julian Bond in Atlanta. He was the communications person at SNCC headquarters. Coreen and I were both on the floor. She was screaming and praying, and I got up in a crouch and reached to get the phone and check Bond's number on my wall. Then I slid back down on the floor with the phone. It was all I could do to dial my numbers in Atlanta.

When Julian answered, I said, "This is Unita Blackwell. Something's going down. It's burning." That's all. You don't have time to hold a conversation when somebody is after you. He knew that I was talking about a cross burning or something happening around the terror of fire. He would call the national FBI and also get the word out to SNCC people in Mississippi.

Julian just said, "I got it."

The next thing I was supposed to do was to call my state FBI office and then the local sheriff. So here I was, still on the floor. I had the number of the state FBI, and I called and told the FBI man what had happened. And he asked, "How tall is the cross?"

I told him that I had no idea. "I am down on the floor," I said, "and I'm not about to get up now and go outside and measure it." And he went on to ask me a bunch of specific questions like that, and I was lying on the floor.

Then he said, "I tell you what you do: You preserve it." He told me to preserve the cross and he'd be up in a few days to investigate. So then he gave me a lesson on how to preserve the cross. He said get a gunnysack and wrap it around the cross. He asked me if I had a gunnysack.

I said, "No. What does it look like?"

I was on the floor with a cross burning in the front yard of my wooden shack, and the FBI man was describing a gunnysack. This man from the FBI, who couldn't conceive of a cross burning in his yard, did what he was trained to do: He told me how to preserve the evidence. He went straight by the book.

Then I called the sheriff. I had to call several times before I finally got him on the phone. By this time, I was hearing from others that crosses were also burning on the levee, at Clarence Hall's house, and at Henry Sias's house. We also had shortwave radios that we could communicate by, since most people didn't have phones. When I finally reached the sheriff, I said, "Mr. Darnell, this is Unita Blackwell. We have a cross burning in my yard and one is in Mr. Sias's, it's one on the levee and it's one at Clarence's house, and I'm on the floor."

I told him that I had already called the FBI and Atlanta, and I said, "I've been trying to get you." I said I thought he'd want to know, so he could find whoever did this.

He said, "You probably set all the crosses on fire. If you know where they are, you must have set them. I'm tired of this mess. I'm coming down there, and I'm going to put you in jail." He was mad.

I told him, "No, sir, I did not set them, but I sure do know where they are all at."

He hung up the phone; so I had done my job. The sheriff never showed up. Coreen and I stayed on the floor for a good while that night.

※　※　※

In the daylight, the Klan would get a poor black guy to do their dirty work. They could always find some head-hanging-down black man who would do whatever a white man wanted for a little pocket change. One time a black man came into my yard trying to start an argument. He told me later that a white man had sent him. The black fellow was supposed to get me into an argument and then shoot me. The shooting would have been "legitimate" then, in the horrible ways of the day.

When I first looked out the window and saw him outside my house, he was drinking whiskey out of a pint bottle. He was getting up his nerve, but I didn't know that at the time. I didn't sense what he was up to. Then he started walking all over my flowers, mashing them down, and stomping on them. He was deliberately trying to make me mad. And it was working. I loved my flowers, and I walked over toward him and ordered him out of my yard.

He said, "You think you're one of them smart niggers." And he began cursing and carrying on in all kinds of bad language, telling me I was going to get what was coming to me.

I just looked at him. And something said to me, "Forget it. Don't say nothing; just turn around."

So I didn't say a word and walked on back to the house. When I looked around—I was going into my house at the time—he had pulled a gun on me and was ready to shoot me. But I made it into the house.

"Well," I said, "I thank you, Lord. You always take care of me."

I'm often asked how we kept going when so much was working against us. The truth is, once I got into the movement I never thought of getting out. I never doubted for a minute that we were on the right side of the struggle: The vote was right by the Constitution, and freedom was right by God. Freedom ain't free, I'd always heard, so I was expecting to pay a big price. The more violent the Klan types became and the more afraid I was, the more urgent I knew work was—and the angrier I became. The bombings, arrests, the hatred I encountered—the buried bad feelings of a lifetime bubbled up to the surface. Just because I didn't explode with anger in the face of the people who infuriated me didn't mean I didn't have rage in my heart. The madder I got, the harder I worked. My anger was a motivator, keeping me moving during those terrifying early days. Being angry at white people was liberating, too. A person doesn't get mad if she doesn't have a certain amount of self-respect. (Later on, my anger would start to take control of me, and I'd have to work myself out of it.)

The truth is, in such terrible times you have to follow the advice of the freedom song and "Keep Your Eyes on the Prize. Hold On." And sometimes all you can do is pray.

11

Dare to Challenge

A S I EXPECTED, I did not pass the voter registration test the first time I took it, so I tried again the next month, and I failed again. Then one day in the early fall of 1964 I decided I was going in to pay my poll tax anyway, so I'd be all set if I ever did pass the test. The poll tax was another state requirement to keep blacks from voting; voters had to pay poll tax for two years. Since I had to know which voting precinct I lived in to pay my tax, I went to Mrs. Vandevender's office to see a precinct map. This time she seemed upset and nervous. I think the civil rights workers and Justice Department lawyers coming and going in the state all summer had gotten to her.

"Could you give me a precinct map, Mrs. Vandevender," I said.

"Well, Unita. I just don't have one. We don't have anything but land maps. That's all I can give you."

"Well, since I'm here, I'll take the registration test."

She gave me a registration form, and I filled it out. I had this routine down. I don't remember which section of the constitution I had to interpret this time, but I picked some of the words out and wrote down what I thought they meant. Then I looked over what I had written and saw I had misspelled "length." I said, "Oh, my Lord." But I handed it to her—I didn't expect to be registered anyway—and I said, "Well, I misspelled this, and I didn't date the top."

"Oh, that's all right, it's all right, it's all right." And she ran and got the voter registration book and wrote my name in it. I guess Mrs. Vandevender was tired of looking at me.

And that quick, I was a registered voter. I wanted to shout, but I just thanked her and acted like it was an everyday occurrence.

Before the end of June 1964 I had never been inside the courthouse, and by the end of July I was helping set up a new political party in Mississippi: the Mississippi Freedom Democratic Party (MFDP). By the end of August I was on my way to the Democratic National Convention in Atlantic City to challenge the "official" state delegation for seating.

Since the state-level Democrats in Mississippi refused to let blacks participate in their party process, we decided to elect our own slate of delegates in an open process, following all the national party rules. This, we hoped, would demonstrate to the national party that the MFDP was the rightful Democratic delegation from Mississippi. The official—white—state Democrats had turned blacks away from party caucuses earlier that summer; they also had passed resolutions condemning the Civil Rights Act of 1964 (the equal accommodations act, which had become effective the first of July), calling for "separation of the races in all phases of our society," and demanding that civil-rights–oriented U.S. Supreme Court justices be removed from the bench. In addition, almost every delegate elected to attend the Democratic National Convention openly supported not Lyndon Johnson, the incumbent president of the United States and Democratic nominee, but the Republican candidate, Barry Goldwater. Yet those people had complete control of the Democratic Party in the state and proclaimed themselves the rightful Democratic representatives from Mississippi.

Mississippi's white voters had voted solidly Democratic since before the Civil War, but since 1948 they had been pulling away from the Democratic Party in national elections, in large part over the subject of race. In 1948 the Mississippi delegates walked out of the Democratic National Convention in protest of the civil rights stand taken by their party's nominee, Harry Truman, and they formed their own States' Rights Party. They chose Strom Thurmond as their presidential candidate and former Mississippi governor Fielding Wright as their candidate for vice president. The States' Rights Party carried Mississippi by a large margin. Over the next years, an increasing number of white Democrats voted Republican for president and in 1960 gave Richard Nixon an overwhelming margin over John F. Kennedy. This splintering of whites from the national Democratic Party over racial issues laid the foundation of the very white Mississippi Republican Party of today. In the process, black voters who were descendants of the Reconstruction-era Black and Tan Republicans ended up without a party. So in Mississippi there was no political apparatus in either party for black voters to turn to.

I knew nothing about the state's political history at the time. I didn't know a thing about politics at all. Not a single thing. Everything about the political process was new to me. I had never voted. I had never heard of a caucus, and I didn't even know what a delegate was, but I set up precinct and county caucuses in Issaquena County. I had a piece of paper telling me what to do, I could read, and I followed the instructions. And as I learned, I taught the others like me what I knew. The process of selecting delegates to attend the national convention at the time was about the same as it is now in the state Democratic Party. People gathered on a certain day at their voting precincts and elected delegates to their county convention. At the county level, delegates were chosen to attend their district caucus. I found places for the meetings—black churches—and informed people of what precinct they were in and where and when to meet. We had five voting precincts in Issaquena County, and my precinct met at the Moon Lake Baptist Church, the same place we'd been having mass meetings all summer. Our precinct caucus was held on Saturday, July 25. I was elected from my precinct and then elected to represent Issaquena County at the Second Congressional District caucus.

Freedom people from counties all over the Delta convened in Greenville for our district caucus, which we held in a movie theater on Washington Avenue. The Delta was swarming with MFDP folks, and we had great participation. Stokely Carmichael made the arrangements for this meeting, and he had me standing up there in Greenville as the temporary chairperson in charge of opening the caucus!

Stokely told me to follow parliamentary procedure. I had been in charge of many church meetings, but parliamentary procedure was not in the picture there. So I said, "Stokely, you stand by me and tell me what I'm supposed to do next." And that's what happened. Stokely said softly, "The meeting is called to order," and I said loudly, "The meeting is called to order." When he whispered, "The floor is now open for nominations for permanent chairman," I said it right behind him. I was not elected as the permanent chairman, but I was elected to the executive committee of MFDP, and I also got elected as a delegate to the state and national conventions.

When the Mississippi Freedom Democratic Party had our state convention on August 6, more than eight hundred delegates from forty counties were present at the Masonic Lodge on Lynch Street in Jackson.[1] Ella Baker was the keynote speaker at the state convention. She was coordinating the MFDP challenge. Ella knew politics. She was the first woman I knew who really understood politics. She told us we were demonstrating to white Mississippians and all Americans that the black people in Mississippi were ready to be let into the country. "Until the killing of black mothers' sons becomes as important to the rest of the country as the killing of white mothers' sons, we who believe in freedom cannot rest," she said. I had never seen or heard anybody with that kind of powerful voice talking about what black people had to do to get political power in this country. When Ella finished her talk, we were so fired up, all eight hundred of us were marching around the auditorium singing freedom songs and clapping. The Democratic National Convention was a couple of weeks off, but she had me so energized, I would have left there walking that day!

Our challenge lawyer, Joseph Rauh, explained the procedure to us. We would make our argument to the credentials committee of the national Democratic Party. The committee consisted of 108 of the national delegates. If 10 percent of the committee approved our challenge, the issue would go before the entire national delegation for a vote. Then, if ten states asked for it, there would be a roll call of the states with every delegation voicing its vote. Rauh said that many

---

1. The street was named in honor of John R. Lynch (1847–1939), an outstanding black leader during Reconstruction, who served in the Mississippi legislature, the U.S. Congress, and President Benjamin Harrison's administration.

Democrats around the nation were supporting us. He believed that if we could get the challenge out of the credentials committee and onto the convention floor, we would be seated.

Sixty-eight people were chosen to represent the Mississippi Freedom Democratic Party at the 1964 Democratic National Convention. Both Henry Sias and I were elected. All but four members of the delegation were black; more than half were women. Most were grassroots activists like me—Fannie Lou Hamer, the Turnbows from Holmes County (Hartman Turnbow and his wife, "Sweets"), E. W. Steptoe from Amite County, Winson Hudson from Carthage, Annie Devine from Madison County. Aaron Henry and Amzie Moore and several other state NAACP leaders were part of the delegation. The national NAACP didn't support our challenge; they thought we were moving too fast. I thought it was high time!

We elected Lawrence Guyot, a SNCC field director and native Mississippian, chairman of our party. Aaron Henry was chosen chair of the delegation and Mrs. Hamer vice chair. Victoria Gray and the Reverend Ed King, the white chaplain at Tougaloo College, who had been active in the movement for several years, were elected national committee members. Bob Moses and Stokely, along with several other SNCC staff people and volunteers, would also be going to Atlantic City, but they were not Mississippians and were not members of our delegation.

The white power structure in Mississippi did everything it could to knock us down. Guyot, who worked tirelessly getting our party ready for the convention and organizing the challenge, was put in jail right before we left for Atlantic City. He was arrested on some trumped-up charges—it was said that he'd done something to some girl who was underage. The charge wasn't true, and he was later released, but it kept him from attending the convention. (Fortunately, that didn't deter Guyot from providing dynamic leadership to the MFDP for several years and teaching me a lot about politics.) The governor and the state attorney general even got the courts to issue an injunction against MDFP to prevent us from leaving the state. We didn't pay a bit of attention to that. We were going to the convention!

We pulled out of Jackson August 20 on two big chartered buses, heading for Atlantic City—delegates, alternates, and volunteers. Mrs.

Hamer and Aaron Henry and Ella Baker had been speaking around the country to raise money for our trip, and Harry Belafonte, Sidney Poitier, and others had contributed money for the buses. As we pulled out of town, I hardly knew what we were getting into, but I figured I'd learn as I went along, just like I'd been doing all summer. It was just a joyous thing to be heading to challenge the regular Democratic Party. And a mysterious one. I didn't know then about the wheeling and dealing and compromises in politics. I had my mind on getting seated as the official Mississippi delegates. We wanted all the seats, and we would not take less than half.

The trip was going fine until we got up into the hills of Tennessee. That's when the Klan came out. The white man who was driving our bus started slowing down, and we saw some men setting up barriers in the middle of the road up ahead. At first I thought it might have been police or highway people doing work on the road. But when we got closer, I could see it was white men with guns—about eight or ten of them, and they were spreading out across the road. I was one of the captains on that bus charged with making sure that everybody was safe and that our people didn't do anything rash. I was seeing all this stuff happening and trying to figure out what to do. The others in the bus were seeing it, too, and they were shrieking and getting in the aisles, some scared and some just mad. So I started moving down the aisles to try to calm people down.

We were not supposed to be carrying guns, of course. But Mr. Turnbow grabbed my arm and started sputtering.

"They start anything, I have a gun, and my wife—she got one, too."

"Mr. Turnbow," I said, "we are not supposed to have weapons."

He said to his wife, "Baby, get out your gun." And Sweets reached into a paper bag and pulled out a pistol.

"We gonna, we gonna kill up a few of them," he said and got up.

I knew Mr. Turnbow would do it, too. He was from Holmes County and his house, like mine, was a freedom house, where activists stayed. When you went to Mr. Turnbow's house, you had to flash your lights. If you went at night, you'd better start flashing long before you got there because he *would* shoot at you.

The next thing I knew, a petite young brown-skinned woman got up and moved up the aisle, and when I looked around, she was in the seat right behind the driver. Before I knew what was going on, she had pulled a switchblade knife out of her purse and laid it on the front of the driver's neck. All she had to do was hit the button, and the blade would pop out. She told him, "Just move on."

He had started slowing down, and she said, "You better put your feet on the gas."

I don't know whether I was more scared that the Klan was going to get us all or that Mr. Turnbow was going to shoot or that the lady was going to kill the bus driver. And me sitting up on the bus trying to keep us nonviolent for the challenge.

I said to the bus driver, "Mister, you better not stop, because she is going to pull that blade across your throat, and there's some other people on here with guns."

That white bus driver turned blood red. He knew if he moved a muscle, his head was coming off. And down through there we went, picking up speed. When those folks trying to roadblock us saw that we were going to come on through, they scattered like scalded chickens and all their stuff went everywhere.

I felt sorry for the poor bus driver. I've thought about that man through the years. I have never seen anybody so scared in my life. When we got farther up the road, he stopped and made a telephone call, and we soon had a new driver. I don't know where he went, but I bet that was the happiest he'd ever been in his whole life.

We drove straight through without any more incidents. Every now and then we got out and stretched, but mostly we just kept moving. It's a good thing the bus had a restroom in the back. We had all packed lunches, and we slept on the bus. That's the way we always used to do it, because otherwise we might not find a place where black people were allowed to eat. It was even harder to find a place to spend the night. We arrived in Atlantic City on Friday, August 21, after a day and a half on the road. Our hotel, the Gem Hotel, was a mile or more from the convention center. It was not the best hotel, but it was the best we could afford. It was the first hotel I ever stayed in, and we slept five and six to a room. And I was in Atlantic City, New Jersey, trying to get seated as a delegate to the Democratic National Convention.

The old folks used to say, "I don't care if the mule goes blind. I'm going sit here holding the line." I'd been holding that line tight to get here, and I wasn't fixing to turn loose now.

The credentials committee would meet the next day to hear our challenge argument. As soon as we got to Atlantic City, people in our delegation started spreading out and talking to other state delegations to win support for our challenge. We told them about things that happened in our state and how we were denied the right to participate in the political process and then asked them for their support when the MFDP challenge went to the floor of the convention for a vote. I was assigned to two states, Wisconsin and Minnesota, I think it was. I told about going to the courthouse and being denied the right to register to vote and having crosses burned in my yard. I told about how our people were being killed and how we had been denied work chopping and picking cotton and how they put us out of the fields, how we had no money. I told it all. "The white people have taken away everything they could from us," I said, "but they haven't taken away our dignity." My two states voted to support us, and many of the other states our delegates spoke to were supportive, as well.

After the meetings the first night, we all went down to the boardwalk to see the sights. A breeze was blowing off the Atlantic Ocean; I had never been this cool in August. Soon we were singing freedom songs, and a crowd of onlookers gathered, some joining the singing. Throughout the week delegates, volunteers, and supporters gathered on the boardwalk near the convention center keeping vigil and singing freedom songs. Everyone attending the convention had to come by us to get into or out of the center. Herman DeCell from Yazoo City, who was a member of the regular Mississippi delegation, told me years later, when I was mayor of Mayersville and he was a state senator, that he and his wife and three children were entranced by our singing. Their children were so captivated, he said, they turned down a chance to see the Beatles, who were performing in Atlantic City that week, and stayed to hear us sing.

We had had no idea our delegation would get so much attention.

Reporters practically camped out at our hotel and followed us everywhere we went. The Mississippi Freedom Challenge was the biggest
thing happening at that convention.

The credentials committee met Saturday afternoon. Aaron Henry,
Ed King, Rita Schwerner, Martin Luther King Jr., and Fannie Lou
Hamer were scheduled to give testimony on behalf of the MFDP. Mrs.
Hamer and I had become good friends, and before she left for the
meeting, she sat me down in her hotel room and put me right-side
of her.

"Girl, you reckon I ought to tell it?" Mrs. Hamer asked me.

I said, "Tell it."

She said, "I'm going to tell it today. I'm sure going to tell it."

She told it, and the whole country was listening. The television networks covered the hearing live. The other speakers gave strong, elo-
quent statements about how blacks in Mississippi had been denied the
right to take part in the regular democratic process. But Mrs. Hamer
just tore the place down. She told about trying to register to vote and
being thrown off the plantation and having people shoot at her house
and about being beat up in the jail in Winona. The people in that room
and the millions of others who watched the proceedings on television
had never seen anyone like Fannie Lou Hamer—including President
Johnson, who was watching from the White House. He promptly called
a press conference, and the networks abruptly cut her off. That night,
however, they played her testimony over and over. Mrs. Hamer could
really talk—she could really make folks feel what she had been
through—and that day she had the whole country crying and thinking, too. She ended her talk with these words:

> If the Freedom Democratic Party is not seated now, I question
> America. Is this America, the land of the free and the home of
> the brave, where we have to sleep with our telephones off the
> hooks because our lives be threatened daily because we want
> to live as decent human beings?

Mrs. Hamer became nationally famous because of her speech, and she
taught us all. I never will forget that President Johnson broke in with a

message to the people, because he was the only person who could cut off Mrs. Hamer. Every television station across this nation was broadcasting her testimony. Mrs. Hamer had captured the United States, and the president knew it. We were moving—the MFDP was moving. That's the reason why Johnson had to do what he did. He hadn't counted on having any disruptions at his convention.

Some people today may have a hard time understanding why Lyndon Johnson, who had gotten the Civil Rights Act passed that summer, would be against the seating of the MFDP. After all, MFDP—not the regulars—were supporting Johnson; all but four of the regulars were openly supporting Goldwater, the Republican opponent. It was politics, pure and simple—my first look at hardball politics. Johnson, who was unopposed as the Democratic presidential nominee, was afraid that if the MFDP got seated, all the other southern states—including his state of Texas—would walk out of the convention. Johnson knew he had to win Texas to be elected, and he hoped to get Georgia and maybe another southern state or two. He also didn't want a big floor fight about the challenge, which he thought would look bad for the party and work against his election.

So President Johnson used the many resources at his disposal to prevent our delegation from being seated. He put Senator Hubert Humphrey, the well-known liberal civil rights proponent from Minnesota, in charge of keeping the Freedom Democrats from causing a scene that would endanger his election. Besides our challenge, the only other major issue to be determined at the convention was who would be Johnson's vice presidential running mate. Humphrey wanted that job. As majority whip of the U.S. Senate, Johnson had earned a reputation for being persuasive, using tough techniques—and winning. In 1964 he was at the top of his game.

After Saturday's hearing, the credentials committee postponed the decision and started trying to work out a solution that would satisfy both Mississippi delegations and also please the president. This effort went on for three days. At first we heard they wanted to make us "honored guests" who couldn't vote and seat us in the balcony. When I heard that, I said, "We been sitting in the balcony all our lives; I'm through sitting in the balcony." Then Edith Greene from Oregon presented to the committee a plan that would have seated all delegates of both parties who signed a pledge to vote for the national party's nominee. This plan had been used in past years when two delegations challenged seating. The Greene proposal would have been fine with us because we would have signed the pledge and most of the Mississippi regulars would not have. But Greene's plan was defeated in the committee because President Johnson didn't like it.

Then the committee came up with the plan of giving MDFP two seats at large—two seats that, the committee members had already decided, would be filled by Aaron Henry and Ed King. "At large" meant that the votes the two men cast would represent not Mississippi but the nation at large. Also, any regulars who pledged to support the president would still be allowed to vote. The committee called this a "compromise." I may not have been knowledgeable about politics, but I did know that a compromise was supposed to be something that both sides agreed on. This plan didn't seem much like a compromise to me; it looked like Lyndon Johnson was just throwing some scraps out to the dogs.

While members of the credentials committee were going through their negotiations, other delegates were meeting about our situation and trying to get us to accept the two-delegate compromise and not cause a scene. Congressman Charles Diggs, a black delegate from Michigan, had been one of our biggest supporters; but when all the black delegates caucused on Sunday night, he was among the first to fall off our bandwagon. Senator Humphrey was setting up meetings right and left to negotiate with our people, bringing in others to persuade us. Usually Aaron Henry, Ed King, Bob Moses, and our lawyer represented us at the meetings. At first Mrs. Hamer, as vice chair of our delegation, was invited to the meetings, but she was excluded after she told Humphrey to his face that he wanted to be vice president more than he wanted to do what was right and that she was going to pray for him.

The president brought in labor leader Walter Reuther and black activist Bayard Rustin to try to convince us. Then other outstanding black leaders in the country came to press for the president's position—Martin Luther King Jr., Roy Wilkins, head of the NAACP, and Whitney Young Jr., head of the national Urban League, and Andrew Young, director of the Southern Christian Leadership Conference.

Most of these men had been on our side earlier. Dr. King, in fact, had spent a week in July touring Mississippi and rallying people to participate in our MFDP precinct meetings, and he had spoken on our behalf to the credentials committee. But by the time of the credentials report on Tuesday evening, they were all singing the president's song: Take the compromise. They said Johnson's election was the best thing for the civil rights movement, for us in Mississippi, and for the MFDP. They insisted that Johnson needed the MDFP to cool it to improve his chances for reelection. They told us that as president, Johnson would be more inclined toward working for the Voting Rights Act if we went along with his plan and didn't do anything to jeopardize his election. Neither the president nor the credentials committee was going to change its decision, they said, and it was not in our best interest to fight the decision any longer. Something—anything—was better than nothing, they argued.

It got down to the big shots on the president's side talking to the big shots on our side. The poor folks in our delegation—which included most of us—weren't consulted at all. We were just backwards to them—little people out of some cotton field in Mississippi. Both sides went to calling us "ignorant grassroots folks." It's true that the majority of us were poor, uneducated folks out of Mississippi; most of the people in the delegation had not gone above the eighth grade in school. But we were not stupid, and there's a difference between stupid and ignorant.

On Tuesday afternoon Walter Mondale, a delegate from Minnesota, announced on television that the credentials committee had voted in favor of the so-called compromise. Bob Moses was irritated and quickly called a meeting of our delegation at the Union Temple Baptist Church. Before the meeting started, Mrs. Hamer and I were sitting in the vestibule with Bob Moses. I will never forget it. Mrs. Hamer said, "Girl, what you think about this compromise for two seats?" and I said, "Well, it don't make much sense to me, 'cause all us can't fit in them two seats." She looked at Bob, and she asked him what he thought we ought to do. He said, "It's your decision to make. You are the delegates. Do what you think is right." He did not tell us what to do. This was characteristic of Bob.

"All right," Mrs. Hamer said, and she got herself up and walked into the meeting. I came on in behind her. I can see her right now walking, because she had that limp. She went in through the side, and I came straight from the back. It was just our delegation and staff, and our big heads were in there saying the time had come to face reality and take the compromise. Ed King and Aaron Henry, who had started out being against the two-seat compromise, had been won over. Even our lawyer was now pushing compromise.

Three women did most of the talking against the compromise—Annie Devine, Victoria Gray, and Mrs. Hamer. These women with "mother wit" talked straight and tough and emotionally about what we needed—at least half the seats—and about what was right: Two at-large seats was not right. It was a fiery, combative meeting. Mr. Sias, who had been leaning toward the compromise, later said, "When those women got through whooping and hollering, I changed my mind." He told me, "Unita, I didn't want to be just breath and britches." When the vote was put to the MFDP delegation, we voted not to accept it, by 70 percent.

As soon as the meeting was over, we walked out in front and the press people—a dozen or more—were all over us. And Mrs. Hamer started singing—"Go tell it on the mountain. . . . Let my people go." When she got through singing—she was standing there with her head back and they had all those microphones in her face—she said, "We will not take the compromise." And she told them that we had been compromising all our lives. Then she put it out there as only Fannie Lou Hamer could do: "We didn't come all this way for no two seats. All of us is tired."

About five hundred supporters marched with us down the board-walk to the convention hall. Aaron Henry, who had voted in favor of the compromise, stuck with the delegation's decision and led the way. By the time we got to the hall, the credentials committee's decision had been announced by the chairman, approved, and gaveled into history—all in the wink of an eye. Many of the Mississippi regulars packed up and left, and the four Mississippi regulars who pledged to support Johnson were officially seated. Our delegation had been given "honored guest" tickets to sit in the balcony that night—as we had done on Monday night—but several of us decided to go onto the floor and take the now nearly empty Mississippi seats in protest. You had to have a credentials tag around your neck to get onto the floor. Twenty-one delegates from other states had given us their tags. I was sitting in one delegation and somebody else in another one, and we were scattered all over the place. Then gradually we began moving into the Mississippi seats. After an unsuccessful attempt by the sergeant at arms to remove us, the four regulars evacuated their seats, and our whole delegation sat in those seats for the rest of that night's session. We had made it into the convention hall and brought attention to our challenge.

The spotlight was on us that night in the hall. And I had a feeling I had never had before: It was a sense of history. I felt a part of history. I felt free and significant and very much a part of the United States of America. After the session that night, we sang as we had never sung it before. Mrs. Hamer was leading out the words. Most of the freedom songs have clapping, but when we sang "We Shall Overcome," we always held hands and swayed and sang it very slowly. A woman from another delegation who heard us said it was the most haunting sound she ever heard, and "the words seemed to float in the air."

> Deep in my heart,
> I know it's true.
> We shall overcome some day.

The song filled me with hope every time I sang it, but that night I knew it was true: Another level of slavery had fallen away.

Wednesday morning Aaron called us together again to reconsider our vote. This time we heard reasoned arguments from Andrew Young and Dr. King to accept the compromise, but they didn't change any minds. When we voted the second time, the results were the same. Even when I didn't always agree with Martin Luther King on issues, I was drawn in by his personal magnetism. He was a powerful presence in any room and made you want to get close to him. I could sense that he truly loved people, and that alienated me. I didn't want to hear about love in those situations. Mrs. Hamer and I would talk, and we'd be mad at him sometimes because he always wanted to compromise or move too slow. We were SNCC, and we were hot, moving, and ready. Andy Young got his thinking from King, but he was more reachable. Later, when I worked with Andy on the Delta Ministry board, we'd clash over the same kind of thinking—being too safe—and I'd say the churches have to recognize that we cannot water down the issues: We just have to tell the truth. Clashes between angry grassroots SNCC folks and the calmer, more conservative NAACP and SCLC people would continue for several years, and sometimes the organizations seemed to work at cross-purposes. I see now that it took all types of people and tactics to fight injustice and gain equal rights for our people.

When we loaded the buses to return to Mississippi, we were informed that because we had disregarded the injunction not to leave the state we'd all be arrested when we got to the Mississippi state line. The law we had broken was "impersonating a political party." We fully expected to go to jail when we got back home. We made it back to Mississippi, however, without any difficulty. But the whole trip had been some kind of ride.

Even though we didn't win our challenge, the experience didn't feel like defeat to me. We had, in fact, knocked out most of the regulars from being seated, and we had drawn national attention to our new party and to problems within the national Democratic organization. We had stood proud and strong. At that convention I had learned a lot about politics—practical politics—and how political parties operate. I had learned that how people said they were going to vote and how they actually voted were often two different things. I had learned about backroom deals and heavy-handed political power. I found out that a person with poor education could be a major player in the political world, that perfect grammatical speech is not a requirement for leadership. I discovered that I had a political voice and an ability to use it.

I had seen enough to know that your vote can make a difference, that you can support what you think is right and persuade people to change their minds. And that if enough people will get together and stick together, they can change the political landscape. Although we hadn't been successful in getting seated, we had made a difference within our own delegation. And I believed that if we could get our people registered to vote and get them to the polls, voting could make a difference, even in Mississippi.

I hope this nation never forgets the 1964 Democratic National Convention, because we dared to challenge the party and this nation to do something about injustice, and it started a whole new thinking process. We dared to question. Here was a group of people who had never—most of us—been involved in a political process, and we were trying to find out how it worked. We questioned the ways things were being done. We challenged this nation to let us in. The Democratic Party—and America—needed to be challenged into the shock and reality of how it had cut off segments of people, how prejudice had silenced and smothered vast numbers of people. As a result of our challenge, the Democratic Party liberalized its policies about minority delegations. This nation needs to be challenged anew with each passing generation.

We should all dare to question. Dare to question political parties, presidents, local and state officials. This country was founded on the right to question. We must not stand silent when events run counter to the principles of our country, no matter how large or loud or "official" the group on the other side. We have to question because that's the way we remain free. It bothers me today when I hear people who question the president or government policies called "unpatriotic"—the same way civil rights activists used to be labeled "Communist." In November 1964 the *Jackson Clarion-Ledger* published national columnist Jack Anderson's assessment under the headline "Reds in State Freedom Party":

> It is no secret that a few communists have managed to infiltrate the civil rights movement. Four members of the freedom delegation that sought to represent Mississippi at the Democratic Convention, for example, were known to have communist ties.
>
> They raised shrill objections to the slightest compromise, seemed more interested in stirring up trouble than in settling any issues.

It's no surprise that Anderson was unable to name the four "communists" or to identify their "known . . . communist ties," because there were none. "I know 'bout as much about communism as a horse knows about Christmas," Mrs. Hamer once told a reporter. And she used to tell me, "If they ain't calling you a Communist, you ain't doing your job."

* * *

Even though Lyndon Johnson hadn't stood behind seating our Freedom Democratic delegation, I supported him in the November election, as most of us in the MDFP did. A few hard-liners accused us of selling out after our stand at the convention, and Bob Moses himself was so disillusioned after being unable to shake the party establishment that he left the movement the following year, changed his name to Bob Parris, and moved to Africa. But most of us believed we had made our point and now was the time to choose the better of the two candidates running. I believed that Lyndon Johnson was more likely than Goldwater to get the Voting Rights Act passed and support other programs to help black people. It was as simple as that. In retrospect, I see this decision marked the point at which I became a political person—a true believer in the political process.

I was excited about our new state party and about jumping into the Mississippi political fray. That didn't take long. The Mississippi Freedom Democratic Party nominated Fannie Lou Hamer, Annie Devine, and Victoria Gray for the U.S. House of Representatives from their respective districts to run in the November general election. We hustled to circulate petitions to get our candidates listed on the official general election ballot, along with the regular Democrats' candidates. But the regulars controlled the process and said we didn't have enough signatures. So shortly before the official general election, we decided to have our own open "freedom election." To get ready for the vote, the MDFP held "citizenship schools" across the state, and I helped distribute "freedom primers" to new and potential black voters, explaining in simple words and short sentences what MFDP was, what had happened at the national convention, and how both the general and the freedom elections would work.

The Sharkey County sheriff was keeping an eye on us during this time, as the Mississippi State Sovereignty Commission reported: "An automobile, occupied by several people, was observed in the county, and [the sheriff] believed these to be COFO organizers. He stated that the tag number of the car was 288B-147 and belonged to Unita Blackwell. This was a 1964 Plymouth."

* * *

As expected, Goldwater took Mississippi in the general election with 87 percent of the state's vote! I cast my first vote ever at the Issaquena County Courthouse, where six months before I'd been afraid for my life, and I voted for the winner. Just that quick, I'd gone from picking cotton to picking the president! Along with sixty thousand others, I also voted in the "freedom election," in which our MFDP congressional candidates ran. Part of the Freedom Summer program involved setting up parallel open elections for blacks, unregistered and registered, to learn the voting process and create a political structure for blacks in the state, as well as to make a show of strength to white Mississippi and the federal government. SNCC had held a freedom election for governor in 1963. If our freedom candidates had been allowed on the general election ballot in 1964, they would certainly have lost. But, as expected, they won the freedom vote. Our election didn't count. Or did it?

In January 1965 the Mississippi Freedom Democratic Party decided to challenge the seating of the regular Mississippi congressional delegation. The challenge was based on the grounds that the official winners had been illegally elected because blacks had been denied the right to vote. Our freedom election, in contrast, had been open to anyone and everyone. We knew the challenge was a long shot at best, but we needed to use every opportunity to make the public aware of the severity of voter discrimination in Mississippi. We were used to losing, but we were also learning that when you're organizing, even your defeats call attention to your position, and each defeat brings a few more people along.

MDFP presented its challenge argument to the U.S. Congress in January, at the time all members were sworn in. House members voted (276–149) for a temporary seating of the "official" Mississippi congressmen, pending a full investigation of MFDP's challenge. Throughout the spring and summer of 1965, MDFP lawyers took testimony from hundreds of black Mississippians who'd been threatened and prevented from registering to vote. And for the first time ever, white elected state officials—the attorney general, the secretary of state, and others—had to answer questions under oath in public hearings.

In September, I was among several hundred people from Mississippi who rode the bus to Washington to be there when the challenge went before the U.S. Congress for its decision. A couple of days earlier, a subcommittee had voted in a closed hearing to recommend to the House that the challenge be dismissed. Our lawyers were pushing for the women to testify personally on the floor, since there had been no public hearings. We knew then our chances were slim, but we wanted to support our candidates, and the publicity we'd generate certainly wouldn't hurt our cause. About noon the day before the vote, our Mississippi freedom group and sympathizers stationed ourselves on the east front of the Capitol, keeping a silent vigil for twenty-four hours. There were about four hundred of us in all. We broke late in the afternoon to attend a prayer service at the Washington National Cathedral, which the National Council of Churches held for us.

The next day, September 17, 1965, I accompanied Mrs. Hamer, Annie Devine, and Vicki Gray to the House of Representatives, walking through a long passageway formed by the hundreds of people supporting our challenge. I took my seat in the visitors' gallery, along with as many other challenge supporters as could fit in. Representative Charles Diggs, from Illinois, had made sure I got a place; Diggs's family was from Issaquena County and he was related to my husband. As we waited for the session to begin, Diggs and a young black congressman from California, James Roosevelt, came up to talk with me. They wanted us to know that people might be saying all kinds of mean and nasty things in the debate, and they hoped we wouldn't be embarrassed and feel rejected if the three women weren't allowed to speak or if the challenge was defeated.

"What the hell are you talking about?" I said. "You think we won't be able to take it if three Mississippi women get rejected? We've been embarrassed and rejected all our lives."

Speaker of the House John McCormick had invited our three candidates to the floor. I watched with pride from the gallery as Congressman William F. Ryan of New York, the challenge sponsor, escorted my friends to their seats. They were the first black women ever to have floor privileges at the U.S. House of Representatives—and the first black people from Mississippi since Reconstruction. The women were not invited to make statements, and after debate the challenge was voted down 228 to 143.

But as with the Atlantic City experience, defeat didn't feel like defeat to me. It was almost worth the struggle I had endured to see those black Mississippi women seated on the floor of the U.S. House of Representatives. We hadn't won the challenge, but we were in the race, and people knew we were in it for real. When we started out, we were all excited and wanted to reach the finish line quickly. But we had to adjust our thinking. We were discovering that gaining political influence is a process of going step by step. Learning to do anything new and different doesn't happen overnight. And if you don't dare to challenge, it may not ever happen.

12

Things May Get Worse
Before They Get Better

A S I HAD HOPED, President Johnson stepped up his efforts to get the Voting Rights Act passed. In early 1965 the U.S. Civil Rights Commission documented voter discrimination throughout southern states for the president and Congress to use in determining the need for a voting rights bill. (This was going on at the same time the MFDP was making its congressional challenge.) In February, the commission held hearings in Jackson, and I was among those testifying. The hearings took place at the Veterans Administration Hospital. It was a strange place to hold hearings, but when I asked about it, I was told that the city and state wouldn't allow the commission to meet on their property. The VA hospital was the best place they could find. At the time of the hearings, I was in Atlanta attending a SNCC retreat and was called to go to Jackson for the hearings.

This was the occasion of my first flight in an airplane and the first time I ever stayed in a Mississippi hotel. I was skittish about flying, but as soon as we got in the air, a young lady came by and asked me if I'd like a cocktail. "A cocktail? What is that?" I had never heard of a cocktail. "It's a drink," she said. I ordered one right away, and that ended my fear of flying. The night before my testimony, I spent the night at the Admiral Benbow Inn, located on State Street, with Victorian mansions on either side and a swimming pool out back. It was hard to believe that a black person—namely me—was staying in a nice motel in Jackson, Mississippi.

The following afternoon, I testified before the commissioners. They were an outstanding group: John Hannah, president of Michigan State, the Reverend Theodore Hesburgh of Notre Dame, Erin Griswold from Harvard Law School, and Mrs. Frankie Freeman, a black attorney from St. Louis. I told them about going to the courthouse to take the registration test three times before I was registered. After I finished giving my testimony about the difficulties I had had getting registered to vote, Father Hesburgh asked if I anticipated having any difficulty because I had come to the hearings and participated. Here is my answer, as recorded in the commission's report:

> Well, I don't know, because it has got to the place, you know—
> well, the other day we was coming out—we had been to Mr.
> Jackson's house, and was talking to him about coming to a par-
> ents' meeting, and some white guys came up in a truck and
> blocked us and got out and told us all kinds of nasty things,
> "Get out of here and don't come back." That was Wednesday,
> and the Sunday before then, the same truck, they run a lot of
> school kids out because they was down talking to people, and
> [the white men] had a gun and [they were] flashing it, you
> know, and saying, "I could have killed you way back yonder in
> the woods," and all this kind of stuff.
>
> And you just get to the place you know it's going to happen,
> but you've just got to stand up and got to do something.

By June of 1965, elected officials in Mississippi knew there was no stopping the U.S. Congress from passing the Voting Rights Act. (Johnson's voting rights bill was introduced in March, after Bloody Sunday on the Selma bridge.) So the governor and state legislature cooked up another plan. In the early summer as we were gearing up for another voter registration drive, the governor called a special session of the legislature to repeal some of the state's unfair voter registration laws, such as the requirement to interpret the state constitution. That sounded fine, until we discovered his motive: He thought that bringing our laws more in line with northern states would put Mississippi in a better position to challenge the new federal voting rights law. That's the kind of thinking our state did best in those days—scheming and conniving to figure out some way to get around doing what was right for black Mississippians. Even when state officials seemed to be doing right, we couldn't trust them to be right.

To protest the special session, the MDFP organized what was supposed to be a quiet march to the state capitol. I was on the executive committee of MFDP and one of the leaders of the protest. We met the night before with our party chair, Lawrence Guyot, and decided this would be a silent, orderly demonstration. We would walk on the sidewalks, two abreast, rather than down the middle of the street in a large, unmanageable throng.

About six hundred people—black and white, young, old, and in between, including many teenagers—gathered at Morning Star Baptist Church on Monday morning, June 14, to get their instructions and pick up leaflets to pass out. A little before noon we started out on our walk from the church to the capitol, which was about a mile away. We were halfway there when the police approached Guyot and asked if he had a parade permit. We hadn't applied for one, since we knew from experience it was a futile exercise. They already knew the answer, of course, but they waited for him to say no before a gang of police stormed us.

I was walking along by the Sun-n-Sand Motel on Lamar Street when the police came out and started grabbing and hitting us, knocking us down, and dragging us into the street. They had dogs and sticks. The police were beating us, and we were hitting the streets, covering our heads, and curling up to protect ourselves. My son was with me at the time—he wasn't quite eight years old. And I can hear Jerry now, screaming, "Don't put your hands on my mama." He was screaming and holding on to me. He didn't want to turn me loose. I had to get my son out of there. We had planned for this. We were always cautious, and we'd arranged for several women to be available to take children who were walking with their parents, in case something like this happened. They would make sure the children got home or to a relative's house. So I looked over to the side and saw one of the women, and I gave her the eye. She came and got Jerry and several other children and ran with them away from the scene. I'll never forget his screams, and I don't think he will either.

Then they turned all the troops loose on us. They grabbed us and threw us in paddy wagons and in those big caged trucks they picked up garbage in. They just crammed us in on top of one another and took us to the livestock barns at the state fairgrounds near downtown Jackson. Then they snatched us out of the paddy wagons, and when they got us out, they slung us around and threw us up against a concrete block wall. They were beating the men, hitting them upside the head. You could see knots swelling before your eyes, and blood running. They were pushing us like we were horses or cattle or something, getting us inside the barns. The city had called in the game and fish commissioners, the highway patrol, and every other kind of officer they could find in Jackson. They kept bringing demonstrators in all through the day. By the end of the day, 482 of us had been arrested. This went on throughout the next couple of weeks until the federal court made them stop. In all, nearly eleven hundred people were arrested.

Inside the livestock barns, they separated the men and the women. They took Mrs. Ripley and some of the other old people and put them in the jail downtown. They were trying to locate all the leaders of the protest, weed us out, and keep us apart from everybody else. In the cattle barns, they would tell the masses of the people that they could go home if they would testify against the leaders—say that they didn't know why they were there, that we had made them do it. The police were trying to take all the strength of the movement.

I began to spot what was going on, how they were operating. The policemen had brought in some women "Toms" to infiltrate our group to identify those in charge. They would stand and watch to see which ones of us had a big group gathered around us and try to jerk out the leader. We had black and white women holding on to each other—we were in this together—and the police decided that gave us too much strength, so they took all the white ones somewhere else and left nothing but the black women where I was. That first day they removed fourteen leaders, but they didn't get me, not that day or later. I was the only one left from the MFDP who had helped stage the march. I knew those other women needed me, and I had to stay with them. I found the perfect place to dodge the authorities and to take care of the other women at the same time: I moved myself into the bathroom.

I stayed in the bathroom most of the time during the day. Eleven days I sat on a garbage can in the bathroom. That was the only way I could talk to the women in private and try to hold them together. Most of them were young. They would come in and say, "I don't know how my children are. I wonder what my family's doing." And they would burst out in tears. These women knew they wanted to vote, and they believed the march was the right thing to do. But many of them hadn't realized the personal danger and sacrifice that movement work would require of them. They hadn't yet made that soul-deep commitment. So they had a difficult time worrying about their families and handling the horrors they were experiencing in the stockyard. I sat there on that garbage can and said, "You can make it."

Nobody even had a change of clothes. We'd all wash out our underwear every night and hang it up in the bathroom—hundreds of panties, hanging everywhere. Police would pull up the women's dresses. Just a lot of filth went on, you know. Then they brought in doctors, and they opened every one of the women's legs, mine included. We had to undress, and they looked up in our vaginas, put their hands up in there, and stuck things in them. They said they were examining us to see if we had some terrible disease. It wasn't even done privately, but with a whole bunch of women in a big room at the same time. It was terrible to see hundreds of naked, humiliated women all standing in a row. So depressing and sad and repulsive.

We didn't have any blankets or anything to lie on. We slept on bare concrete floors. And the police walked us—kept us moving. They would walk us all night long. Just about time we'd nod off to sleep, somebody would come in and say, "Niggers, move up." And the guards worked in shifts to keep us awake, to harass and torture us. They would go to hollering at one or two o'clock in the morning. They'd say things like "Something is stinking in here. Do you see any niggers?" Then they would come in and move us again.

They would keep us up all night. And when we tried to take a little nap in the daytime, they would get us up, and then they'd turn the hoses on us. They'd say we were filthy, and then they'd bring in disinfectant and spray it over us. They would empty a big container of disinfectant on the floor, and then they'd spray it with water and it would get all over us. It would get all in your eyes. I tried to get out of the way, but if I got too far away, somebody would be standing there with a stick hitting me.

One day when they were moving us around, one woman just refused to move. She said, "I just ain't going to move no more." So one of the policemen grabbed this woman. Now this was a big woman. The man's name was Red; he was one that really loved to torture us. And Red was planning to drag her off, but she reached up and grabbed him between the legs and caught hold of his testicles. Red throwed up his hands and lost his stick. She took his gun, everything, Red just gave it up. He was trying to scream, but that man couldn't say nothing. He was in a mess. He buckled down and went to his knees. I can see Red now, his eyes bugged out and going down. Red had harassed this woman till she couldn't take any more.

And so Red was laid out; and then we all went to hollering and laughing, because we couldn't do anything else. We made a circle and Red was in the middle. Red was hurting so bad, he couldn't walk, couldn't even get up. So when the guard came to see what the commotion was about, he missed Red at first. It was five minutes before he found him, down on the floor.

And then the reinforcement troops moved in. They moved in and cocked their guns. And I thought: I have gotten your message. I glanced over at the other women and gave them a look and a gesture that said, back off, because they're fixing to shoot us. And those women understood the message. The police were going to let us all down that day. But we backed off.

And then they came in, and they beat that woman. They closed in on her and held her down, and they spread her legs open wide and beat her between the legs. They just moved in on her. They beat her and they beat her and they beat her. Just beat her, savagely. They were calling her an animal, and worse. And I was thinking, the only animals around here are the police.

After eleven days of this insanity, we were released. A group of women from the North—black women, white women—had come to the state with a program called "Wednesdays in Mississippi," to support civil rights organizers. When they saw the evidence of brutality, they called upon the National Council of Churches to help out. Not long after that a fifty-thousand-dollar bond was posted on our behalf, and they let us all out. I'll be forever grateful for their aid.

Before that horrible experience—even with all the other things that had happened to me before and to others—nobody could have made me believe that such savagery could go on in the United States of America, savagery carried out by law enforcement under the direction of elected officials. When I hear all these things that are happening now—al-Qaeda terrorists, our own "war on terrorism," and the torture our own people inflicted on Iraqi prisoners—it feels so strange because black people in Mississippi went through this. I don't think most people today—younger people especially—have any idea the price that ordinary black Mississippians have paid. Sometimes today people look at those who got through all this, and in spite of it managed to have a little success, and say, "Them people think they something." They don't know what kind of hell we been through. I can hardly bear, even now—forty years later—to think about it.

President Johnson signed the Voting Rights Act into law on August 2, 1965, making it against the law to deny an eligible black person the right to register and vote. I was proud that I had been a part of gaining these rights. In an inspiring address to both houses of Congress that day, President Johnson expressed ideals I think every generation of our citizens and our leaders needs to hear anew:

> The central fact of American civilization—one so hard for others to understand—is that freedom and justice and the dignity of man are not just words to us. We believe in them. Under all the growth and the tumult and abundance, we believe. And so, as long as some among us are oppressed—and we are part of that oppression—it must blunt our faith and sap the strength of our high purpose.
>
> Thus, this is a victory for the freedom of the American Negro. But it is also a victory for the freedom of the American Nation. And every family across this great, entire searching land will live more splendid in expectation, and will be prouder to be American because of the act that you have passed that I will sign today.

Not long after the president signed the Voting Rights Act, I was among a group of two hundred civil rights leaders and activists invited by the president to Washington to plan a White House conference titled "To Fulfill These Rights." The conference, which would take place the following spring, was supposed to address ways to translate the ideals of racial equality into reality. When we got there, the meetings seemed part of the president's PR campaign to smooth things over with civil rights leaders, but we went further and called for the president to "act now"—not wait until the spring—to enforce the Civil Rights Acts of 1964 and 1965 and to crack down on discrimination in housing and education, jury selection, and law enforcement. I don't think much came out of our "planning." To tell the truth, I went to so many meetings like that in those days, I don't remember many specifics of the sessions. But I have vivid memories of my first visit to the White House.

President and Mrs. Johnson held a reception for us shortly before the start of our work. We all got together and went over to the White House. I wanted to act dignified because I was in the White House, and this important man had just signed the bill saying we had done right in fighting to vote. The president and his wife, Lady Bird, were standing there in the big hall. A young lady was standing in front of them, telling us what to do. This was the "receiving line," she explained. I was supposed to speak to the president and tell him who I was. If he reached out to shake my hand, I was to shake his hand and then Lady Bird's hand. I had never been in a receiving line in my whole life. But I did all right, I guess.

Then we walked into another room and kind of made a circle, standing around the room. I had never been in any setting this fabulous and fancy. When I had worked in rich white people's houses and waited on them, their houses looked nice but nothing compared to this place. I was standing there, kind of in shock, gazing at the chandeliers and the fancy heavy curtains and thinking, I wish Aunt Rosetta could see this fine room. And I looked across the room and saw bottles and bottles of whiskey, all laid out. I could walk right over to them if I wanted to, or a waiter wearing a bow tie would come over to me and say, "What would you like to drink?" And he'd pour me a shot of whatever I wanted and bring it to me. I could drink whiskey or whatever, right there in the White House, in front of the president of the United States. I'd take me a little sip and walk around.

I stopped drinking a long time ago, but in those days I liked to take a drink. I had never seen that much liquor. Mississippi was a dry state. Of course, we could find something to drink in Mississippi, but we'd usually be on the stoop of somebody's house drinking or in some little place around the corner. In the background I came out of, we didn't have big cocktail parties.

The president served ribs—Texas barbecued ribs. And those were the best-tasting ribs I've ever had. They had the ribs cut so we could pick up one rib at a time. And they had napkins—cloth napkins—everywhere, so we wouldn't get barbecue sauce all over us or on the furniture. Two fantastic things were happening to me in the White House. I could drink legal whiskey in the White House, and I was eating the best ribs that you'd ever want to taste, while the president of the United States was standing right there with me. Since then I've been to the White House many times to see presidents and first ladies, but this was the most amazing thing that had ever happened to me up to that time, and I'll never forget it.

Growing up, I'd heard my family talking about "dirty low-down Hoover starving us to death," and they'd say Franklin Roosevelt cared about us. But before that day in the White House, I couldn't relate to the president of the United States as a person. That day, I struck up a conversation with President Johnson.

Some of the people started leaving, and several of us from SNCC were still standing around talking. Those bottles and bottles of that good "seal" whiskey—not moonshine—were still laid out on the table, and some of them hadn't even been opened. I was standing there looking at those bottles everywhere, and I thought it would be nice to get me a fifth of this whiskey and take it back to Mississippi and show those people what I got at the White House. I had a big purse, but it was in the coatroom. So I just picked up a fifth of whiskey and put it under my arm. I looked around at the president so he could see what I was doing, because I didn't want the president of the United States to take off behind me for stealing whiskey from the White House.

With the whiskey under my arm, I walked right on over to the president and said, "If y'all ain't going to drink this whiskey, ain't no use of it going back to the kitchen. I would like to take a bottle of this whiskey back to Mississippi." He looked at the bottle and looked back at me with his eyebrows sort of raised, but not in a disapproving way.

"Mr. President," I said, "you know Mississippi's a dry state, and the folks are right now debating about legalizing whiskey. If we can stand here in Washington, D.C., in the White House, right in front of you and everybody else, and drink legal whiskey, I'm going to let them folks at home know that it's all right to have legal whiskey." I told the president—I could see he was trying not to laugh—"Now, I want you to know that there's plenty of whiskey stills in Mississippi and they are illegal. But I will speak to the situation when I get back."

About that time somebody came up and handed me my purse, and I stuck my whiskey in it. On my way out, I turned around and said, "You had some mighty good ribs, Mr. President, and I thank you very much." He didn't mention the whiskey, and I didn't either. The president just smiled.

13

Focus on What Matters Most

FROM THE TIME the movement came into my life until today, one road has led to another. When you find something that gives your life meaning and moves you and makes you feel alive, you know you're barefootin' in the right direction. Once I got the vision in sight that black people in Mississippi could improve our own conditions and that I had ability and talent and drive to help, all I wanted to do was focus on those possibilities. There was so much to do, and many things were happening at once. Our people needed a living wage to get food and clothes and a decent place to live. We needed better educational opportunities for our children. In 1965, along with my activities with the MDFP and the congressional challenge and demonstrating for the Voting Rights Act, I decided to focus on the education of our children. Since I only finished the eighth grade, I was especially touched by the struggles of children in school. The future of our children—my own son's future—was at stake. Their future is everyone's future. Our children and their education matter most. We have to take care of our children.

On Friday, January 29, 1965, thirty students at Henry Weathers High School, the Issaquena County high school for blacks, wore SNCC buttons to school. These were little round pins, about an inch in diameter, with a black hand and a white hand clasped and the letters "SNCC" above them. The principal, E. O. Jordan, called several male students into his office and told them to remove the pins. According to the students, Mr. Jordan told them they couldn't wear the buttons because the white folks didn't like the artwork showing black and white hands clasped. Mr. Jordan, who was black, said they could not attend school "wearing buttons and creating a disturbance unless the Superintendent of the School Board overrules me." He also said that one of the students called him an "Uncle Tom."[1]

The following Monday, when 150 students wore buttons and were distributing them to other students, Mr. Jordan gathered the students in the cafeteria and told them all they couldn't wear the SNCC buttons. The next day 200 students wore buttons, and Mr. Jordan said if they didn't remove them, they would be suspended. By the end of the week, he had suspended 300 students.

This was a serious matter to me. I always worked with the kids and tried to help them, and I had given these pins to students who wanted them. I wasn't trying to stir up a rebellion; I wanted our young people to have a symbol to help them feel that they were just as good as white children—that they mattered—and that white and black people could live in harmony with each other. So I talked with the students and with some of their parents. The kids assured me they weren't trying to create a disturbance and didn't want to create a disturbance; they just wanted to wear their pins. Soon students in the elementary school—including Jerry, who was a second-grader—were wearing SNCC buttons, too.

I wanted the students to return to school, but I also believed they should be able to wear their buttons, if they didn't create a disturbance. Several other parents and I went to see Mr. Jordan and tried to meet with the white superintendent and the Sharkey-Issaquena school board. The officials wouldn't consider our argument. We also asked one of the black high school teachers, Ms. Killens, who wasn't as pushy as the rest of us, to talk with Mr. Jordan, to mediate between the parents and school officials. She got nowhere, either; in fact, her contract wasn't renewed at the end of the year. The principal announced that any student who remained home for twenty days would be sus-

---

1. From briefs filed with the U.S. Court of Appeals for the Fifth Circuit.

pended for the rest of the year. After that, all the kids walked out—about six hundred from both schools—in a boycott.

To me, the matter was about more than buttons. Jerry started first grade in 1963, and I wanted him to get a better education than I'd been able to get. It was long past time to get rid of the split session that closed black schools in the spring and fall so children could work in the cotton fields. We desperately needed good, well-paid teachers and better school facilities, including up-to-date textbooks instead of the old, torn-up, scribbled-on textbooks that the white schools had discarded. We would never get any of these things, I believed, without black principals who were willing to stand up to the white superintendents and white school boards and aggressively plead for our children's benefit. Principal Jordan had never been a strong advocate. He was a yes-man who, I believed, was more concerned about keeping his job than helping our children. If he had truly cared anything about our children, he would have said long ago to the superintendent of education, "You make sure that these children have the books they need. If not, I will not take the job."

Jordan's response to the SNCC pin incident, I felt, was just another sign of his fear and weakness. Before my voter registration work, I saw such problems as impossible and hopeless. But I'd discovered that black people do have the ability to make change. I was an organizer now, and I wanted to get something done. We had a serious situation on our hands. We had to stand up for our children. Although my work had begun as a way to improve education for students in black schools, it led to the desegregation of the Sharkey-Issaquena schools.

So I called Marian Wright, who was with the NAACP Legal Defense Fund in Jackson. A recent graduate of the Yale Law School, she was a faithful source of wise counsel, compassion, and hope. "Thank God for Marian," I've said many times. I could always count on Marian to look into our problems and do the right thing. I asked her: "What are we gonna do about our children?" She said our students had been denied their First Amendment rights—freedom of speech—and we needed to file a lawsuit. Clarence Hall and I went to Jackson and met with Marian and the other NAACP lawyers, who explained what was involved. In the lawsuit we would ask the court for an injunction to compel the school to allow the students to attend school and wear the buttons.

Marian said that in the same suit we should also address the larger issue of the poor quality of education of black children, since Mississippi still operated "separate but equal" school systems more than a decade after the *Brown* decision. There was, however, no indication that opportunities in the black schools would ever be equal to opportunities for whites. Therefore, we would ask the federal courts to prohibit the school district from operating "compulsory racially segregated schools."

First we needed to get supporters among the black parents to sign petitions requesting that the schools make changes. These petitions would go to the school authorities, who would have a chance to respond. We went back and talked to the people in Sharkey and Issaquena counties. People were mad and several hundred parents signed petitions asking that authorities do the following things: begin desegregating the schools; make the quality of curriculum and instruction equal in white and black schools; abolish the split school term; and, finally, allow students to wear freedom pins to school.

On March 6, we sent the petition to the school boards of all Issaquena and Sharkey county schools. The school boards did not respond, and we filed a lawsuit on April 1. My son's name was listed first on the suit, so the case is known as *Blackwell v. Issaquena County Board of Education*. His daddy was listed with him; we had so many names I left my name off. There were 196 other plaintiffs, and the defendants also included all other school boards in the two counties.

On May 17, when the school year was almost over, the district judge, Harold Cox, turned down the request for an injunction concerning the freedom pins.[2] But, of more lasting importance, he ruled at the same time that black students in Issaquena County could not be prohibited from attending white schools beginning in the fall of 1965, and he ordered the schools to submit a desegregation plan to comply with federal law. *Blackwell v. Issaquena County* was one of the very first desegregation cases in Mississippi. (It was set up as an open case

---

2. In July 1966 the U.S. Court of Appeals for the Fifth Circuit upheld the previous judge's decision on the grounds that the students were disrupting the educational process and the principal had the right to make decisions regarding order in his school.

to be enforced on an ongoing basis, and today, after all these years, lawsuits in those counties are still filed in its name.)

The Sovereignty Commission files show that white parents had at least two meetings about the boycotts and other "agitative work which outside people have been carrying on in these two counties and which is being sponsored by COFO." According to the files, after we sent our petitions to the school officials, about seventy-five to one hundred white citizens gathered to discuss the situation. The commission learned from the parents and duly reported that "white slouchy beatnik-looking people"—two women, Valery Hogan and Elizabeth Fussco, and four white men—were in Rolling Fork; and "also Eunita [sic] Blackwell, colored female of Atlanta, Georgia, is in the area at work, and two negro males from Chicago." The investigator somberly concluded his report with this analysis:

> I have not been able to determine thus far whether any of the ones mentioned herein are members of any subversive organization or if they, themselves, are Communists. They are, however, following the Communist line in creating cells from which to work in a peaceful community stirring up discord and trouble among the races.

What Liz Fussco, Valery Hogan, and I were actually doing—in our "Communist cell"—was setting up a school to educate the children who had been kicked out. Many of the students who boycotted had gone back to school before the twenty-day limit, but about fifty children, including my son, did not, and we had to get busy figuring out how to educate them. The previous summer SNCC workers and teachers had established "freedom schools" for black students in many other parts of the state—a concept created by Charlie Cobb—but we didn't have any in Issaquena County. So now we set up freedom school classrooms in churches and homes throughout the county to teach our children. I took the lead in organizing these, finding locations, and spreading the word about them to parents in the area.

SNCC put out an urgent call across the country for volunteer teachers, and we ended up with some of the best teachers in America—highly educated, caring people, most of them white. The teachers were amazing, and we saw how our children were learning and really seemed to be enjoying it. This was the first time most of those black children had ever been around white people, except for working as their field hands or babysitters. And the children had fine textbooks to study, because people from up north sent books and school equipment. In no time we had put together a good educational system for our kids, much better, in fact, than they would have had in the public schools, white or black. Thirty-five years later, Jerry still talks enthusiastically about his freedom school experience—how considerate and kind his teachers were, how they didn't try to pour information into his head in a strict, controlling way but got him involved in learning, and how much he learned. The students learned reading, writing, math, and science through activities and problems from their everyday experiences.

In addition to teaching the regular school subjects, the freedom schools were teaching students to believe they could make something of themselves. Poor Mississippi Delta blacks had never understood freedom, and I wanted our children to learn that black people have as much right to freedom as white people—freedom to vote, yes, but also freedom to live out their dreams—and to pass it on to others. The freedom schools were helping the children to discover that reading and education can be fun and exciting and unlock the door to a better life. They were learning about African American history, too, and discovering that they had a heritage to be proud of.

It was a struggle to get through all this, not just with the school people, black and white, but also with some black parents who were afraid to rock the boat and became agitated at those of us who were trying to get something done. I didn't come down hard on those people, because I understood where they were coming from. Gradually other parents began to become less fearful and get more involved. In the summer many more students wanted to attend freedom schools, and we had to get more teachers. Older teachers, university professors, came to Mississippi and spent their summer teaching our children. After that, we had freedom schools every summer until the time of complete desegregation in 1970.

It was my responsibility to keep the schools going and the money coming in. I'd get people together, and we'd write letters to those who had contributed to other civil rights projects. I made speeches around the country about the freedom schools and our needs. Our needs weren't great—just books and pencils and paper. We didn't pay the teachers—most of them volunteered their time or were SNCC staff people who worked for nearly nothing. We had come up out of the dirt with nothing, but we were creating schools by getting people from other parts of the country to make donations of their money and time to help us. And our children were learning to believe in themselves and take an interest in school.

By 1970 the freedom schools had ceased operation, but in the early 1990s, the Children's Defense Fund, under the direction of Marian Wright Edelman, rejuvenated the concept as part of the Black Community Crusade for Children (BCCC). Now eight-week summer freedom schools operate in low-income, high-crime neighborhoods in more than twenty states. (Freedom schools are part of BCCC's "No Child Left Behind" program, created long before President George W. Bush latched on to that title for his presidential campaign.) When I was mayor of Mayersville, I had freedom schools in our community again, but there are none now. Every year, Marian invites me to come to the Alex Haley Farm in Tennessee and talk to the young people training to be freedom school teachers and mentors. It's a thrilling experience for me and always takes me back to the excitement and promise of those early years and renews my hope for the future.

Judge Cox's May 1965 ruling on *Blackwell v. Issaquena*, that segregation of public schools could no longer be mandatory, ordered the Sharkey and Issaquena county schools to allow all students "freedom of choice" in determining where they attended school, beginning with the 1965 fall session. All schools would remain in operation, but any black student who wished must be allowed to attend a white school. Since Issaquena County had no white schools, black children who wanted to attend a white school would have to go to nearby Sharkey County, as the white Issaquena students did.

Before the start of the fall session, I was among a group of frustrated black parents who decided to exercise that choice. By this time I was very knowledgeable about the educational programs in both black and white schools. It was clear to me that in a white school our children would have better textbooks, more highly educated teachers, more advanced work, additional courses, and better facilities; and, without the split session, they would spend more time in school. We had a rally at one of the black churches to motivate other parents to send their children and to give each other encouragement and support. Clarence Hall was leading the discussion about how and when we would enroll our children. We decided that we should all enroll our children on the same day, and Clarence announced what day that would be. I always watched people in these meetings to see if anything unusual was going on. As the meeting was winding down, I noticed one woman get up and leave. I knew the lady, and I knew that she worked as a cook for one of the white school officials. I was sitting near the back of the room near the aisle, and as she walked out, I looked straight into her eyes, and I could tell from her look she was a snitch and was going to go straight to her boss's house to let him know what we were planning.

As soon as she got out of the room, I went up to Clarence and whispered in his ear that we needed to change our schedule. As organizers in those sensitive times, we didn't ask questions—we just trusted and followed each other. So Clarence told the group we needed to change the date for enrolling our children, and we'd let them know later what day it would be. Those attending the meeting didn't ask for an explanation, either. They trusted their leader. Movement work was built on trust.

Sure enough, on the date we had originally announced we would enroll our children, the white schools were ringed with police and had dogs waiting for us. But we didn't show. Little successes like that kept us going.

A few days later, when we did take our children to the white schools, no one was expecting us. Pauline Sias, Minnie Ripley, and I went together to take my son, Pauline's daughter, and a couple of other children to Rolling Fork Elementary School. Mrs. Ripley's daughter was grown, but she went with us for moral support. She was always with us, whenever we did anything. The white folks at the school looked up and there we were, walking onto the schoolyard with our little black children. A white woman came running over to where we were. I don't know who she was, but, Lord, I will never forget the look on her face.

She came right up to me, and she screamed, "Nigger, nigger, nigger, go back where you belong."

I said, "Ma'am, I am where I belong."

She was cursing us and shrieking, "Take those nigger children back home."

And our children were hearing all this. Jerry was only eight years old.

I was so angry, but I just looked at that woman. The situation was similar to the one at the courthouse the first time I tried to register to vote, but this time I was much angrier and not afraid. I was enraged. I didn't argue, but this was the most difficult time I'd ever had trying to keep my emotions under control. Mrs. Ripley could tell how upset I was, and she was worried that I was getting ready to fight or somebody was going to shoot, so she just went to singing her favorite hymn:

> I need thee;
> Oh, I need thee.
> Every hour I need thee.
> Oh, bless me now, my Savior.
> I come to thee.

And she kept on singing it, over and over, till things had cooled down and the white woman left. Then we went inside and registered our children without incident.

Jerry was supposed to be in the third grade, but because he was black, the school officials assumed he was slow and made him repeat the second grade. They made the same assumption about the other black child in his grade. Besides being humiliating to Jerry, this meant that the schoolwork was incredibly boring. But Jerry and the other child got the last word a few years later when the school established a program for gifted students: Both boys easily qualified for the program, and they graduated with honors from Rolling Fork High School.

About fifty other black students in the two counties enrolled in the previously all-white Rolling Fork schools under the "freedom of choice plan" in the fall of 1965. Freedom to choose was about the only freedom the students had. They were harassed, called names, and shunned by the other students at school. Jerry came home with stories about thumbtacks on his seat and barrages of spitballs thrown at him by white bullies. He later admitted that he didn't tell me all the mean and ugly things he had endured. The white administrators did everything possible to keep the black children separated from the white ones, no matter the cost. In some schools, they put black children together and taught them in completely segregated classrooms. The black children had to eat together in the cafeteria when no white students were there. The school even ran different school buses for those few black students, so the white kids didn't have to be on the bus with them. It's so sad to think of the money and time those white school administrators and teachers put into this effort to "protect" the white kids.

As a mother, I worried about my son and hated for him to experience the isolation and humiliation and harassment, but I felt it was something we had to do, for the benefit of his education and the future of other black children. As we had broken down the voting barriers, we had to knock down the walls restricting our children. But I did a lot of praying for Jerry. The old gospel song "Jesus Is My Captain; I Shall Not Be Moved," revived and revised in the sixties by Pete Seeger, helped guide me through these days:

> Just like a tree that's planted by the water,
> We shall not be moved.

The persecution didn't end with the children in the schoolyard. During this time, there was more terror in Issaquena and Sharkey counties than we had experienced during Freedom Summer. If registering to vote had enraged the white community, putting our black children in "their" schools to "mix" with their children brought out whites' deepest hatreds and fears. These always came down to interracial marriage: If blacks and whites went to school with each other, they would marry each other, and that would ruin the white race. White businessmen and farmers retaliated against black parents by canceling credit, evicting them from homes. The Klan was attracting huge numbers at meetings, and they were burning crosses in our yards. A white friend told me about a Klan meeting happening one night just outside Rolling Fork, right near the highway, and out of curiosity I drove over there to see for myself. There they were, the people in their robes, out in the open for anyone to see.

Acts like those prevented many black parents from sending their children to white schools or allowing them to stay. Many "freedom of choicers" didn't stick it out in the white schools that first year, but my son did, as did the Sias child, and Clarence Hall's children, and a few others in elementary school. The only black Issaquena student who didn't give up going to Rolling Fork High School that first year was Thelma Lee Harris. The Klan not only burned crosses in her family's yard, but when she was coming in from school one day, a gunman on the levee shot at her. Thelma was not badly hurt by the shooting and went on to graduate from Rolling Fork High School the following spring. The Sovereignty Commission was on Harris's case, but the commissioners' report doesn't mention the shooting or the crosses that were burned in her yard. Instead, their inquiry focused on the burning question of whether she'd had an illegitimate child! The investigator was unable to confirm that notion.[3] (And for good reason: It wasn't true.)

"Freedom of choice" desegregation continued in Issaquena County for four more years, and Jerry and several other black students continued to choose the previously all-white schools. After a couple of years, the agitation against the black students subsided. When Jerry was in the sixth grade, the courts ordered massive desegregation of students and teachers in the middle of the year. (*Blackwell v. Issaquena County* was among the many school desegregation cases that brought about that decision.) As happened in many other Delta public schools, most white students in Sharkey and Issaquena counties fled to "seg academies"—hurriedly organized, lily-white private schools—leaving the "desegregated" public schools with nearly all-black student bodies. Jerry's graduating class in 1976 consisted of only a handful of whites.

Growing up, I had learned that my future hinged on education, even if the bar wasn't set very high. Thirst for education among poor

---

3. Report dated September 22, 1965.

Delta blacks was at a fairly low level—the desire to read and write and do simple arithmetic—but it was always there. Even for those who worked in the fields, being able to write one's name and understand numbers was important. As an adult, I knew how limited I was by getting only an eighth-grade education. To me education meant freedom—or at least the possibility of freedom—from cotton fields and poverty. Education meant freedom from control by white people and freedom from dependency on them. For that reason, many white people I knew in the Delta didn't like the fact that some blacks could read, although they also complained about our ignorance.

Once when I was working in the home of a white person in Helena, I picked up a book and started looking through it. When the white man of the house saw me, he said, "What are you looking at?" His tone of voice and question were meant to be intimidating.

"I'm just looking at this book," I told him.

"Well, do you know what it says?" he asked.

If I said no, I'd be seen as ignorant; if I said yes, he'd think I was uppity. So I just answered, "Well, sometimes I do, and sometimes I don't."

Mississippi Delta black people have made progress in their education during my lifetime. Today it's rare to find a black adult younger than sixty who can't read and write. And white people don't intimidate blacks openly because of their lack of education. More than two-thirds of black students in my area graduate from high school. Yet many of the schools in the Delta are depressing reminders of the past. Few white students attend the public schools in Issaquena and Sharkey counties, or in the other Mississippi Delta counties. In our district, 97 percent of the students are black. And they are poor: 95 percent are eligible for the free school lunch program. Of those who graduate, more than 80 percent complete the vocational program. The high school has no advanced placement courses.[4] Delta public schools face

4. South Delta School District (all Sharkey-Issaquena public schools); *Mississippi Report Card, 2000* (Jackson: Mississippi Department of Education, Office of Accountability).

many of the same problems the all-black schools always faced: low self-esteem and poor standardized test scores among students; lack of parental and community involvement; unimaginative teaching and harsh disciplinary measures; some board members serving at the will of whites who send their own children to private academies. Are we better off now? I think so, but we still have a long way to go.

In the last decade a few bright lights have begun to shine on our schools. Nonprofit groups such as CREATE, Barksdale Reading Institute, and the Rural School and Community Trust, as well as local grassroots groups, have begun working to improve the quality of education for Delta children and bring parents and the community into the picture. I believe that the future of our schools depends on involvement of people in the community at the grassroots level and on educational programs that follow the freedom school model—caring, creative teachers who encourage learning by discovery and experience.

My SNCC mentor and Freedom Summer director, Bob Moses, is now such a teacher in Jackson, Mississippi. Through his Algebra Project, he teaches math to middle and high school students through real-life experiences in their community, and he brings their parents into the process. Just as Bob taught me and other poor uneducated blacks in the 1960s that we could take charge of our own lives and change the world around us, he is challenging black students to empower themselves through algebra to create a meaningful, fulfilling future for themselves.[5] Any school that offers an education like that is a freedom school.

---

5. *Radical Equations: Civil Rights from Mississippi to the Algebra Project* (Boston: Beacon Press, 2002), by Robert P. Moses and Charles E. Cobb Jr., describes and explains the philosophy of this program.

14

Risk Your Heart for What Is Right

I N THE SPRING OF 1965, as we began to see how freedom schools were giving such a boost to the children and communities after the SNCC button boycott, I learned about another educational group taking shape—the Child Development Group of Mississippi (CDGM). It was based on a very simple idea: "Why can't we take little children and start them off early so they'll have a head start when they get to the school." Dr. Tom Levin, a New York psychologist who had previously organized the Medical Committee for Human Rights, which brought doctors into the state to provide medical help to our people during Freedom Summer, believed that poor black preschool children needed educational opportunities.

Levin began working with the Reverend Art Thomas and others from the Delta Ministry to develop plans for a community-based early childhood education program, to be privately funded. The Delta Ministry was an outreach organization established by the National Council of Churches at the end of Freedom Summer to further the work of the civil rights movement in Mississippi. After the COFO coalition fell apart in 1965, the Delta Ministry and the Mississippi Freedom Democratic Party were the main groups doing civil rights work in the state. They worked both separately and together on projects. As a board member of both groups, I was actively involved in their activities. I was especially excited about the plans for creating preschool programs for our children.

This was an idea whose time had come. President Johnson's "War on Poverty" had led to the creation of the Office of Economic Opportunity, directed by Sargent Shriver, to administer programs for poor Americans. One of the early OEO initiatives was a preschool program called Head Start. When Polly Greenberg, an OEO Head Start analyst, heard about CDGM's plans, she persuaded Dr. Levin to apply for federal Head Start funding. Working through Mary Holmes Junior College, an all-black school in West Point, Mississippi, CDGM became one of the first Head Start groups in the nation and the largest one that OEO funded that summer.[1]

With the first OEO grant, CDGM set up an eight-week program for the summer of 1965. The federal money, according to OEO guidelines, required that the poor people themselves govern the local groups that used the money. The programs, Shriver said, should incorporate "maximum feasibility of the poor." We took him at his word and that's what we set up. (Later on, I would take Mr. Shriver to task over what "maximum feasibility" was all about.) I was hired as a congressional district developer to get the Head Start centers opened in the Delta and set up committees to run them. This was my first full-time job that paid a regular salary. I made eighty dollars a week, as I recall.

Local black people were hired as teachers, aides, cooks, and administrators. Teachers earned forty or fifty dollars a week; that's three times what they would have made working in the field or as a domestic. A good many of them couldn't get that work anyway, because they had been involved in voter registration and no white person would hire them anymore. The fact that they were being paid for the first time by someone other than "Old Master" meant something to them. I knew that feeling well, too. All teachers, aides, and administrators attended training sessions sponsored by OEO and CDGM.

The first year CDGM operated eighty-one Head Start centers in twenty-six counties. These centers were usually set up in churches or other places we had used during Freedom Summer; these places also were often the sites of MFDP meetings. Minnie Ripley, Pauline Sias,

---

1. Polly Greenberg's book *The Devil Has Slippery Shoes: A Biased Biography of the Child Development Group of Mississippi* (New York: Macmillan, 1969), is a detailed history of CDGM.

and Dorothy Carter helped set up and run the Mayersville center at Old Pilgrim's Rest Church.

In addition to teaching little children, ages three to six, their ABCs and numbers, the centers gave the children two hot meals a day and medical attention, which most of them had never had. Parents were encouraged to come to the Head Start centers and get involved in their children's education. We also had discussion groups and classes for parents in the evenings. I knew several adults who went back to school as a result of these programs and today are working in good jobs and making good lives for themselves and their families. So the centers provided a "head start" for parents, too.

Parents and other volunteers helped us set up and run our centers. Mr. Dukey White and his buddies brought tires and a wagon wheel and created playground equipment. Women in the community brought food from home—a skillet of bread, a pot of peas. Mothers started little groups to help the teachers out. Black people in black communities gave their time and whatever resources they had. There was a giving spirit among the people about Head Start. CDGM centers truly were about our black Mississippi Delta people for the first time being totally in charge of running and staffing an educational program that was not controlled by the white establishment. The CDGM centers were a source of personal support and community pride for blacks.

We had started to pull together with hope. The teachers and aides were going to workshops in other parts of the country, for the first time in their lives traveling out of their familiar surroundings and getting together with people from other places to talk about their work, about their common problems and dreams. They came back from training sessions with enthusiasm about their own lives and about what they could do for the children. And they came home and worked their hearts out for the children. I saw what it did for children to have people caring for them and saying, "You're wonderful." The children were so happy to have little toys to play with. These people were truly in poverty but now, through their own work, saw what more life could offer.

※　※　※

CDGM drove the white establishment in Mississippi wild. They couldn't believe that federal money was coming straight to black people in Mississippi who were developing community education and helping our people. The biggest complaint was that the federal government was using taxpayer dollars to finance civil rights "agitators." It was true that many of those involved in CDGM had worked in the movement. We were people who had been inspired by the movement to take charge of our own lives, to better our own conditions. The idea of CDGM was built on some of the same principles that SNCC had fostered—people in communities working to help themselves. CDGM was a way of continuing our work for a better life. Since SNCC had the best statewide organization and best community organizers, many of us who had been SNCC organizers became involved in CDGM, although SNCC itself did not sponsor or endorse the program. Some SNCC people even opposed it because they had lost faith in the federal government to do right by black people.

When we started Head Start, white people in the communities wouldn't rent buildings to us, and local businesses wouldn't sell us supplies. Many local banks wouldn't even cash the checks of Head Start staff people. We tried to buy food and supplies from local businesses, but they made it very difficult, if not impossible. They didn't trust us to pay and wouldn't give us credit. We had to go to Greenville or Vicksburg to get food and other supplies. Sunflower Foods in Greenville always sold to us. And since we had to get most of our food from them, when the Sunflower people saw us coming, they had smiles on their faces!

Money really does talk, so it wasn't long till the people in Rolling Fork and Mayersville realized we had good money and it was flowing sweetly. They hurried up and got so nice to us. "Y'all need to buy from local people," they said, like we never had been run off from local stores. Money has changed many a mind. Head Start was an economic blast in the small, very rural counties like ours, and it did wonders for the children and parents.

I didn't work at our center in Mayersville. My job was to organize the people in the district, to find additional funding sources for supplies and such, and to raise hell. And I did have to raise some hell. Before it was over, I had to take our case straight to Washington to help keep our funding. As soon as the first CDGM Head Start dollar came into the state, Governor Paul B. Johnson Jr. and our U.S. senators and congressmen started trying to get rid of CDGM. Senator John Stennis was the one leading the charge to pressure the Office of Economic Opportunity not to continue funding us. Stennis was the head of the Senate Appropriations Committee, which controlled the funding of OEO, so he had real pressure to apply. He also had the investigative fervor and full support of the Sovereignty Commission in the state. Stennis accused CDGM of mismanaging federal funds and called for an investigation. Auditors came down and pored over the books. They determined that, out of a grant of 1.5 million dollars, only five thousand dollars had been misused. Stennis didn't let up, however, and funding for a six-month Head Start program was delayed. OEO also called for the removal of CDGM's founder, Dr. Levin. But many centers continued to operate because volunteers worked without pay and people donated food.

By the beginning of 1966, we still hadn't gotten our funding. Shriver was dragging his feet, buckling in response to continued criticism coming from Stennis and others in Washington. So we loaded up two buses full of CDGM children and teachers and parents and went to Washington to attend a hearing the House Education and Labor Committee was holding on the matter. What a scene—forty-eight four- and five-year-olds paraded into an ornate, walnut-paneled hearing room and plopped down on the thick carpet with their crayons and drawing paper. One little boy was pulling a quacking Donald Duck, and another child had a live mouse in a cage. The *New York Times* called it a "romper room lobby." We had our little kids clapping and singing:

> *We are marching up to Washington.*
> *We want our Head Start School.*
> *Please don't refuse us.*
> *We want our Head Start School.*

We had about twenty-five adults with us, and several of us spoke about how we had lost faith in the poverty programs, that all we got was promises. It was just like the hearings you see on television—a long table with microphones—and I sat there and told the members of the committee that "we need our money now, not maybe next week, next month, next year." Two weeks later CDGM received 5.6 million dollars for 125 centers for six months.

But now the governor of Mississippi and other state officials wanted some of this money. So white people in communities all over the state figured out a way to set up local Community Action Programs (CAPs) so they could apply for Head Start and other antipoverty money and prevent CDGM from controlling it. The communities would set up a biracial CAP committee, which generally consisted half of white men whose idea it was and half of "Uncle Toms" they had handpicked.

In April I went back to Washington for the convention of the Citizens' Crusade Against Poverty. This was a group organized by Walter Reuther of the United Auto Workers union to help grassroots poor people get antipoverty funding and draw attention to the pressure southern congressmen were putting on OEO. For a day and a half we sat in a fancy banquet hall at the International Inn and listened to bureaucrats talk about the War on Poverty. The second day Sargent Shriver gave the luncheon speech, and about halfway through it, the folks in the audience let him have it. There were boos and hoots from the poor people—a thousand of us—who had come to the meeting from all across the country. Then the people took the floor themselves, and Shriver had to listen for a while.

I stood up to protest the new white groups in Mississippi who were applying for antipoverty money. "The federal government ought to be ashamed of itself," I told him. "The same men who pay us three dollars a day and are bent on putting people off the land—that's the men who are on the poverty committee." And I questioned him about what happened to those big ideas of "maximum feasible participation" of the poor he had talked about. The conference participants stood and applauded when I pleaded to Shriver: "Help us to catch up. If you don't, we'll run off and leave you." But Shriver was not moved.

The criticism of CDGM never let up, in the state or in Washington. In the fall Shriver prompted the creation of a statewide community action group to get himself out from under criticism. Shriver got in touch with Mississippians Hodding Carter III and Aaron Henry, who put together a statewide biracial group known as Mississippi Action for Progress (MAP). They called upon the white Yazoo City industrialist

Owen Cooper to be the chairman. MAP was essentially a coalition of liberal white Mississippians and NAACP blacks. OEO funded most of MAP's proposed programs and did not fund most of CDGM's. Carter and Henry weren't bad men—in fact, I liked them both a lot (and Shriver, too)—and they were sensitive to the needs of the people, but they weren't "the people." The same divisions that had come out at the 1964 Democratic National Convention were at work here.

We fought passionately for CDGM for another year or so and received funding for fourteen counties, including Issaquena. In five counties that weren't funded, the communities continued their Head Start programs with volunteers and grants from the Field Foundation. CDGM's last grant ran out at the end of 1967. MAP took over most of the Head Start programs.

Losing our Head Start programs was a tremendous blow for many poor people in the black community. I took it very personally, as a slap in my face. I was angry and saddened and sickened over the whole matter. Many in the white establishment had frequently pointed their fingers at poor people with no education, so we started Head Start in our communities to begin solving that problem. They said we couldn't keep up with money, which was found to be mostly false. They said we didn't know how to manage and administer the program adequately. It's true: These skills were not part of the backgrounds of most rural blacks, and maybe we did need some more training. But instead of working with us and helping us reach the next level, the finger-pointers pulled the rug out from under us. And as soon as they found out there was money in it, they took it over. They always said, "Pull yourself up by your bootstrap." So we did. And what happened? First they snatched the strap, and then they took the boot.

When CDGM lost its Head Start funding and control went to the white community, we lost our heart—the spirit of community and togetherness. That kind of spirit is a lot harder to build than a new school.

❖ ❖ ❖

The CDGM experience, like all of my movement activities, greatly enlarged my own community. CDGM brought into my life two of the best friends I've ever had: Dr. Josephine D. Martin and Robert J. Schwartz. Jo was a child psychiatrist in New York and a member of Tom Levin's Medical Committee for Human Rights. She came as a volunteer in the summer of 1965 to help CDGM set up our health care program for our Head Start children. Jo and Bob stayed about a week in Mayersville. We drove around the Delta, and Jo examined children at several Head Start centers.

On the surface our friendship seems unlikely—a poor black Mississippi woman and two Upper West Side New Yorkers, one a child psychiatrist of Cuban descent and the other a Jewish investment banker. But such is the magic of friendship. Jo and Bob were, in fact, very special people. Jo devoted much of her medical practice in New York to helping troubled adolescents and homeless families, and she had long been an activist in social and civil rights issues. Bob was an investment banker who had pioneered the concept of socially responsible investing and became very active in promoting arms reduction and world peace. Together they were an interesting and unusual couple. Each possessed a strong social conscience and generous spirit, and they were passionate about their work to create a more just and democratic society. By the end of the week, we were fast friends, and we've remained close family friends throughout the years.

In 2002 Bob published his memoirs, *Can You Make a Difference? A Memoir of a Life for Change*, telling about the fascinating and fulfilled life he's had working as an economist with the Treasury Department in Washington and on Wall Street, and in the world peace movement. I'm especially grateful for his memories of his and Jo's first Mississippi visit, because I had forgotten the specifics of everyday occurrences that so defined the times, which he vividly describes:

> I'll never forget the moment we arrived. From what was hardly more than a shack like those we had seen on the road, emerged a large woman who, without even saying hello, told us loud and clear to move the car off the road and onto the sparse grass adjoining the house. We did so, I thought.

"Look, I said off the road. A side of the car is still on the road. Do you want us arrested?"

She clearly was someone used to being in charge. I quickly got back in the car and moved it farther onto the grass. Only when she was satisfied that the car was parked in a safe place did we go into the house.[2]

After my none-too-gracious welcome, I'm amazed they stayed long enough to become friends. Fortunately, Bob and Jo did stay, and they became emotionally involved in the lives of people here, as Bob recounts:

> One afternoon, five very excited young girls ran to the house, shouting, "Miss Blackwell! Miss Blackwell! We have to see you!" They said they had been on [a certain planter's] field giving the workers voting registration forms when he came out with a shotgun. He told them to leave and never to come back, or he would shoot them. The girls were concerned because they had not finished distributing the forms, and asked if they should go back now.
>
> Jo and I were absolutely astonished by the dedication of these young people who were willing to risk their lives to further black voting. No doubt they would have done so if Unita had given them the go-ahead. Speaking in a reassuring maternal voice, she told them not to go back now, [the man] being "all hot and bothered," but that they had done a wonderful job, and "I'm not going to forget that, but just you wait for a better time to go back."[3]

Bob and Jo took a special interest in Jerry, who was eight years old at the time. They wanted Jerry to know white people who were good and kind to him, and they made arrangements for him to visit them in

2. Robert J. Schwartz, *Can You Make a Difference? A Memoir of a Life for Change* (New York: Lantern Books, 2002), p. 176.
3. Schwartz, *Can You Make a Difference?* pp. 176–77.

New York later that summer and attend summer camp in Vermont. When I put Jerry on an airplane in Greenville that first year, to fly to New York by himself, my husband thought I was sending our little boy into outer space. But I was thrilled to see my son so happy. Jo and Bob met him at the airport and drove him to the camp. They sent him to camp every year until he finished high school and became a counselor. Jerry met boys of many ethnic and religious groups and economic levels. It made me so happy to see how Jerry's eyes were opened to the world. Every year on Parents' Day at the camp, Jo and Bob would drive up to visit Jerry. I was able to go one year for Parents' Day to see Jerry and the friends and camp he loved.

Just as they introduced Jerry to a wider world, they wanted me to know about New York and its cultural advantages. The first time I went to the Metropolitan Museum of Art, Bob and Jo took me. Over the years, I went with them to operas, ballets, Broadway shows, and fancy restaurants. Occasionally, I could open a New York door for them. Once when I was there, we went to a play starring Ruby Dee. I had gotten to know Ruby through the movement, and she invited us backstage after the play. Later they hosted a lovely dinner party for Ruby and her husband, Ossie Davis. Bob and Jo became like family to me. Besides being my friend, Jo was my doctor, confidant, and counselor. Bob introduced me to the world of Wall Street. Their home was always open to me, and they supported many of my projects and activities. I grieved when Jo died in September 2000 after a lengthy bout with cancer, but Bob and I stay in touch. I have CDGM to thank for their friendship.

Although CDGM ceased to run Head Start, most Mississippi communities in the state have Head Start programs today. They play an important role in the lives of many poor young children in Mississippi. The stigma whites attached to Head Start has mostly disappeared in our state. So it was depressing when our current governor, Haley Barbour, said, "Some of those kids in [Head Start] would be better off sitting up on a piano bench in a whore house than where they are now." I wish the governor had been in Rolling Fork, where I was invited recently to speak to Head Start staff, teachers, and community supporters in the new library. There was a crowd of black professional people and white community leaders, too—big farmers and bankers—who take pride in the program and respect each other. That day, I felt a spirit of community that uplifted me and reminded me of the original spirit of CDGM and the movement—open, communal, and full of faith that progress is possible.

15

Be Willing to Take Bold Action
(and Cry Some, Too)

THE WAR ON POVERTY was a war but not always the kind we had hoped for. In August 1965, the federal government established a new program, Operation Help, to provide twenty-four million dollars' worth of surplus food—cheese, flour, cornmeal, and such—to poor people in Mississippi over the winter of 1965–66. This food was called "commodities." But by the end of January, the poor people in Mississippi had not gotten any of the food. A plan for distribution was still tied up in disagreements between Washington and the state of Mississippi, which was in no hurry to help out poor black folks. People were downright hungry.

The median annual income of blacks in the Delta in 1964 was $465.[1] Plantation workers were furnished places to live—a shack with cracks in the walls and floor, no indoor plumbing of any kind, and one electric wire. Because mechanical cotton-picking machines and chemicals had taken over many jobs, over two thousand people moved off plantations in 1965.[2] Several hundred others were kicked off because they had formed a labor union, the Mississippi Freedom Labor Union, and staged a strike for higher wages. A tractor driver made six dollars a day, and a field hand made three dollars a day. Their days were ten

---

1. U.S. Department of Agriculture, 1964.
2. Freedom Information Service.

hours long during cotton season; the rest of the year most didn't work at all and didn't get paid. They'd gone on strike, demanding $1.25 an hour, which then was minimum wage for industry and retail shops. (At that time farm labor was not included in the national minimum wage provisions.) A couple of the farmers agreed to raise their workers' pay by one dollar a day, but others told them if they wanted to work at all, they could work for what they'd been getting.

The sad truth was that the workers really couldn't pressure the farmers much. Farmers didn't need as many people to get out their crops. Farmers were using mechanical pickers more and more to pick the cotton that black people had picked by hand, and they were spraying herbicides to kill weeds that black cotton choppers had gotten rid of before. A two-thousand-acre farm with one hundred families working on it in 1940 would have needed only ten to twelve families in 1965. To make matters worse, the federal government was paying farmers not to plant cotton.

So lots of black people in the Mississippi Delta went from low wages to no wages. They had no job, no houses, and no ways of getting them. Nobody else would hire them or even rent them a house. They set up tents and created "Strike City" on a little plot of land owned by a black man, at Tribett, just outside Leland and about forty miles north of Mayersville. The winter of 1965–66 was one of the coldest on record in Mississippi. And the commodities they were supposed to have received were sitting in a warehouse somewhere. Something had to be done.

Out of these problems came the Poor People's Conference, which was held January 28–30, 1966, in Edwards, Mississippi, about thirty miles west of Jackson, at Mt. Beulah, formerly the site of a black junior college and at the time the headquarters of the Delta Ministry and CDGM. (SNCC had also previously used the buildings.) The Mississippi Freedom Democratic Party, the Delta Ministry, and the new Freedom Labor Union cosponsored the conference. The Delta Ministry had been trying for some time to get the commodities distributed and had given away clothing collected from churches across the nation. By this time SNCC had nearly phased out its work in the state, but many Mississippi grassroots SNCC people were working through the MFDP and other organizations.

About seven hundred people came to Mt. Beulah for the Poor People's Conference. The old college was designed to house about two hundred. The main building was a big white antebellum house where, it was said, slaves had once been sold from the porch. In an auditorium seating two hundred fifty people, hundreds more packed in, lining up on both sides of the auditorium to speak into two microphones. They told their stories about having no food, no place to live, pleading for help. These poor people were angry, more so with the federal government than with Mississippi. We were used to getting ignored and left out by the state, but we thought the federal government would keep its promises. The government was acting like the old cow that would give a good pail of milk and then kick it over, as the old folks might say. And that's putting matters lightly.

Speakers began proposing ways to get the attention of Washington, like a march on Jackson and camping out on federal land. We sent a telegram to President Johnson during the conference, asking him to help us find jobs and food and housing. The president didn't respond. People were getting madder and madder, talking about burning down commodities warehouses and launching into out-and-out warfare. And that's when we came up with the idea of taking over the old Greenville Air Force Base. There was logic behind it: The Air Force hadn't used the base for more than a year, and empty buildings where pilots and others had lived were sitting there unused. Our people needed a place to stay, and the Air Force buildings were going to waste. Commercial airlines used the airstrip for flights in and out of Greenville, and the Air Force talked about giving the property to Greenville but had never done so. It was federal property, and we thought that by occupying it, we might finally be able to get the attention of the president and get some relief. It was a daring idea, we knew, but it was nonviolent and wouldn't hurt a soul. And we needed to make a bold statement to draw attention to the problem and get results.

Several people voiced their concern that trespassing on federal property was a federal offense that could land us in the federal pen. Some thought the plan too dangerous, too radical, and they decided not to participate. But many of us were charged up and ready to go. I was one of them. I was frustrated and angry that our poor people had been treated unfairly. There wasn't a doubt in my mind that the government was wrong not to do whatever was necessary to get the commodities to the poor people who desperately needed them. We were dealing with serious problems—not only homelessness but hunger, a life or death issue. In the last two or three years I'd learned about what government is supposed to do. The Declaration of Independence says that our government was established to secure the people's God-given right to life—to say nothing of liberty and the pursuit of happiness. Life. One purpose of the Constitution is to "promote the general welfare" of the people. Feeding the hungry was about life, and certainly about the general welfare. I believed feeding our hungry people was imperative enough for such a drastic move, and if we were breaking the law, I was willing to risk the consequences.

At the close of the meeting several carloads of poor black people and a handful of civil rights workers decided to make the move onto the Air Force base. Sunday night we loaded up our cars and went in a caravan to Greenville to spend the night in a community center there. I was involved in strategy and planning and stayed up all night. Some people were really scared and couldn't sleep. I tried to calm their nerves and went over what we were going to do. I also had to make sure everybody stayed inside. We couldn't have anybody going out and talking. Our plan depended on us making a surprise move.

Before dawn the next day, January 31, I got everybody up—there were forty-one of us—to carry out our plan. We piled into seven cars and headed out shortly before sunrise. It was a freezing cold Monday morning—about as cold as it ever gets in Mississippi. Ice was on the road; there were patches of snow on the ground. We drove six miles north on Highway 1 to the old Air Force base. The first car—an old Volkswagen van with a white driver—went through the gate, and the gatekeeper smiled and waved. I imagine he thought the occupants were going to catch a plane. But then the van turned toward the buildings instead of going straight to the airport. I was in the second car, and we drove right on in, following the van. By this time, the gatekeeper was waving and yelling, "Y'all going the wrong way." The rest of the cars went right on by him. He couldn't do a thing to stop them.

We drove to a big gray wooden building; one of the men in the first car pried open the door with a screwdriver; and we all piled in with our blankets and food. There was no heat in the building, and I sure was glad I had on a raggedy old fur coat that had come in one of the boxes of clothes church people from the North had sent down to us. There were still a few military people on the base, and one came over.

"What do you people think you're doing breaking into a U.S. military base?" The group had asked me to be a spokesperson for them. So I told him: "We have a lot of folks here who don't have anywhere else to go. You've got an empty building here. Our people are hungry, and we need help. We need the government of the United States to come to our aid. We've got a tragic situation here."

He was calm and didn't respond directly to me. He just told us to leave. But nobody made a move. The local police and the sheriff came out, but they didn't make any arrests.

Around noon the head of the FBI for the state came. He knew me because he had been the one to investigate the cross burnings at my house. He came over to me.

"Unita, why didn't you tell me what y'all were planning to do?"

And I said, "Well, if I had told you, then you would have tried to stop us."

He said, "Well, maybe we could have negotiated something." He wasn't confrontational or nasty about it; he was just doing his duty in a straightforward manner.

My answer was just as direct and polite: "It's time the world knows what's happening to us in Mississippi."

The world soon would find out, but not before four more carloads of our demonstrators came rolling in. The police, the sheriff, the FBI, and the Air Force men were all standing there watching. No one had even closed the gate! The new group brought a couple of wood stoves and some food. And people from all around the area were driving by to see what was going on.

None of the officials or their lawyers seemed to know who was responsible for the air base. The city owned the land, the federal government owned the buildings, and all of it was in Washington County. A young lawyer from the Justice Department eventually came, and he told us that we had violated federal law but the government wouldn't prosecute if we left right away. But we couldn't leave without making our point clear. "Most of our folks didn't have anywhere to go. That's the problem," I said.

Newspaper reporters and radio and television crews descended. All three national television networks came in the afternoon. And they were all interviewing me. I told how we didn't have jobs or food or clothes, and there I was in my fur coat. It was a raggedy old coat, with one side split up to my armpit, but you couldn't tell that on television. We laughed and laughed about that later on that night. The people told me I needed to take my fur coat off the next time I went on television.

That night whole families kept coming in support, some through the gate and some over the fence. By nighttime we had about one hundred people in that big room, and we had locked ourselves in. It was a sight to behold. The electricity was off in the building, and we burned candles and kerosene lamps. I tried to keep people entertained. I started leading songs, and we were singing and telling stories, trying to keep warm. I stood up and told about going to the White House to see President Johnson and Lady Bird, the year before all this. When I brought up the whiskey, the folks just howled. I'm telling you we were having a great time that night.

Then about midnight we heard airplanes circling. One lady screamed, "Maybe the president is coming to help us." But I thought to myself, I doubt that very seriously. Throughout the night we heard several more planes circling, and then landing, one after another, maybe a half dozen in all.

The next morning the sun was shining, but there was no one in sight. Just before noon, we looked out and saw soldiers, dressed in fatigues and carrying billy clubs, marching toward our building. There were about one hundred fifty men—a lot of them black. The general in charge came inside, followed by reporters and TV cameras. IIe said, "You've violated the law." Then he said he was concerned about our health and safety: "Without running water or sanitation facilities this building is both a fire and health hazard." We told him that this was nothing new. We had never had running water or bathroom facilities. Then the general said if we would all write down our grievances, the president would have the Agriculture and Justice Departments consider them carefully. I spoke up.

"We have been sending pieces of paper up to Washington for three years now, and it ain't done no good. If that's all you got to say, I guess we'll just stay right here."

He announced that the commodity money from Operation Help was being released that very day. Then he said he was there to see that we left the building. Twenty minutes later, the troops broke a window-pane, unlocked the door, and escorted us out. There was no beating and dragging; the troops were respectful of us. And we didn't put up a fight. We knew they had the power, and we had gone as far as we could.

We had made our stand. We exposed our situation on national tele-vision, and we knew Washington was looking. The federal troops understood our anger, and they carried out their duties. How different this was from the scene the previous year in Jackson, when the police had thrown us in the livestock barns and tormented us day and night! This is what a demonstration is supposed to look like, I thought. We had taken our lives in our hands, and it took the U.S. armed forces to move us out. This was powerful stuff.

We didn't stop pushing, though. At a press conference the day after we left the air base, I said I believed the federal government had proved that it doesn't care about poor people. "We, the poor people of Mississippi, is tired. We're so tired of it, we're going to build for our-selves, because we don't have a government that represents us." With the help of the Delta Ministry, the Poor People's Conference borrowed money, bought four hundred acres of land in Washington County, and created Freedom Village (originally known as Freedom City). I was not closely involved in establishing Freedom Village, but Clarence Hall and Jake Ayers and others struggled mightily to provide housing to families who wanted to live there and farm. Eventually the federal gov-ernment did provide some money for housing. For a decade or so fam-ilies raised soybeans and operated the Delta Brick Factory.

Our demonstration at the Greenville Air Force Base in January 1966 raised the consciousness of some people regarding poverty in Mississippi. Not long afterward, the commodities were distributed, and government officials started talking about job training and housing for our people. It would be another year, however, before those in Wash-ington really saw the depth of our problems in Mississippi.

In 1967 Robert Kennedy, then a U.S. senator, came to the Delta and saw the poverty firsthand. Kennedy was one of four members of a Senate subcommittee looking into our CDGM Head Start program and other antipoverty issues. They came to Jackson to conduct hearings. Since I had been one of the people involved in CDGM, I was there for the hearings the day Marian Wright testified. And then she invited the senators to see the Delta. She asked me to help her make the arrangements and accompany her and the group. She wasn't as familiar with the Delta as I was. I got in touch with Amzie Moore in Cleveland, Mississippi, and he said, "Sure, come to Bolivar County." The senators' tour was put together on very short notice. Besides Kennedy, Senator Joseph Clark of Pennsylvania was along and Peter Edelman, who worked for Kennedy and later became Marian's husband.

So off we went to the Delta. We hooked up with Amzie, and he took us out to where the people lived. There was a row of the regular one- and two-room shotgun shacks—nothing out of the ordinary for black housing at the time. Old porches with holes between the planks. Some of the houses might have had a window or two that was good, but most of the time there was something over the window, a piece of paper or cardboard, to keep the cold and rain and bugs out. The folks were sitting inside waiting for us.

Senator Kennedy went from one house to another, and I was right there with him. I saw the look on his face when he walked into those houses and saw the little children with the skinny legs and bloated stomachs and the whole thing. This was the first time, Robert Kennedy said, that he'd seen poverty of this level with his own eyes. Senator Kennedy said that he didn't know that this was going on in the United States of America. He was thinking he was in some other country. He was shocked and hurt by the scene. It was pitiful, and these were people who chopped cotton and picked cotton and worked hard. But they didn't have any money left for food and nowhere else to go. We went from house to house, and tears welled up in Bobby Kennedy's eyes.

When I drove Bobby Kennedy to Memphis and put him on a plane, he said he would never again be the same. I saw him again the following year when he was campaigning for president. He just kept saying, "Unita, I thank you for helping me to see the drastic needs of Mississippi Delta people." A few months later the Senate subcommittee published its report describing the hunger and disease the senators had seen in Mississippi, and Mississippi governor Paul B. Johnson Jr. held a press conference to refute its findings. "Nobody is starving in Mississippi. The nigra women I see are so fat they shine," he said.

Today when I think about those terrible times and pitiful people, I cry. It's painful for me even now, because I know that some of those children might have not made it; or, if they did, they were probably deformed. And that was the Mississippi Delta for many black people in that time. I've cried many days because of the pain of our people. There's an old Dr. Watts hymn that helps to relieve the sadness and give me the strength to keep going:

> *I don't know why we have to cry sometimes.*
> *I don't know why we have to weep and moan.*
> *But I love the Lord;*
> *He heard my cry,*
> *And pitied every groan.*

16

Carry On

FANNIE LOU HAMER, Amzie Moore, and I were sitting around one day talking—just the three of us—at Mrs. Hamer's house. It was toward the end of 1966 or early 1967, as I recall. We were remembering what we'd been through and wondering what was coming next. It's hard to believe how much had happened from 1964 to 1967. In 1964, I was stuck in poverty and trapped by the color of my skin in a pointless existence. Then the movement came along, and my mind opened up. I started trying to register people to vote. I said, OK, I did that; now I'll try the next thing that comes along. I didn't have a plan, but I had desire and daring and nothing to lose. In 1967 I was still struggling financially, my skin was as black as it had ever been, but my life had meaning.

By this time, the Mississippi SNCC and CORE and COFO groups had broken up, and all the "outside agitators" were long gone. Bob Moses, disillusioned after the 1964 convention, had gone to Africa to teach school. Stokely Carmichael had taken over as head of SNCC in 1966 and grown impatient with nonviolent resistance. He introduced the term "black power" in a speech in Greenwood in June 1966, after James Meredith had been shot on a march from Memphis to Jackson. After that, Stokely's SNCC had no presence in the state. Just us home-grown agitators were left to carry on.

"We got to keep our people moving," Mrs. Hamer said. "We can't stop and rest now."

"We've gone from standing up to the power structure to breaking it down," I said. "Can we go to the next level?"

I didn't doubt for a minute that we could or that we would, and neither did the others. We had to. It was up to us.

"We know we've got to keep getting our people registered and to the polls, and we need to get people in office, now," Amzie said. Amzie had been fighting for voter registration for years before Mrs. Hamer and I got involved. He had worked with Bob Moses to get Freedom Summer organized.

We agreed that we had to find a way to keep teaching our people about government and how they can work within government to make their lives better—all our lives better. We wanted to keep pushing voter registration and participation in our government. We discussed the need to teach others about local government: what the city council, the board of supervisors, and the justice of the peace do. We had to train our people to organize and provide leadership. We've come so far, we said. We don't want to fall back. We want to build on our progress.

What we needed to do was bigger than all of us. We had to help our people help themselves.

That conversation was the start of MACE—Mississippi Action for Community Education—a nonprofit, minority rural development organization to help educate and empower poor people in the Mississippi Delta. The three of us came together and said that we needed to start something ourselves, and we created MACE. I named it that first day. We had our name, and we had our mission: "Helping people help themselves." We contacted some of our friends from Holmes County and Madison County, and they were interested in helping start this organization to continue educating our people in voting and politics. We were off and running.

We immediately got in touch with Ed Brown, who'd been a SNCC project director in the state, and we asked him to come back and serve as the first director of MACE. Ed Brown was working in Washington for the Citizens' Crusade Against Poverty, and they allowed Ed to come right down. Then the four of us got busy and set up a board of directors from all over the Delta, mostly other grassroots people—fifteen of us. We found a place for an office on Eighth Street in Greenville and convinced the owners that if they'd let us use the building, we would pay our rent.

At that time MACE didn't have a dime, but our first decision was not to use federal money. We wanted to do voter registration, which the government classified as political action and therefore not eligible for federal money. We didn't want to find ourselves in the same struggle we'd had with CDGM. We said we'd raise the money ourselves, just the way SNCC had done. If we could imagine it, we believed, we could do it. And we did. The Citizens' Crusade Against Poverty contributed to get us started.

We wanted MACE to represent the needs of low-income people in Delta communities from the grassroots up. Under Ed's leadership, MACE set up associate groups in fourteen Delta counties. Each county had five groups (one group for each "beat," or political district in the county) that met every other week to discuss local issues and concerns. Those groups each sent two representatives to the county organization, which selected one member of the MACE board from its own county. I was on the first board and remained a board member for many years, as the organization developed and expanded its vision and its work.

Ed Brown got MACE organized and its programming under way. By 1969 we began trying to create jobs and economic opportunities. Because MACE was a leadership training organization and involved in support for political and social rights, we formed a separate organization, the Delta Foundation, which would be better able to deal with lending agencies. One of our very first ventures to create jobs was Fine Vines, a blue-jeans manufacturing plant. We set it up in the old Greenville Air Force Base, the place our Poor People's Conference had taken over three years earlier. By this time, the buildings were owned by the city of Greenville, which leased them to Fine Vines, Inc. At the time, I was also a junior consultant with the Ford Foundation, which provided funds to the state of Mississippi's Research and Development Center to do feasibility studies for Fine Vines.

Fine Vines provided many jobs for people who came off the plantations, and MACE sponsored training sessions and workshops for them. Those workers could do very fast work because they were used to picking cotton. Fine Vines became the main supplier of women's and children's blue jeans for JCPenney. Fine Vines was in business until recent years, when, like so many other U.S. manufacturing companies, it became unable to compete with foreign companies.

Ed Brown left MACE in the early 1970s.[1] I went to all kinds of meetings and programs trying to keep MACE going, and at a Citizens' Crusade Against Poverty workshop I met Charles Bannerman. Charles was a New Yorker and had never been to Mississippi, but I persuaded him to come to Greenville and try us out. Once he got here, he loved it and never left. Charles told everybody, "That's the best thing Unita Blackwell ever did in her life." He became MACE's second director.

Charles started in immediately working on fund-raising to broaden our base of support, focusing on foundations. I became the board member who would talk to the foundations. I knew several people in private foundations. Charles would bring in foundation people and have me talk to them, or I'd go with him places to raise funds. Soon we had grants from several foundations. Under Bannerman's leadership, we regrouped to accept federal funding. Charles Bannerman was a smart man. He directed MACE for a long time—until he died of cancer in 1986.

In recent years MACE had some problems with management, but now things are under control. That can happen when an organization grows and changes leadership several times. It sometimes gets too satisfied with its own success and forgets to cross the *t*'s and dot the *i*'s. You've always got to be careful with the details, especially those involving money. And you've got to remember the big picture and always keep your main purpose in clear view.

I'm proud that we were able to create an organization that has helped so many people help themselves for nearly forty years. We trained hundreds of community organizers and assisted them with educational, health, social service, economic, and community development needs. MACE helped four communities get incorporated and secure

---

1. Ed's brother, H. Rap Brown, the militant activist who took over SNCC after Stokely Carmichael left and later joined the Black Panthers, was shot and captured by New York police during an armed robbery. Ed wasn't militant like his brother, but he was concerned for his family and resigned from MACE to be with them.

needed services, and my town, Mayersville, was one of these. MACE helped groups establish job training and credit unions, get small business loans and housing. In 1976 we hosted the Delta Blues Festival on the site of Freedom Village, to celebrate and preserve an important part of Delta culture. It became an annual event, still ongoing. Every September thousands of people from throughout the world come to hear Delta blues music performed in the land where the blues began.

And all this has happened because three people said, "It's up to us" to help our people. And because many, many others worked to make it happen.

By the fall of 1967 more than 180,000 black Mississippians were registered to vote. It was up to us now to get black candidates elected to office. The Mississippi Freedom Democratic Party was active, and I was active in the MDFP. There were 108 black candidates on the ballots in state and county races that year. We worked hard to get black candidates on the ballot, and I wanted to do my part. So I ran for justice of the peace in beat four of Issaquena County. "We sure do need some justice," I said, "and Lord knows we need some peace."

At that time every beat—there are five in every county—had a justice of the peace who served as judge and jury for all the small crimes and disputes between people involving under five hundred dollars. I had observed how often blacks were at the mercy of the justice of the peace. I remembered the sad situation of Bob Fitzpatrick when the men beat him up: The JP arrested Bob and not the thugs who attacked him. Black people were arrested for any little thing—like standing in the wrong place or talking too loud—and sent to see the JP. For black people, going to "court" meant going in the back door of a white man's house—that's where JPs held court—being found guilty, and paying whatever fine the JP wanted to set. Working in cahoots with the sheriffs and highway patrolmen, justices had their own little kingdoms out in the rural counties. Each JP also had a constable working with him in his beat to find lawbreakers, serve papers on them, and haul them in to pay their fines. JPs were paid a portion of the fines they collected, so the more people they found and the higher the fine, the more money they made. I lost the election by three votes.

Twenty-two black candidates, however, were elected to office in our state. Most significant of all, a teacher from Holmes County, Robert Clark, an MFDP candidate, won a seat in the Mississippi House of Representatives. He was the first African American to serve in the Mississippi legislature since Isaiah Montgomery, who'd been the personal slave of Jefferson Davis's brother and also founded the all-black Delta town of Mound Bayou. Clark would go on to serve with distinction for thirty-six years—nine consecutive terms, the longest continuously serving legislator in the state's history. He served ten years as speaker pro tempore. As chairman of the education committee, he guided the passage of Governor William Winter's education reform bill, which was the most progressive and important legislative program of the last fifty years. Today, Mississippi has about nine hundred black elected officials, the highest number of any state.

The year 1968 was another presidential election year, and I was again a delegate to the Democratic National Convention, but this time I got a seat. Our delegation, known as "Loyalists," represented a merger of MFDP, NAACP, and a group of liberal white Mississippi Young Democrats, led by Hodding Carter III. At first Mrs. Hamer and I didn't want to go along with the Loyalists. We felt the Democratic Party didn't provide enough representation for poor blacks, but then we decided if we didn't participate, poor blacks wouldn't be represented at all. It was up to us to go and speak up for poor people. Aaron Henry led our delegation of 50 percent black, 50 percent white Democrats. This time Hubert Humphrey, who was running for the presidential nomination, supported us, and the seating question was settled before we ever got to Chicago. Since 1964, the party had made rules requiring racial diversity among the delegations. The regulars didn't stand a chance.

This was the infamous Chicago convention with demonstrations and violence over the Vietnam War. President Johnson had escalated the war, which was such an unpopular position that he didn't run for reelection. Vice President Humphrey inherited Johnson's pro-war position and had the nomination sewn up, defeating the peace candidates, Eugene McCarthy and George McGovern. But many of us wanted to get a peace plank in the party platform. Hundreds of students and others opposed to the Vietnam War came to town and camped out in Grant Park to protest the war. Mayor Richard Daley called out the cops—twelve thousand of them. Five hundred demonstrators were arrested and beaten, and two hundred were wounded. The whole country saw the hideous brutality on television, but I saw it with my own eyes when Mrs. Hamer and I drove across town to an Operation PUSH rally. The whole Jackson fairgrounds episode came back to me as in a nightmare. Oh, no, not again! As soon as we get a little sun shining one place, a storm cloud busts out somewhere else.

Another heavy cloud hung over the 1968 Democratic National Convention and over the whole country—the assassinations earlier that year of Martin Luther King Jr. on April 4 and Robert Kennedy on June 5. Their violent deaths, within the space of two months, stunned and horrified our country and devastated me. Dr. King had inspired me to believe in my rights as a person and as an American and to demand better treatment from my government, even though I didn't always agree with his strategy. Robert Kennedy had taught me that I could trust our leaders to do the right thing. I had stood beside these men and looked into their eyes and seen for myself their compassion and understanding and the burdens and the dreams they carried. Their deaths were a blow, but their legacies lived on. With the wise guidance of these men and others, our nation finally had begun to address the problems of civil rights and poverty and transform the lives of many Americans, including my own life.

Just four years earlier, in despair, I had followed two young SNCC workers in the cause of justice and a better life. I faced the opposition and stood my ground and fought it down. I had gone from following to standing up and protesting and on to finding ways to solve our own problems and make our political system work for black people, for all people. I had seen black Mississippians gain the freedom to vote and be elected to public office, serve on juries, and go to better schools. I had seen our people begin to believe in themselves, as I had begun to believe in myself. I'd grown in self-confidence and self-respect not only as a black person but as a woman. Like many other women in the movement, I discovered that I could be a leader.

I had learned a lot about freedom, too. When I started out as a freedom fighter, I believed that all my freedom was in somebody else's hands. And a lot of it *was* controlled by others—white people, who made the laws and enforced them, who sat on juries and served as judges, who hired and fired us and owned most of our houses, who ran our schools and owned the stores where we bought our groceries. So I went to work fighting against that control, and we were making progress. I was discovering that freedom doesn't happen by getting rid of the control of other people, by having others free us. *Getting freed* is only the beginning. Freedom has to happen on the inside, too. To be free we have to take control of our own lives and become responsible for ourselves, not rely on other people to take care of us; we have to become productive. It's up to each of us to free ourselves from whatever holds us back and keeps us from being the best we can be. And this is true regardless of a person's race or gender or religion or social standing.

Frederick Douglass said, "Freedom is a constant struggle." I had a feeling that I was only beginning to understand what he meant. But I was ready and eager to take on whatever uncertainties and challenges lay ahead. The spirit of freedom was in my step. I had come this far barefootin', and nobody was going to turn me around now.

Part III

Movin' On

1968–2005

17

You Don't Always
Have to Fight to Win

WHEN I GOT INTO THE MOVEMENT, the movement was
my life. The truth is, the movement gave me a life. It was a
close, communal experience. If it hadn't been, I wouldn't
have made it through. Just four years earlier, I prayed for something
that would breathe life into me and give me a purpose. But after barefootin' in the movement, pushing hard and seeing some walls tumble
down, I gained some confidence. I had learned so much that I hadn't
known before, and I wanted to do and see and learn as much as I
could. I was no longer content just to protest and react; I was beginning to come up with ideas of my own to solve problems and make
things happen. I was beginning to feel my own rhythm.

By 1968, I had barefooted my way into a new job and a new brick
house. Dorothy Height, the executive director of the National Council
of Negro Women (NCNW), hired me to help develop and carry out a
national housing program that would help make it possible for poor
people to buy homes. As NCNW community housing coordinator from
1967 through 1975, I continued to live in Mayersville, although my job
involved frequent travel around the state and the nation.

Miss Height had begun coming to Mississippi during Freedom Summer with a program she helped organize called Wednesdays in Mississippi. In the summers of 1964 and 1965, teams of prominent black and
white women from the Northeast and Midwest came to Mississippi to

meet with women in our state. They called the project Wednesdays in
Mississippi because they always came on Tuesday evening, spent all
day Wednesday talking with people, and left on Thursday. It was very
bold at that time to bring biracial groups, no matter how prominent,
into this state. Some of these women had helped get me released from
incarceration at the fairgrounds in 1965.

That program gave way to Workshops in Mississippi, which sponsored sessions around the state where Mississippi black women could
identify and tackle some of their main problems. At these workshops,
Miss Height discovered that one of the most pressing problems was
housing, and NCNW hired a housing specialist, Dorothy Duke, to
explore possible solutions. Dorothy Duke was white, and Miss Height
needed a black woman to work in partnership with her. I had been to
one of the NCNW workshops, and Miss Height had met me. She spoke
with Mrs. Hamer, who recommended me for the job. I was in Greenville
attending a MACE board meeting, and Dorothy Duke came and got me
out of the meeting to discuss the project with her and Miss Height.
At the conclusion of our talk, Miss Height said she thought I would
be a good person to work with Dorothy Duke on a national housing
initiative.

"I don't know a thing about housing, Miss Height," I said.

"Well," she replied, "you know about what it's like to need a good
house."

"Now, that's the gospel truth," I said.

I knew firsthand about the disgraceful housing situation for poor
people in the Delta. Very few poor people in the Delta owned a home.
On the cotton farms, the people lived in shacks that belonged to the
landowner, if they hadn't been thrown out. I had worked to find places
for people to put their heads down after farmers threw them out of
their houses. In towns, most black folks rented no-count houses
owned by white people. The house Jeremiah and I had been living in
wasn't much, but at least we owned it. And I had struggled for a couple
of years to get a loan from the Farmers Home Administration to build a
new brick house for my own family. We already owned a large lot to
build it on, right next door.

At first Jeremiah said, "Why do we need a new house? How are we
going to pay for it? We can't get a loan."

FHA lends money for people to build houses, I told him. "Why can't we get one of those?" By now, with my understanding of federal government programs, I knew Jeremiah and I should be eligible for a construction loan from the Farmers Home Administration. Providing low-interest loans to rural people who can't get a bank loan was the purpose of the FHA. We didn't make a lot of money, but he had a job with the U.S. Army Corps of Engineers, and I was working as a junior consultant for the Ford Foundation on projects in the area.

He said, "OK. If you want a new house, you go try to get a loan and see what happens."

So I put on my best dress and my best manners and headed out to the Rolling Fork FHA office. Well, I found out right quick that a woman couldn't get a loan without her husband. It had nothing to do with having money or job—only that I was a woman. I couldn't even *apply* for a loan without Jeremiah. He had to sign for it.

So now I had to convince him to do it. Sometimes Jeremiah locked into a position just to get me arguing with him, so I left the subject alone for a day or two. Then I casually said, "It's a shame our little boy can't have a warm bath every night before he goes to bed." Then I took Jerry aside and told him his daddy was going to get him a house with a bathtub. Jerry was excited and thanked his daddy. Jeremiah was softening.

"If you will sign the papers," I said, "I'll pay for the house." That did it. He couldn't refuse.

We headed out to the FHA office together. Jeremiah did the talking. He told the man why we were there, though I'd talked to that man so many times, he already knew. Instead of getting down to business, the man started joking around with Jeremiah. White men had a habit of doing that kind of thing with black men. On the surface it sounded friendly, but it was really a put-down. This went on for a while, and I could see Jeremiah getting impatient and irritated. (I call that his "white folks rising up in him.") I thought to myself, Oh, Lord, he's going to start cussing the man, but Jeremiah remained cool and began asking all the right questions to find out what we needed to do.

I jumped right on the job, gathering and providing FHA with the information and documents the man had asked for. But FHA kept dragging its feet and giving us the runaround. For example, I wanted a *brick* house that wouldn't go up in flames with one match and didn't require as much maintenance as a frame house. The FHA man told me they couldn't lend money for brick houses, just frame ones. Now, I couldn't determine any way a brick house could be a liability, so I knew they were playing games with me. At that time, black people didn't live in brick houses, and I think they believed a brick house was too big a status symbol for black people to have. I finally had to file a lawsuit against them for discriminatory practices in order to get our FHA loan approved.

Jeremiah, Jerry, and I moved into our brand-new three-bedroom, one-bathroom brick house by the end of 1967. Jerry immediately filled up the bathtub with hot running water, and I went around the house flipping light switches on and off. Jeremiah turned on the central heat. We were one happy family.

By the time we moved into our own new house, I was working with the National Council of Negro Women on a national housing program. Up till then, nearly all federally funded low-income housing was for rental projects. Families who rented had no incentive for keeping up their homes, and if their income rose above a certain level, they had to move out. We knew that there's a lot of dignity connected to a family buying and owning a place they can call their very own. We wanted to find a way for poor people, who couldn't qualify for bank mortgages, to put their money toward a house they could eventually own and never have to move out of as long as they fulfilled their obligations. We believed that home ownership would actually decrease the need for federal subsidies over time.

NCNW first presented its idea for funding home ownership to the Department of Housing and Urban Development. HUD initially said the idea was "too people oriented" and suggested we go to the Office of Economic Opportunity. The people at OEO loved the idea and set up meetings among NCNW, HUD, OEO, the Mississippi Research and Development Center, the National Association of Housing and Redevelopment Officials, the Mississippi Home Builders, and Mississippi developers, contractors, lending agencies, and city and county officials. When Miss Height and I—two black women—sat down with these Mississippi people—most of them white men—I believe it was the first time white leaders had ever met with black people *as equals*

to solve problems of poor black people in our state. And with us was a
southern white woman, Dorothy Duke. I don't think they quite knew
what to make of us. I'm certain they had never spoken with a black
woman with the confident, businesslike manner of Miss Height. She
spoke directly and didn't sidestep issues or beat around the bush, but
she was always "ladylike" and usually wore a hat. Dorothy Duke was
professional—polite but persistent. And then there was *me*, the civil
rights worker who was supposed to be a raging militant. But of course I
wasn't. I listened carefully to the tone of their voices and watched the
looks on their faces to figure out what they were thinking. Then I'd
speak up with realistic, practical suggestions and comments, which
were all just the "mother wit" I'd been brought up with. We explained
how the plan we were developing would benefit the Mississippi business community as well as the poor people who needed housing. It
would bring millions of dollars into the state economy. We were successful in convincing the business leaders of the value of our program,
and they gave us their support. We were off and running.

Miss Height was a remarkable woman to work for. She was—and
is—smart and dignified. She brought me from the world of a grassroots
organizer-activist into professional life. Miss Height believed in me and
saw potential in me. And I thank her for that. From her manner I
learned much that would help me in dealing with people. She taught
me, by example, that if I approached people, even the most highly
placed leaders, on their level as an equal, most of them would receive
me as an equal. This raging SNCC freedom fighter was learning how to
fight a different kind of battle now. When Miss Height entered a room,
she commanded respect, and she always respected other people. She
always called me Mrs. Blackwell. Sometimes Miss Height would ask
me to sit with her during meetings she attended and tell her what I
saw and heard. She said that I have a gift for intuitively understanding people—what people really meant when they said or did certain
things. I knew I always had hunches about people, but I'd never
thought of them as a gift. Miss Height introduced me to many people in
Washington. Mrs. Nixon worked with us on housing issues when she
was first lady, and occasionally we had committee meetings in the
White House. I first met President Nixon when he came by after one of
our meetings.

After the meeting in Mississippi, Miss Height, Dorothy Duke, and I went to see HUD secretary Robert Weaver. Secretary Weaver assigned HUD general counsel Joseph Burstein to work with us to see if we could put a program together. (Burstein had developed a home owner- ship program for the Bureau of Indian Affairs.) As I was sitting up there in his fine Washington office with this man asking *me* to tell him what I thought he should do, I couldn't help wishing that those FHA men in Rolling Fork who'd given me the runaround could see me now! Once we got the go-ahead from HUD and the others, Dorothy Duke and I worked out the details with Joe Burstein; he was a brilliant thinker and a fantastic man. We presented our ideas about the needs and concerns of poor people, and he found the legal means to accom- plish them. Then in his calm, soft-spoken way, he would explain the plan to the HUD officials and persuade them of its value. It was a thrilling, exhilarating creative process. We were designing something that had never existed before to address the needs of poor people and, at the same time, working around the concerns of community power structures.

Turnkey III, the program we developed with him, was a lease- purchase plan, subsidized by the federal government, enabling poor people to buy into the ownership of their own single-family homes. This is how it worked: A local housing authority had to initiate the process with HUD; upon approval a local developer was chosen to build the houses; local lenders provided financing for the construction loans, which were guaranteed by the federal government; the devel- oper then sold the houses to the local housing authority. The federal subsidy went to the housing authority. The home buyers paid no down payment, but they agreed to provide maintenance work to keep up their homes—"sweat equity," we called it—and pay a small amount of money each month to the housing authority; the amount was figured on a sliding scale, according to their income.

We needed to make sure Mississippi's Senator James Eastland wasn't going to interfere with getting the program through Congress. Eastland, who was one of the most powerful senators, usually voted against antipoverty projects, and we didn't need a repeat of all we'd gone through with Senator Stennis on CDGM. (Stennis was the "lib- eral" of the two!) We wanted to let Eastland know what we were working on and get his support, if possible. Like my granddaddy used to say, "You don't try to handle a one-eyed mule on his blind side." Since Eastland was from the Mississippi Delta and my senator, I said I would see what I could do. Knowing the senator wouldn't give me the time of day, I found out who his chauffeur was and went to see him. (I wish I could remember his name.) I asked him to speak to his boss about our housing program and how important it was to Mississippi. It wasn't long before I got a call back from the chauffeur, who reported that Senator Eastland had just nodded positively. He said that meant Eastland would not oppose it but did not want to go on record as supporting it. That's all we needed from him. Senator Eastland was a powerhouse and could have destroyed the project with one statement, but he didn't say a single word, for or against it. Appropriations for Turnkey III sailed through Congress.

The pilot project for Turnkey III was in Gulfport, Mississippi. My first trip to Gulfport was one I'll never forget. Dorothy Duke was down there working with the housing authorities, city officials, and the bankers and contractors—all of them white. I was to go down and talk to them about the project from the perspective of the home owners— their needs and responsibilities. Dorothy Duke had told them that a consultant from Washington, whose approval would be necessary for the project to go forward, was coming to meet with them and that, as a matter of fact, she was black. These local white men had never dealt with a black person—a black woman, at that—on this level. So Dorothy led them to believe I would be coming from Washington. To prepare them for my visit, she explained that I was a professional woman and they'd have to say "Negro," not "nigger" or "nigra" or even "colored." (We hadn't yet become African Americans—or even black people.) And she practiced with them saying "knee-grow" over and over, having them touch their knees on "knee" and stretch their arms up high on "grow." She told them that I would have to sit in the front seat of the car and they had to call me *Mrs.* Blackwell.

Instead of simply getting in my car and driving to Gulfport, which would have been the easiest thing to do, Dorothy had me take an airplane from Greenville to Gulfport. So I flew in from "Washington," and Dorothy and two Gulfport businessmen came to pick me up. The man driving opened the car door for me, put me in the front seat, and was so polite. The other man and Dorothy sat in the back. Everything was going fine. It was "Mrs. Blackwell" this and "Mrs. Blackwell" that. They said we would drive by to see where they were planning to build the housing units. On the way, the man driving was pointing out houses in Gulfport. He'd say, "There on the right are houses that white people live in." We'd go down the road, and he'd point out a "knee-grow" business or residence. So I guess he got pretty comfortable with me, and we were just chattering away. And then, before he thought, he said, "Now, over there is where some niggers live." That poor man turned red as he could be; he was so embarrassed. I just went on talking and acted like I hadn't heard what he said. I knew, of course, about Dorothy's attempts to "train" him, and I could hear her snickering in the backseat, and I had a hard time keeping a straight face. If the man had made that statement deliberately and in an arrogant, insulting manner, I might have been offended, but he'd been trying so hard to make a good impression. We were both on a fast track to learning how to work with people of a different race and get things done. Good will goes a long way. Dorothy and I laughed about that incident many a time.

Gulfport opened its first two hundred detached homes, called Forest Heights, in late 1968. We had insisted that they be brick to reduce maintenance costs. Those houses are still there, and those home owners have taken great care of them. We put emphasis on developing community spirit and pride, and I worked to set up a cooperative skills pool among the residents, in order to cut maintenance costs. Home buyers pooled their skills and services—plumbing, heating repair, carpentry needs, whatever—and swapped them with each other. One woman might babysit for another in exchange for getting her hair done. One man who knew carpentry would make repairs on his neighbor's house in return for plumbing help.

In 1969, when Hurricane Camille devastated large sections of the Gulf Coast, one of the few areas not destroyed was Forest Heights. The residents took homeless people into their homes after the flood and helped greatly in getting food and medicine and supplies to people. Forest Heights suffered little damage because one of the residents, Ike Thomas, went out into the storm and closed the floodgates on Turkey Creek, which runs on the edge of the development. When HUD secretary George Romney toured the area after that terrible storm, he asked Mr. Thomas why he risked his life to save the houses. He said it was because for the first time in their lives, they had something of their own. When HUD made a film about Turnkey housing, it was called *Something of Their Own.*

Most of the original residents of Forest Heights were still living there in 2005, when Hurricane Katrina blasted the Gulf Coast. They had fully paid mortgages and deeds to their houses—truly something of their own. But the residents, many quite old, couldn't afford to evacuate or were physically unable to, and this time they weren't able to hold back the water, which rose within their homes to three and four feet. As a result the home owners faced serious medical and financial problems, in addition to the damage to their homes. Despite all this, they had not lost hope for their community, as former President Bill Clinton reported soon after the storm:

> In Gulfport, I visited the predominantly African American community of Forest Heights. It's a proud neighborhood, where most residents own houses they've lived in for decades. The entire area was devastated by the hurricane, with debris scattered everywhere and blue tarps covering what were once roofs. I met with members of the community under a canopy in one resident's yard, and everyone agreed that they loved their neighborhood the way it used to be, when multiple generations lived together and Forest Heights had a strong community spirit. Because they weren't in an area previously identified as being at risk of flooding, few had any flood insurance, and so no money was being made available to help them rebuild. Most residents just wanted to be given a chance to rebuild their homes and to restore Forest Heights' way of life.

After developing Forest Heights in Gulfport, we put in 264 units in the Delta town of Indianola, town houses in St. Louis, hundreds of units in Dallas, Oklahoma, and North Carolina. We worked all over the country and arranged for thousands of low-income families to own their own homes. By the end of the project in 1976, we had built 8,761 homes. Dorothy Duke handled all the technical details of getting the houses in the ground. As the community organization specialist, I dealt directly with the prospective home buyers to set up home buyers associations, and I organized training programs to teach people how to manage and maintain their homes.

Dorothy and I were a great team, if I do say so myself, and we had a good time. She understood the white power structure, and I understood people. So when we came up with projects, we could hash them out and figure out what would work or not work and how to handle them. We were both on new ground because we were creating a program from scratch and we were women. Any two women would have had a hard enough time, but a black woman and a white woman running around the country together coming up with ideas that folks were always telling us we couldn't do—people didn't know what to make of us.

Dorothy Duke was the first white woman with whom I could discuss racial problems honestly and openly; I could reveal my own opinions and not feel that they would be used against me. She was the first white woman I could argue with and be comfortable about it. I always knew where she stood. Dorothy and I both were very opinionated people, and we would clash sometimes. She was very persistent, and it was hard to say no to her. We would get to arguing about some housing issue or strategy. She would come right out and say things to me like "Lord, I'm so tired of you black people, I don't know what to do." And I would laugh and say, "I know the feeling. I can't take being shut up in a room full of white folks but just so long." But our disagreements were never personal, and we worked out ways of getting things done together. It wasn't just two women working together. It was two cultures. Two people with different backgrounds who had learned to function in different ways. But we always knew the differences were cultural and not personal. And we'd laugh and enjoy each other's company as much as we argued.

Our problems were not with each other. Any troubles we had concerned overcoming public resistance to housing for poor people—poor black people. Many times community leaders said the program sounded like a wonderful idea, "but not in our neighborhood." We were dealing with the same old song of prejudice and fear: "Poor folks won't take care of their houses, and our property values will go down," or "I made it without a government handout, and those poor folks just need to get up and work for a living." We'd explain how home owners had to maintain their own property up to certain standards, which was not the case with federal rental housing projects. Then we'd talk about how these housing developments would bring money into their towns to developers, construction workers, bankers. "Money, honey" was usually the best strategy: Money has solved many a racial conflict.

We ran up against a different twist on the resistance theme in Indianola, Mississippi. Jack Harper, the chancery clerk and a civic leader, had learned about the program from Miss Height at a workshop she held in Indianola, and he had convinced the establishment there to build some Turnkey houses. He had builders and banks lined up. The white people were on board, but the black people weren't. Dorothy Duke and Mr. Harper were trying to get the project under way, and she told him I'd be coming to work with him on some things. In Gulfport, Dorothy had been able to tell the white businessmen that I was a Washington consultant. But that wouldn't work in Indianola, which was only a couple of counties over from where I lived. This was Sunflower County, Fannie Lou Hamer's county, and they knew me there. Mr. Harper told her they weren't going to fool with "that radical Unita Blackwell." He said they were having enough problems with the local blacks.

"Well, if you can't talk to her, there's nothing more we can do, because the project won't fly," Dorothy said.

After Dorothy explained that I worked in partnership with her, Mr. Harper finally agreed to talk with me.

Mr. Harper was also head of the chamber of commerce, and it was in that capacity that he was working toward housing. I was in there to build houses, and we needed to be on the same wavelength. When I arrived in town, there was a black boycott of white businesses. Mr. Harper asked me, "How're you going to get this housing done? There's a mess down there with those black folks. They are against us [white people]; they won't even talk to us. You civil rights agitators have made sure that they don't talk to us."

The only black people Mr. Harper seemed to feel comfortable talking to were the "yes-people" he had always talked to—the ones who would go along with whatever Mr. White Man wanted. Mr. Harper thought he had to fight black folks who weren't yes-people. He thought—and a lot of white people made this mistake—that the others wouldn't listen to him. And they wouldn't have, as long as they felt like they were being told what to do. So, in Indianola, we were dealing not only with a black-white division; he had managed to split up the black people. And that had set up more problems. When the problems are long embedded, you have to fight to shake old ways loose, as we had learned in the movement. But in a case like this, people need to create a harmonious situation to get things done. When you set up divisions, it backfires. It will do so every time. So I told him: "Don't deal with the ones who're saying nice words to you, the ones who're telling you what you want to hear. That won't get you any- where. It will only harden up the division. You need to talk to the people who are giving you the problem and listen to them." I said he needed to be getting cooperation among all the black people: "When you create strife and confusion, it always comes back to you," I said, "Now, Mr. Harper, wouldn't I look like a nut trying to split up the white folks in my community?"

Mr. Harper understood my point, and he asked me who he should talk to. I gave him names, he called them to a meeting, things began to move, and we got those houses in the ground. A black Delta woman, an old freedom fighter, was leading white people in the Mississippi Delta—it's shocking even now to think of it. Mr. Harper and I became friends, and over the years he has done a lot to keep that town moving.

It had taken me years to come to the place that I didn't get angry with people like Mr. Harper. My first years in the movement, I was seething with anger. You have to have some anger to get involved in a movement. Mrs. Hamer used to say, "Child, don't let white folks get you so upset. Don't pay no attention to them. They're sick." She'd try to get me laughing, poking fun with her stories. Gradually it began to sink in that my fury wasn't hurting the white folks I was mad at, but it was eating me up. My anger was taking away the very freedom I had worked for. It was no longer the kind of anger that motivated me; it was holding me back. I knew I had to free myself from it. "Try to let up off yourself. Don't take things so hard," my mother would tell me; "Wear life like a loose garment." As I grew into believing more in my own abilities and dignity as a human being, I got my angry spirit under control.

I came to find out that one of the most liberating things that can happen to you is to face the opposition calmly, declare your position, and come out feeling good about yourself. We have all name-called each other in anger. Through the years, I had seen that some of the most "radical" people were the ones who sold us out, and some of the hard-liners have managed to do good things after all. I look at results. I want to know what you can do and if I can trust you. Then I can decide how far I'm going with you and where I'm not going. That's the way I think, and I've gotten a lot of work done that way. You don't have to water down the message; I gave it to people straight, but sometimes just a little at a time. I found out that rushing into a group I'd never met before with ultimatums never works, or not for very long. To work with others to solve problems or to persuade people to consider new ideas and new ways of thinking, you have to listen to people and try to understand where they're coming from, what their concerns and needs are. And then give them some wiggle room and time. When you're solving problems and negotiating through people's differences—whatever they are—everybody needs to feel recognized; everybody wants to come out looking good.

Even at my most angry I never hated white people. None of my family hated whites, and that's the way I was brought up. I hated the way I'd been treated and the way I was always having to look out for snakes and be uncertain and afraid. But I had grown to see that people can change. It's not easy to free ourselves from beliefs and attitudes that have controlled and guided our lives since childhood. But when they're no longer applicable, I think we must do so, to become mature, free people. If I could expand my own horizons and understanding as much as I had, I had faith that others could do so, too. My faith became more steadfast as I saw people willing to open their minds and respect each other and work together. When that happens, there's almost no limit to the good that can be accomplished for the betterment of the whole society.

I have to confess that I was more successful at creating harmonious situations in the professional world, among people I didn't know, than I was in my own house. I had been working nonstop at home and around the country—being a mother and a wife, an activist and a professional woman. I always managed to work my trips around Jeremiah's work schedule and my son's school activities—the way many women have done for years. But keeping up such a hectic pace took a toll on my personal life. When I was home, Jeremiah and I were arguing more and more, about every little thing, and I was drinking too much. As I've said before, the man was a talker and he loved to argue, and in those days, I gave as good as I got. As I'd become more involved in movement and professional activities, our household routines had changed. All of a sudden people were looking for me, asking me questions about what to do or what I thought. It didn't get intense until after we got a telephone. Jeremiah'd answer the phone, and the caller would want to talk to me. And he'd say, "Well, I'm here. What is it?" And the caller would say, "No, we don't want to talk to you; we want to talk to Unita." And this started competitiveness between us. And it got worse and worse. Even though Jeremiah had been supportive of my work in the movement—because he always was an independent thinker—he was still a man who considered himself the head of the household, and my new professional status wasn't easy for him to deal with. He just couldn't believe that I was the woman he'd married. I don't want to put everything off on Jeremiah, because much of what was going on between us was about me. I had changed on the inside. I guess I was blooming into the person I really was or wanted to be— someone who would make decisions on my own and not be hampered.

By 1970, I had come through several stages of self-development. The civil rights movement had been a crash course in psychology and self-analysis. The women's movement was taking hold all over the country—women's lib, as we called it then. And like thousands of women, I was more aware of my equality with men, and of my power. I never had been a woman who wanted to sit over in the corner and not say anything. But the civil rights movement and then the women's movement pushed me along. I needed some peace and joy in my life that I couldn't find in my marriage. Or in my work.

Although my job gave me a lot of satisfaction, and I felt confident and capable and productive, I carried my personal unrest with me. So I tried to drown the turmoil and fill the void by drinking whiskey and partying. Since I'm not a person who can drink just a little bit, that only made matters worse, both at work and at home. I decided to free myself from alcohol and marriage both in 1971.

It wasn't easy to do either of those things, but I've never been sorry I did. I found myself more able to move toward the joy and peace I needed, and I became more free and responsible and fulfilled. I was discovering that freedom has many layers, like an onion or a cabbage head, and becoming free is an ongoing process of peeling them off, one by one. For me it is a spiritual journey, which draws upon my deepest faith in the divine source and brings me closer and closer to my own spiritual core.

I haven't had a drink since 1971, and Jeremiah and I remain friends to this day.

18

Open Your Eyes to Other
Worlds, Other Ways

ONE JANUARY MORNING in 1973 I got an unexpected call
from Shirley MacLaine.

"Hi, Unita. This is Shirley. How are you?"

"Oh, just fine," I said. I was thinking, what is Miss MacLaine up to
this time?

I hadn't heard from Shirley since the 1968 convention in Chicago,
when she was a George McGovern delegate from California. I had
introduced her to Fannie Lou Hamer and Hodding Carter and the
other people in our delegation. (I think Hodding was flabbergasted
that I knew Shirley MacLaine.) I have pictures of everybody standing
there smiling at the movie star. We had first gotten to know each other
when she came to see me in Mayersville during movement days. I'll
never forget Shirley's visit—it was the fall of 1964, and she stayed at
my house about a week. And what a week it was.

John Lewis, head of SNCC, had come by my house with Muriel Tillinghast and another young woman from SNCC, as well as a visitor he
wanted me to meet. He said her name was Shirley MacLaine. The
name didn't ring a bell. I didn't know anything about her other than
that she was from outside Mississippi and had come down to check on
our civil rights activities. We had people like that coming by all the
time. I figured she probably had given SNCC some money. She was
wearing a pair of leather pants and a silk blouse. I had never actually

seen silk before, but as soon as I saw it, I knew it had to be silk. I thought, this child must be mighty rich.

We were talking and she was looking around my house, and she said, "What can I do?"

"Well, you can go out and pump some water."

John jumped up and started out with her. And I said to myself, what is his problem? Why is he running out there with her? So I went out back and saw John trying to help her.

I said, "You don't know how to pump water?"

She said, "No. I never have done this before."

Then Muriel Tillinghast came out, and she and John said they would handle the water and Shirley could go back inside with me.

On the way we stopped at her car to get something. I was really thrilled to see her car because it was new and bright—it just gleamed—and had very fancy hubcaps with spokes and whitewall tires. She said it was a rent-a-car. I had no idea that people could rent cars. There were some shiny metal boxes in her car, and we got these out and carried them into the house. I didn't know what they were, but I later found out they were tape recorders. They had great big ones back then. We took them into the house, and she asked me where a plug-in was. She was looking for wall outlets. Well, I had one socket with a plug hanging from the ceiling in the front room and another coming down from the ceiling of the other room. I showed them to Shirley, but she said we couldn't plug the equipment in there. We sat around talking, the four of us, trying to figure out how we were going to get those boxes plugged in, and then they all spent the night at my house.

The next day John and I left and went to a meeting in Jackson. Shirley and the others stayed so they could try to get her recording machines plugged in. We were going down the road, and John said, "Unita, do you know that woman is a movie star? That's Shirley MacLaine, and she's a big star. But don't tell anybody she's here."

At that time I didn't know much about movie stars. Most of the movies I had seen were cowboy shows on Saturday. The only movie actor I remembered was Tom Mix and some actress who might have been in a movie with him. I remembered him because he always rode a white horse, and there was a difference between a black horse and a white horse. The black horse was the bad horse that the bad man rode, and the white horse was the good horse that the hero rode. Shirley didn't look like she fit into that picture. I just knew Shirley MacLaine was a rich somebody, because she had on pure silk and leather pants and the others were running around waiting on her. That was different because we didn't wait on one another; everybody did their own piece in the movement.

When we got back from the meeting, they were fastening the machines up. She had a transformer or battery or something they plugged in from the top of the house. The wires and things were hanging everywhere. We were all sitting around talking, and I didn't know we were being taped. It turns out she was taping for her book *Don't Fall Off the Mountain.* In the book, which was published in 1970, she described being at my house. Here's part of what she wrote:

> In Issaquena County about one and a half hours from Jackson, Mississippi, I stayed with a woman named Unida [sic] Black-well. . . . For hours we sat drinking beer and philosophizing about the suppressions of women. . . . They put up with too much, she said—not only black women, but all women, because they had bought the myth that they weren't equal to their male counterparts. . . .
>
> In Unida Blackwell's house there was only one bed [for guests]. The SNCC workers and I slept in shifts, usually four in the bed. Unida's son, Joshua [sic], slept in the living room in a chair. . . .
>
> During those days with [Unita], whenever we drove in daylight around the countryside to talk to people about registering, there were always a few of the guys along to keep an eye out for sheriff cars. And whenever one was spotted there was a yell and I was pushed to the floor. To avoid a lot of trouble it was better to keep me out of sight. For seven days and most of the seven nights all of us lived together. I'd purchase food at the neighborhood white-run market, so high-priced that I was out of money by the end of the week. We ate together, drank,

talked, cried, and laughed together. It was a time of communi-
cation I'll remember always.[1]

When I asked Shirley why she called my son "Joshua" in her book,
she said she liked the name Joshua better than Jerry. I came to find
out Shirley could do wild, funny things.

She did very generous things, too. Shirley spent a lot of time with
Jerry while she was here, and he was crazy about her. When she got
home, she sent him a coat called a Windbreaker. I had never seen one
of them. We weren't into those kinds of things then. And later on—I'll
never forget—she sent me a suit, a tweed suit. It was a nice suit. My
mother held on to it for years because a movie star bought it.

After Shirley left, we went looking for Shirley MacLaine on
television—my mother and friends and I. When she was on television,
she looked different. The name announced for the program would be
Shirley MacLaine, but when she'd come on, she might be a nun or whatever. Mrs. Hamer would call me and say, "Girl, what has that movie
star done to her hair now?" We also had not known how makeup could
change the way you look. But we learned. Shirley taught us a lot about
movie stars. I think she learned some things from us, too. She's an
adventurer, and she found a new and different world in Mississippi.

Shirley MacLaine's telephone call that January morning in 1973, eight
years after her visit, would open up the entire world to me.

"We're going to China," she said.

"Well, how nice. Oh, that's very nice."

"Did you hear what I said? *We* are going to China."

"Wait a minute. What 'we'?"

She said, "You, if you can go, and me and several other women."
She explained that the Chinese foreign minister had invited her to
bring a delegation of twelve women to visit China. "I'm putting a group

---

1. Shirley MacLaine, *Don't Fall Off the Mountain* (New York: Norton, 1970),
   p. 63.

together," she said, "and I want you to be a part of it. I hope you're available."

"You mean the *real* China?"

"I know it's startling. All your expenses will be paid. Think about it and let me know."

So I hung up and she hung up, and then I called my mother. My mother had put up with a lot of things, and she had come through fine. But every time she looked up, I was into something else. So I called her up in Helena to tell her what I was going to do now. She asked me how the weather was. We'd just had a big ice storm in Mississippi.

I said, "Well, listen, Shirley called me and we're going to China."

And she said, "I'll tell you the truth, this weather is something else." She kept right on talking—you know how mothers are, they don't really hear you sometimes.

So I said, "Birt, Shirley called me."

"What? You're talking about that movie star?"

"Yes, that's the one. We're going to China."

And she said, "What China, baby? You mean, *China,* China?"

"Yes, ma'am."

She said, "Honey, I tell you what, you hang up, and you call me back."

Then I called my boss, Miss Height, at the National Council of Negro Women. "Miss Height, Shirley MacLaine just called me, and she wants me to go to China with her. I want to know if I can get off from work to go."

And she said, "What China are you talking about, Unita?" She's very educated. "Do you mean the People's Republic of China?"

"Yes, ma'am."

"Well, I can't talk right now. Can you hang up and call me back later?"

So, that was my start. Everybody was in a state of shock that here I was, poor cotton-stocking child, on her way to China.

The word hit the local paper before it even hit the streets. The next week after my phone call from Shirley, the *Deer Creek Pilot* had a front-page story about my trip. This was the first time we'd ever seen a black person on the front page of the paper, except one fixing to be carried off to jail. The headline read: "Unita Blackwell going to Red

China." And all of a sudden it dawned on me: I was going to a Communist country to interpret communism, and people in this state had been calling me a Communist for years. They had called me a Communist when I wanted to register to vote. They called me a Communist when I tried to get our little children a better education. They called me a Communist when I wanted to help people get enough to eat and find houses for them to live in and when I said we wanted help from programs that were funded by our government. I thought, well, I sure do want to find out what a Communist looks like.

President Nixon had gone to China the year before, 1972. And I'd seen that trip all over the television: the president and first lady at the Great Wall of China. He and Zhou Enlai, China's premier, issued the Shanghai Communiqué, pledging to normalize relations between the United States and the People's Republic of China and agreeing that there was only "one China" and that the island of Taiwan was part of it. (After Mao Zedong's Communist revolutionary army had taken over mainland China in 1949, the United States had recognized Taiwan—the island where the Nationalist Chinese had fled after Mao got control of the government—but not the People's Republic of China.) Before Nixon went to mainland China in 1972, few foreign individuals or groups had been allowed to enter China in years. And, in fact, not many others would travel there until 1979 when the United States and China established diplomatic relations. I was heading to Communist China behind the president of the United States.

When the people around Mayersville heard about my trip, some of them said that the Chinese people might not let me out of the country and that I might end up in jail. They all asked the same question: "Ain't you scared to go?"

"It couldn't be no worse than what I already been through," I said.

A month after my fortieth birthday, I flew out of Greenville to Memphis and had a good visit with my daddy before going on to New York to meet up with Shirley and the others in the delegation. I had my first passport, a small suitcase with the few items of clothing Shirley had told us to take, and not a clue about what was to come. I was barefootin' to

China. As soon as I got off the plane in New York, a woman with a camera that had a long nose on it got right down in front of me and stuck it in my face. She was filming all our group as we arrived. That's how I discovered that our whole trip would be documented day and night for a movie. From the airport we went to Shirley's Manhattan apartment to meet the others. There were twelve women in our group—Shirley MacLaine, myself, five other "typical American women," a twelve-year-old girl, and four young women filmmakers; two of them met us in Los Angeles.

The first woman I met in New York was Pat Hansen. She stepped into the room with her black hair all fluffed and piled up on her head and said, "Hi, y'all. I'm from Port Arthur, Texas, and I supported George Wallace." Like we were supposed to think that was something great. She was a typical southern white lady, and she told me that she liked "colored people." She asked me about some of the "colored conditions" in Mississippi. And I told her I wouldn't dare call her house and ask her how the white people were doing in Texas. She said, "Oh, I didn't know that." And she didn't. A lot of people really don't know.

Then came Rosa Marin, a professor from Puerto Rico. She was speaking Spanish, and I don't know a word she said. And here came a tall, white-headed, very plainly dressed Long Island woman named Margaret Whitman. I soon found out that she was a Republican and her husband worked down on Wall Street. Twelve-year-old Karen Boutilier was from Wisconsin, and she told me that she was going to sleep with me, me and her new purse, and that we were going to play cards all night. I told her I didn't play cards. There was one light-haired young woman, who ran and grabbed me and said, "I just love you, I love you!" This surprised me because I couldn't figure out what I had that she loved. She was one of the film crew for the movie Shirley was making. The four film people were Claudia Weill, Cabell Glickler, Nancy Shreiber, and Joan Weidman. By now it had hit me that I'd accepted a trip to China on the other side of the world, to be gone away from home for a whole month, and I had no idea who I was going with or whether we'd all get along.

This group of us flew out the next day to California and went out to Shirley's house, where I stumbled into the other two women going on our trip. I decided it was about time that I started asking questions, because we had a strange crew here. First, I met Dr. Phyllis Kronhausen, and I asked her, "Now what do you do?"

She said, "I run a museum."

"Well, what kind of museum is it? What's in your museum?"

"Well, sex."

Come to find out I was dealing with a sexologist. She had a sex museum, the only one in the country. I was sitting there with a sex lady. She talked about sex just like we would talk about what we're going to eat for breakfast. Lord, have mercy, I thought, I need to move outside to get some air and try to calm myself down. I was glad I hadn't had a drink since 1971, because if it hadn't been for that, I'd probably have been drunk by then.

When I got back inside, in came this American Indian, dressed in a costume with turquoise jewelry, and ribbons and beads hanging all around her, and I was thinking, she must be worth a fortune. When she came to the door, up went her hand and she said, "Woo, woo, woo," and began singing. She brought out a little drum, and she danced all around all of us, beating the drum and sprinkling yellow stuff from a little bag. When she slowed down, I said, "Now, honey, are you on your way to China?" She said, "I sure am." I said, "Me too." She told me her name was Ninibah Crawford, and she was the daughter of a Navajo chief. I thought, my God! What a group!

But soon I loved every one of them. Shirley MacLaine knew what she was doing when she picked these women from different cultural and economic, social, and political backgrounds, who knew nothing about each other's way of life. It wouldn't be long before we'd all be in a world that none of us knew anything about, and we'd get past our own differences and learn about each other's humanity as we learned about the Chinese people. But we didn't know that or anything else the next day, April 16, 1973, when our unusual group boarded a TWA airplane and took off with the movie star.

We couldn't fly directly into the People's Republic of China. We went through Guam and Hawaii; then we flew on to Hong Kong, located on the southeast coast of mainland China and at that time a British colony. The streets were crowded with more people than I'd ever seen before. People were pulling rickshaws with other people sitting up in the back, and grown people were riding bicycles. Street markets sold bright-colored clothes and anything you might think of. The sounds and smells were exotic and wonderful. It was just like I had stepped into a movie.

Over the next three weeks, we visited three large cities in eastern China—Canton (Guangzhou) on the South China Sea, Shanghai on the East China Sea, and Beijing in north-central China, in that order—and we traveled in the rural areas around those cities, to villages and communes and factories. Canton was not far across the border from Hong Kong, but we had to take two trains to get there—one train to the border of the People's Republic of China to go through customs and a second one into Canton itself. The first train was packed with people, all talking and excited, and it was going *da da da boom boom* and swaying back and forth. I looked out the window and saw my first water buffaloes.

At the Chinese border we first went through British customs, and when we came out of the far side of the building, there was a bridge into the People's Republic of China. We walked across the bridge while our film crew ran around furiously with those long-nose cameras zooming in on us arriving in China. When we got to the other side, we were at the Chinese customs center, a large building with huge paintings of Chairman Mao and Chinese people covering the whole wall, and brightly colored flowers growing all around. And that's when you knew you'd left the British side, the wide-open, clashing commercial world that you knew something about, and entered a world about which you knew nothing.

The first people I saw were two fellows in green military uniforms with red armbands and a red star on their caps. They were standing very straight and trying to look serious and tough. These were the Red Guards. I looked closely and saw that they were young and baby faced and their skin was radiant and healthy. I thought I might have seen a little glimmer in their eyes. I was scared to death, anyway. So I just looked straight into their eyes and smiled at them, and they looked down and smiled, very quickly, at me. Yeah, I'll get along all right in China, I thought.

The Red Guards took my passport. And I wouldn't see it again until I left China. It was a strange feeling to hand over my passport, which I'd gone through a lot of trouble to get, another situation where I didn't know what to expect. Inside the customs building, we met the two guides who would be with us for the entire trip. (In addition, we'd pick up interpreters in each place we went.) The Chinese seemed flabbergasted over all our luggage and film equipment. (I think Americans keep everybody else in the world moving.) They let us and our stuff on through. Shirley MacLaine went in first as the celebrity, but little did any of us know that soon Hollywood stardom wouldn't matter.

We got on a Chinese train, and loud Chinese music was playing but everything else was calm. The train ride itself was smooth. We sat in little booths facing each other, and there were real lace curtains on the windows. They served us tea in pretty little pots, which was the beginning of a whole lot of tea serving and drinking over the course of the trip. And then we went into the countryside, and I saw rice growing in paddies with water running through them. It was in the spring of the year. There were gardens of vegetables, and flowers were growing in with the vegetables, just the way we used to do in the Delta, and it was beautiful.

I was very happy to see a group of black people on the train, because I hadn't seen any so far and I wasn't used to not seeing black folks. But then I heard them talking, and I couldn't understand one word they were saying. Cabell Glickler, our film director, spoke French, and she said that's what they were speaking. She and I went over to talk to them, and she found out they were from South Africa and were going to the International Trade Fair in Canton. They would be the last blacks I saw for quite a while and the first black folks I'd ever seen that I couldn't even talk to.

When we got to Canton and checked into the hotel, I was running around trying to find a room key. I didn't know that in China there was no use for a key. People didn't lock up anything because people didn't steal from each other. The hotel room was nice and cool but not fancy; it was clean but not sanitized and bleached to death. There was a mosquito bar over my bed, and boom, it brought back memories. I hadn't seen a mosquito bar since I was a child living on the plantation. I soon found there would be lots of things that brought my childhood memories back. I sat on the bed and discovered it was a featherbed. I hadn't slept on a featherbed since I stayed with Big Mama in the country. From my window I could see the Yangtze River. I could identify with that big old river because I'd lived beside the Mississippi River all my life. But I was in a city that was two thousand years old when Christ was born. Now that was mind-blowing for me.

Early the next morning, before we all headed to the trade fair, the People's Revolutionary Committee met with us. They explained that China was organized into farming communes, factories, and residential areas, and they told us that families worked in production teams and street committees. They were focused on very recent history, giving us facts and figures about industry and progress since 1969, the end of the Cultural Revolution, to reactivate Mao Zedong's strictest Communist teachings and do away with the middle class. No mention was made of the violent revolution itself, when universities were closed, the most creative and intelligent Chinese people were forced into manual labor on collective farms, and millions of young people became Red Guards, storming through towns and cities and killing thousands of people. Although the violence had ended by the time we arrived and Premier Zhou Enlai was reaching out to the United States and other countries, all the Chinese had to study *Quotations from Chairman Mao Tse-tung* in weekly community meetings.

I was surprised to find out that most of the Chinese people didn't belong to the Communist Party. Only about nine million out of eight hundred fifty million people belonged to the Communist Party (many of the people I met called themselves socialist-thinking people). The Chinese Communist Party, started in 1921, is the regime that governs them. I asked, "Well, how do you become a member?" And the lady committee head said, "You have to work to get into the party. You have to show yourself worthy and be approved." I thought to myself, well, I know a little about that.

I soon discovered that signs and posters presenting Communist ideas were plastered everywhere. Our interpreters translated some of them for me: "Practice Birth Control for the Revolution." "Art Comes from the Struggle: The Working People Are Masters." "Work Hard for the Continuing Revolution to Accomplish Even Greater Victories." There was no chance anyone would forget Mao. Gigantic pictures of him were everywhere, and they welcomed us to the Canton International Trade Fair.

The fair consisted of displays of industrial and agricultural products to showcase and promote Chinese industry and agriculture to buyers from around the world. As I wandered around, I came upon a Chinese woman standing at a booth with roots and leaves just like I'd seen growing up in the Mississippi Delta. I could hardly believe my eyes: Laid out there on her table were cockleburs and dandelions and mulberries and mint leaves and thistle and dock weed and honeysuckle vines! Through my interpreter I spoke with the Chinese lady, who explained that these plants were used in China's "scientific medicine."

When I was a girl, Big Mama used to pick the same plants and use them to make tea and preparations to get rid of colds and flu, improve digestion, induce labor, treat burns and cuts. I knew Big Mama's concoctions worked on us, but in Canton, China, I found out that my grandmother was scientific. As I was standing there talking, reporters from the *Hong Kong News* were listening and taking notes and making photographs. The next day one of Shirley's friends, the chief of police in Hong Kong, called and said my picture was in the Hong Kong paper. The caption read something like, "Black American woman and Chinese woman discuss herbal medicines that they both use, and they're worlds apart."

Canton is in the southern Delta part of the country, and the Chinese food there reminded me of what I ate in the Mississippi Delta—deep-fat fried foods and greens. The Chinese would pick a chicken and cut it up in little pieces and fry it up crunchy. Oh Lord, it's so good. And they ate neck bones and little dumplings and pork ribs with a sweet sauce. I was amazed at how the same culture had cut clean across the world. I was already a little homesick being so far away from people I knew, and all these reminders of home made me happy and lonesome at the same time.

People everywhere dressed in grays and khaki and blues. This was the Communist-style dress, loose-fitting pants and shirts, which everybody wore so no one would stand out above anybody else. The only real difference in dress between the officials and the peasants seemed to be the texture of the fabrics. They wore clothes they could work in, because there was a lot of working going on in China. Even when the women dressed up, they wore pants. I saw only a couple of women in dresses on the whole trip. They didn't need more than two outfits—that's the way they lived. They didn't buy a whole lot of anything.

I wanted to learn about Chinese education, and I talked to the children in day care centers, kindergarten, and higher grade levels. They learned politics at an early age, and they sang about and danced to honor Chairman Mao. But the thing that most impressed me was the love shown by the teachers, which surely must have left the children sure of themselves. The children I met in China were told that they were the jewels of the country, and they were treated that way—as precious. Unlike the adults, the children were dressed in the most colorful outfits I've ever seen, with flowers and dots, in bright reds and blues and greens. The Chinese seemed to put everything they had into their children.

In Shanghai we went to the Children's Palace, a big building where children came after school for games and sports and creative projects. One child came running up to me with a little doll that had an African hat on, which she had made herself. I was overcome with emotion. I still get emotional when I think about it, because I was so lonesome, and she presented me with a gift of friendship. I had never been in a place before where there were absolutely no black people—a whole country, I mean. And this little Chinese girl had molded an African hat for me. Shirley was standing there, and she could tell I was about to cry. She said, "Hold that tear," and motioned for Claudia Weill to come over and photograph me. It was like being on a movie set. I'm sure Shirley was used to "holding" tears, but this was a new one for me.

In China my black skin was a novelty. People wanted to *look* at me. Once there was a sea of people standing out in front of the hotel, waiting. Shirley came out and waved at everybody, and they waved back, but they still just stood there, looking up and waiting. Then someone said they were waiting for Unita. When I stepped out, they gave all they had; they roared. I smiled and waved just like a movie star.

Most people in China hadn't seen an American black person. They loved the fact that I was black and different. The black people they had seen were from Africa, so they called me an African and considered me important. This was the first time that I thought of myself as

African—that I ever *felt* African. I knew history, of course, but had no personal knowledge of my African roots. As a black person in the United States, I hadn't always felt as American as the white people I knew seemed to feel. All of my life I never knew where I belonged; my grandmother used to ask, "Who really *is* our people?" In China I found a sense of belonging to my ancestral home, and I became a citizen of the world.

But I was homesick and really wanted to see another black person. In Beijing I got my chance. Beijing is the seat of the revolutionary government; the Great Hall of the People and Tiananmen Square are there. We were riding in our van on the broad crowded avenue leading to our hotel, and we saw a long black diplomatic limousine coming toward us. When the car came even with our van, I looked inside and saw a black man in a business suit. He saw me at the same time and leaned out and yelled, "Hey, sister." I jumped out of our van, and he bounded out of his car, and all of the traffic stopped still while we hugged each other in the middle of the busiest street in the world. Nobody was in any hurry. We were the most important thing happening. We wanted to speak to one another, and everybody recognized that and they stopped. Isn't that beautiful? Then we each got back in our vehicles and went our separate ways. I never knew who he was. It was that kind of trip.

Shirley and all of us were interested in the roles and work of women in China. The women's movement in the United States had been gathering steam with the introduction of the Equal Rights Amendment to the Constitution in 1972 and the *Roe v. Wade* decision in January 1973, ensuring a woman the constitutional right to choose whether to terminate her own pregnancy. We were told that Chairman Mao said that women are the "other half of the sky" and should have pay and opportunities equal to men's. We wanted to know if this was actually happening in China, so we visited farms and factories and went into the countryside and talked to women. They told us how their lives had been during the revolution a few years before, how their children had died, how they didn't have food or medical treatment, and how so many of their children had been born dead. Life was much better for them now, they said. They all had jobs, their families had food, and the men were treating them better. Shirley and some of the other women asked questions about their sex lives—personal questions. The Chinese women were so embarrassed; they couldn't talk about it. I felt so sorry for them.

In Beijing, when Shirley and the rest of the group attended a Women's Day program in Tiananmen Square, I had to stay in the hotel with a cold. I called it a "Chinese cold" because we had experienced so many climate changes in such a short period of time. At the hotel I received a visit from a lovely and compassionate Chinese woman who had met the others earlier in the day and heard I was ill. She said her name was Teng Ying-Zhou. I didn't know anything about her other than she was a nice Chinese woman who came to see how I was. So I was amazed to learn later that Teng Ying-Zhou was, in fact, Madame Zhou Enlai, the wife of the premier of China and a national leader in protecting the rights of women and children.

In our travels in the rural farming areas, I met Chinese farmworkers—peasants, they were called—and I identified with them. I found out that I, too, was a peasant. They would discuss their work and ask questions of us when we attended their revolutionary committee meetings. Shirley encouraged them to talk to me. They could sense that I understood what they were going through. They told me about their cooperative farm system and explained that they shared equally in the profits of their labor. Even though they didn't have much, they had enough to live on, they said. (By my next visit, only five years later, the communes were gone and farmers were buying land to farm on.)

While I was in China, I immersed myself in Chinese ways, but when we returned to Hong Kong to spend a couple of days before we came back to the States, I was jolted back to the realities of home by two pieces of news. The Watergate story had broken open. Nixon's four top aides had resigned, and plans were under way for a full investigation of the president's role in the burglary of the Democratic Party headquarters. The other news was personal. When I called my mother to tell her I was on my way home, she informed me that my daddy had died a couple of weeks earlier. I was so thankful I'd gone by to see him before I left for China. My mind was spinning and my emotions were running wild, and I returned to Mayersville in a daze.

✢   ✢   ✢

My first trip to China was mind-boggling, and it took me a long while after I returned home to put all the pieces together and make sense of what I had seen and heard. China is a gigantic country—about one-fourth of the land area of the entire world. It has four thousand years of recorded history. Before I went to China, I said I wanted to find out what a Communist was. But once I was there, it wasn't the politics but the people that affected me. I saw that a person living in China loves and laughs and cries and needs friends and values family, the same way we do in this country. People are people—rich or poor, black, white, or yellow; American, Chinese, African, or Iraqi. And people need help all over this world. And that is the message I brought home from my first trip to China.

Since then, I've made sixteen trips to China. I've also traveled to India and to many countries in Africa, Europe, and Latin America. I could never have imagined when the movie star came to Mayersville that she would have such an influence on my life. That's what I like about barefootin': You never know who might come along and give you a ride.

My first trip to China opened my eyes to the rest of the world—to the need for friendship and understanding with people who live differently from us. Books, television, and movies provide ways to peek at other countries, but nothing compares to being in another land and viewing life from someone else's perspective. It's like getting new eyes and learning to see all over again. And when you get home, you have new eyes for seeing your own familiar world, too.

19

Think Big *and* Small

THE NATIONAL COUNCIL OF NEGRO WOMEN housing
initiative—and my job—ended in 1975, and I welcomed the
chance to spend more time in Mayersville. Jerry was a senior
in high school in 1975–76, and I loved being able to attend all his foot-
ball and basketball games and tennis matches. Jerry had grown to be
six feet five inches tall, and with his big Afro he looked even taller. He
was so handsome in his cap and gown when he graduated with honors
from Rolling Fork High School in May of 1976. Jerry's graduation was a
very emotional time for me. Even though I'd never doubted that he
would graduate, after all we had been through I was elated and grateful
to know that, as a black male, he would have a chance for a good life.
In my time, I'd known so many fine young black men who'd had to
drop out of school to help support their families, limiting their possibilities for the rest of their lives. In the fall, he entered Mississippi
State University to begin his freshman year in college.

The year 1976 was memorable for other reasons, too. We incorporated Mayersville, and I became the first black female mayor in Mississippi. In 1976 Mayersville still had no paved streets, no police
department, no fire department. We were a bunch of folks living out in
the middle of nowhere with nothing. We didn't even have a town water
system that would bring water into people's homes or a sewerage system that would take it away. There was a spigot down in the center of

town, one little water line. It was sort of like a faucet, and it was running all the time. That's all that was there for the community. People could take buckets and get water and carry it home, if they didn't have a water pump at their house. If you wanted indoor plumbing, you had to run your own lines. Most white residents had put in water lines and septic tanks for their own houses, but most black people still had a hand pump and an outhouse where waste went into an open hole in the ground. Imagine what this was like in a small town with all the houses close together and the windows open. We needed basic services. Our town was tiny, but our problems and needs were enormous. We had to think big.

By 1976, I had already been looking into ways to provide the services for two or three years. From my organizing and planning experience, I knew federal and state money was available to help communities like Mayersville get these services, but we had no organized political group eligible to apply for the funds. I was at a MACE meeting one day talking about Mayersville's problems, and all of a sudden it hit me: We needed to incorporate Mayersville so we could get government money. I didn't have the foggiest notion of how to set up a town, so I suggested, "Let's get some grants and see if we can incorporate Mayersville. If it works for Mayersville, we can try it in other small communities in the Delta." So MACE got a grant from the Mott Foundation to study the possibilities. The consultants told us the basics and got us started. First we had to get the approval of the residents. At my request, Larry Farmer and Charles Bannerman from MACE came to Mayersville and talked to several men in our community about incorporation. That's the way it was done: Men went to other men. A couple of Mayersville fellows agreed to take charge of the process, but a couple of years passed, and the men still hadn't gotten anything moving on incorporation.

Farmer came to me and asked if I would work on it. Since I had the time, I said, "I'll see what I can do to get things moving." I set up a series of public hearings to discuss the issue with our people. "Public hearings" was the government term, but to me they were mass meetings. I was using the same process we'd had during the movement to get people registered to vote and later to set up freedom schools and

CDGM and to desegregate the public schools and take over the Air Force base. The difference now was we were getting rights for all residents, black and white.

At the first meeting, August 19, 1976, I explained that if we got incorporated, we could apply for and receive federal and state funds to improve our community. I couldn't promise a lot, because at that time I didn't know all the details of what would be involved. I put the question to the people who had come to the meeting: Do you want water and sewer systems and paved streets in Mayersville? We need to show our support and willingness to work for our community, I said, because it's easier to ask others to help you when there are visible signs you are trying to help yourself. I also made it clear that the effort to incorporate Mayersville was not a black effort or a white effort but an effort of all the people, black and white, to improve our community. The Mayersville population was about 80 percent black.

More than a hundred people came to the first meeting and endorsed the incorporation attempt. We organized as the Mayersville Citizens for Incorporation, and the group appointed me to form a biracial committee to oversee implementation. I appointed three black members—Mildred Fleming, Robert T. Williams, and Margaret Marshall—and two white members—Mary Vandevender, the chancery clerk, the same lady who had denied me the right to vote, and Herbert Harmon, the postmaster. I assumed that the chancery clerk and the postmaster would be the most knowledgeable ones, but they did not know any more about incorporating a town than the black folks did. That realization cut down feelings of being left out among the black members. We were all learning something new.

Working on a biracial committee itself was new for most people. We were all in a new experiment together. There was a need to learn, sometimes painfully, not only how to incorporate a town but how black and white people could work together as equals. This was twelve years after Freedom Summer. Although black Mayersville residents were voting and a few were even being elected to offices in the county, there had never before been a real give-and-take meeting of the races in our town. We were still dealing in a climate of racial tension, and sometimes I felt like I was on a tightrope trying to balance the needs and ways of blacks and whites in our community. At first the black members wouldn't talk openly in front of white people, but gradually they opened up; and the white people, who were used to being in charge, discovered that their black neighbors had something to offer. Few people in my own community were aware of the experience I'd had problem solving or the negotiating with whites in my national housing job. Now I was working with my people in my town, and I really wanted this project to succeed.

We asked Willie Bailey, a young Greenville lawyer, to serve as our legal counsel, and I found an engineer to complete the land survey. We needed at least one square mile of land within the boundary of the incorporated town. The state agriculture department made aerial photographs of the area. Then we had to figure out where to draw the boundary lines. I had to convince the big farmers surrounding me to let us include their land within the town limits. They were concerned about the taxes, of course. I got in touch with a tax specialist—a good friend of mine in Pennsylvania—and he flew in and looked at the land and the state laws. He explained that we should tax the houses, not the land. That's what we did, and the white farmers finally went along with it, although they were skeptical that we knew what we were doing.

Seven or eight women agreed to walk the streets, knock on every door of every house, black and white, conducting a census, discussing the need for incorporation, and answering questions. They counted 470 residents within the one square mile of land we had mapped out. They took a petition with them for the residents to sign their approval. I talked to a lot of people myself. Since many of the white residents had their own water system and septic tanks, I figured they might not stand to gain as much as black folks. So I explained the issues to them from their perspective: "You know how bad those filthy old outhouses smell, and they carry disease. Don't you think we need to get rid of them and make our lives more healthy and pleasant?" When I talked about being able to get funds to improve our town, they knew I was telling the truth because they had seen me getting government and foundation grants for over a decade. It turned out the white folks were just as interested in getting these services as the blacks. Ninety-seven percent of all registered voters signed the petition for incorporation. In September our citizens group elected the biracial committee as a temporary board of aldermen. I was chosen temporary mayor to serve until the following spring, when regular municipal elections were scheduled.

About the same time, a group of white farmers led by a young man, Jim Mabus, were trying to get a water system for the area through HUD. They knew I had government contacts and experience with federal grants, so they asked me to work with them. Since they also needed black representation to appeal to HUD, they asked me to serve as chairperson of the Mayersville Utility District. I went to work on that project at the same time we were getting incorporated. As soon as we were incorporated, the water system would belong to the town of Mayersville.

In December 1976, the judge signed our incorporation papers, and the new water system was completed and turned over to our new town. All at once we had a town and our town had water! I was jubilant. We'd had a problem and we'd come up with a solution—a simple solution. I've found that some of the most profound ideas and most creative solutions to problems are really very simple.

The big incorporation celebration came the following month. On Saturday, January 29, 1977, nearly 100 percent of the population of Mayersville came together at the Issaquena County Courthouse to commemorate our little town. State dignitaries and federal officials, newspaper reporters, television crews, and guests from New York, Chicago, and Washington crowded into the courtroom. Every seat was filled and little children sat on their parents' laps; people sat in the aisles and stood two deep around the walls. I took my seat with the other speakers and dignitaries in the jury box and looked out over the overflowing crowd of blacks and whites. It was a beautiful thing to see people come together like this in our community and to hear speakers talk about what we'd done and what we planned do to help each other.

The speaker of the Mississippi House of Representatives, C. B. "Buddie" Newman, was a longtime resident of Issaquena County, and he talked about the early history of Mayersville. He'd been one of the first people I contacted when we started the incorporation process. I said to him, "You know, Mr. Speaker, it doesn't seem right that *your* county seat is the only one in the state that is not an incorporated town. We need to change that situation." He agreed, of course, and helped us.

It was a joyful day. Everybody was smiling and talking to each other. I pledged to do everything I could as mayor to maintain and build upon our progress. Gospel choirs sang spirited verses of praise and thanks, and everyone clapped and sang along. Then we all moved into the sunny, crisp winter afternoon to drink punch and eat cookies on the courthouse lawn. The Henry Weathers High School band played "The Star-Spangled Banner." It was a dazzling and festive occasion—a spectacular beginning.

In June, Mayersville held regular elections, and officers were elected to serve a four-year term. I was elected mayor. We didn't have a town hall or other office space, and we ran the town from my living room. My salary as mayor was one hundred dollars a month, if we had it. We started out with nothing. Our annual tax collection was eighty-five hundred dollars. My job was to create something out of nothing—to come up with ideas and find grants and get money to run our little town. I got assistance in these matters from MACE and from the Center for Small Town Development, a nonprofit organization formed and directed by Harvey Johnson, who later became mayor of Jackson.

In my first term (1977–1981), Mayersville got a half-million-dollar sewerage system and paved streets. We also improved the water system, adding an elevated water tank, a chlorinator, a new well, and more distribution lines. We would soon address drainage problems. Everything didn't come from the government, either. We were given the use of an old building downtown as a town hall. Progress went more slowly than I wanted it to, but we were making headway. I knew enough about the government and politics to know things wouldn't happen overnight. I was eager to get better housing for our people and fire protection and a police department and playgrounds and ballparks for the children. These would all come in time. As it turned out, I had twenty years of service as mayor—four consecutive terms, to 1993, then a final term from 1997 to 2001. I was on the board of aldermen during the intervening years.

One of the things that made me happiest during my first term was that blacks and whites were talking to each other. As mayor I had many opportunities to practice the skills I had learned working on housing with diverse community groups. The white people found out they could talk to me; I would listen and follow up. Before, they had seen me as a rabble-rouser, a troublemaker. But they discovered I wasn't trying to stir up problems; I was trying to create a harmonious community where we could get things done.

There's a season for everything, the Bible says. In the mid-sixties, protest and confrontation were necessary to change long-held practices. In the seventies, we needed to build togetherness and foster a giving spirit. To make a small town achieve its potential, you need everybody. When a blind person carries a crippled person who can see, both of them get where they're going.

Jimmy Carter's term as president of the United States coincided with my own first term as mayor of Mayersville. I was fortunate to have an advisory role in the Carter administration, so during those four years I bounced back and forth from Washington to Mayersville. I found out that advising the president of the United States was not too different from advising the citizens of Mayersville. In both places we were thinking and dreaming and talking about things the government could do to help people and figuring out ways to make them happen. There's no job too big to benefit from a small town person's perspective, I discovered, just as there's no town too small for thinking big.

Hodding Carter III (from Greenville, Mississippi, and not related to the president) had gotten me involved in the Carter campaign in 1976, and I worked from the precinct level up to get Carter elected. I met him during his campaign, but I didn't know him personally. Soon after he took office, he established the Presidential Advisory Committee on Women and appointed me to that committee.

Bella Abzug, the colorful former congresswoman from New York who always wore a hat, chaired the committee. Bella was one of the gutsiest, smartest, funniest, wildest, most wonderful women I ever knew. She had long been involved in civil rights. As a young lawyer she had come to Mississippi in 1950 to defend Willie McGee, a black man accused of raping a white woman, and she spent one night locked in a bus station restroom hiding from the Klan. I had met her in the sixties, and we later worked together in Democratic Party politics. She was a great champion of women. "Women have been trained to speak softly and carry a lipstick. Those days are over," she said. Committee meetings with Bella were full of fire and fun, and we got things done, too.

Each person was assigned to a subcommittee—education, welfare, housing, health, child care, for example. It was suggested that I work on welfare. I realized at that particular time that the person making the suggestion wasn't being racist but knew that blacks folks were tied to a lot of the problems with welfare. I was not against fighting for welfare, but I had never been on welfare. I had worked on housing nationally and also had had difficulties myself trying to get a house to stay in, so I said, "I don't mind serving on that issue, but I'd rather work on housing." And I talked about discrimination against women trying to get a loan to buy a house: Single and divorced women couldn't get a loan, and even a married woman couldn't get a loan without her husband's signature. Bella appointed me to the housing subcommittee.

The purpose of the subcommittee was to come up with recommendations for legislation the president could take to Congress. When the women's bill was written, it included the provision that women could not be discriminated against in getting loans for home mortgages. And that was my contribution. This, like many other things I'm credited with, was merely the result of the predicament I was in. Lindy Boggs, congresswoman from Louisiana—the mother of political commentator Cokie Roberts—handled our bill on the Hill. When the men weren't progressing with the bill, she said, "Oh, you guys have forgotten this little old something here, and I know you want to see about the ladies." She pushed it through, and it passed. Most of the time, to get things done, you have to know how to say it the right way.

Bella and President Carter had some disagreements over his economic policies, and the president removed her as chair of the women's committee. Initially I said, if Bella goes, I go. But she came to see me and asked me to stay on and fight. Carter was, after all, the first president ever to address women's issues directly, and I wanted to support him. Lynda Johnson Robb, Lyndon Johnson's daughter, became our new chair, and we continued with our agenda. Lynda was a very different but excellent leader.

The United Nations designated 1979 the International Year of the Child (IYC). Following that lead, Congress established the National

Commission on the International Year of the Child to study the needs of children in our country and abroad and recommend to the president and Congress ways of addressing those needs. Jean Young—the wife of Andrew Young, the U.S. ambassador to the United Nations—chaired this commission. I was privileged to be appointed to this group, along with distinguished members from academia and high-powered civic leaders. Bill Cosby also served on this commission. We'd be meeting in a formal setting in the White House discussing world hunger or some other weighty matter, a situation where you shouldn't laugh, and Bill would roll up a little piece of paper and throw it at somebody—just like a kid in school. Then he'd sit there as if he hadn't done a thing.

These advisory groups met several times a year in the White House, and President Carter would sit in on some of the meetings, so I got to know him. He never created a fanfare around himself, but in meetings with him, I was always aware that he was president: He was firm and persistent. He also had an inner spirituality I could feel. He reached out and touched me with his spirit of compassion and with his honesty. He had no deviousness about him at all.

I was in Washington later for a women's advisory committee meeting in 1979, when I received a call at my hotel from an assistant to the president inviting me to a meeting with Carter the next day at Camp David. The president was convening a small, diverse group at Camp David to discuss ways of dealing with the energy crisis, someone would pick me up at the hotel and take me to the White House, and we'd go to Camp David from there. The assistant told me I was not to tell anybody where I was going. He also told me not to bring a camera, because no photographs were allowed at Camp David for security reasons. In fact, I was forbidden even to describe Camp David to other people after I had been there. The secrecy added to my excitement, and I didn't get much sleep that night. I couldn't imagine what was going to happen.

The next morning a black car arrived and zoomed me off to the White House. The driver took me around to the back of the White House—the Ellipse—where two helicopters with presidential seals were waiting on the lawn. Helicopter One was for the president. I was with eight or nine others in Helicopter Two. This helicopter deal was a big shock because I had no idea I'd be riding a helicopter to Camp David. I hadn't ever ridden on one before. The president took off first, and then we took off. I sat by Governor Richard Riley of South Carolina, and we became good friends. Of course the helicopter was so loud we had to shout at each other. Very soon we were in the mountains. Our helicopter hovered as the president landed on the mountaintop, and he walked off. Marines standing at attention saluted him, and he saluted them back. When I got off, I saluted them, too, just like the president had, and they smiled with their eyes. Then we went into the meeting place.

There were only about a dozen people—fifteen at most—at the meeting, specialists in various subjects from throughout the country. I wish I had kept records of all the people I've met, because I can't remember their names. I was there to represent women's issues, but I also spoke for rural America. Most of the other participants were men, so I tried to have a little fun with them, about how they couldn't even get their socks on without women. They laughed. I was the one who took all the stiffness out of everybody, and they started to loosen up.

The president led the discussion, and we spoke only when he called on us or when he gave a nod for our response. The discussion centered around the energy crisis—the importance of conserving energy and ways the country could do so. I talked about the importance of fuel for farmers who grow our food and about our nation's dependence on them. The meeting went on all afternoon and into the evening. We had lunch and dinner at Camp David, and the helicopter delivered us back to the White House that night.

The following week, when President Carter addressed the nation about the energy crisis and other matters, he included something I had said: "And I like this one particularly from a black woman who happens to be the mayor of a small Mississippi town: 'The big shots are not the only ones who are important. Remember, you can't sell anything on Wall Street unless someone digs it up somewhere else first.'"[1] The Associated Press quoted my remark in the story about the president's

---

1. President Carter's address to the nation on July 15, 1979 (the "Crisis of Confidence" speech).

speech, and soon media people were trying to find out who that black woman mayor from Mississippi was. They found out, and for weeks I had calls from people all over the country. The Mississippi farmers loved what I said. The head of the Mississippi Farm Bureau got in touch with me as soon as the comment hit the papers. He said, "We knew the president had to be talking about you, Unita. Who else could it be?" They were excited that I had gone to bat for the Mississippi farmers.

I always stood by the "little" people—the ordinary people—in the small towns and neighborhoods of this country, the folks who make our country run. Those at the top need us to put them there, and we have a responsibility to make sure they know our needs. The larger the arena of power, the greater the need for getting and understanding the view of the least powerful person there. From the street corner in Mayersville all the way to the White House, the power of the nation is in its people.

The next time I saw President Carter was on Air Force One. He was campaigning for reelection and had arranged to fly to Mississippi on one of his campaign swings. Senator Stennis was supposed to be with him on the plane, but he had become ill. Since I was the vice chair of the Mississippi Democratic Party at the time, I was asked to take Stennis's place. Again, I happened to be in Washington, and one of the president's aides called and told me to get on a plane and head south to meet the president and ride on Air Force One to Jackson with him. I flew down and boarded Air Force One in Memphis, where he was campaigning en route to Mississippi.

Air Force One is not like a commercial airplane. It's more like a very nice house and beautiful office. Johnny Cash and June Carter Cash were on the plane, campaigning with the president, and we talked about our backgrounds and how far we'd come. The three of us agreed that nothing but the grace of God would have brought us to where we were. The president came in and sat with us, and we chatted about what I was supposed to do in Jackson. The White House photographer took a picture of the president and me sitting on the plane together, and the president sent it to me later.

The flight to Jackson was less than an hour, and I was sitting on Air Force One with the president when it landed at the Jackson airport. Everything was cleared off the tarmac; there was nothing anywhere near the plane. The door opened, and the president stood in the doorway. Then I came after him. I had been instructed on what to do. I stood there a minute for pictures with the president, and then I walked down the ramp behind him. At the same time, the president's bulletproof car rolled down from the back of Air Force One and came around to where we were standing. I got into the limousine with the president of the United States as press photographers ran around flashing pictures.

The chauffeur drove the two of us into town to the Governor's Mansion. Governor William Winter and Mrs. Winter greeted us. Hundreds of people gathered on the lawn and the sidewalks and out in the streets to see and hear the president. President Carter spoke from the front steps of the mansion. Johnny Cash and June Carter Cash sang. I didn't say anything. The program didn't last long, and as soon as it was over, I rode back to the airport with the president to give him a wave and a send-off to his next stop.

I stayed in Mississippi. I was home. A cotton-chopping, cotton-picking black child from Lula, Mississippi, raised up with absolutely nothing, who hadn't been allowed to vote, couldn't even look white people in the eye, had represented the state of Mississippi in welcoming the president of the United States to *my* state.

20

Tolerance Is Trust

S HIRLEY MACLAINE'S DOCUMENTARY film about our trip to China, *The Other Half of the Sky,* aired on nationwide public television in the spring of 1975; her book about the trip, *You Can Get There from Here,* was also published that year. So I became an instant expert on China. As soon as the film was shown, I received a flood of invitations to speak from groups all over the country. I made talks about China on the East Coast, on the West Coast, and in dozens of places in between. Although I had spoken publicly in civil rights settings, my China talks around the county marked the beginning of a secondary career as a public speaker, which I continue to enjoy. I also discovered a role I could play in working for world peace.

In the course of speaking and meeting others interested in China, I discovered a wonderful new organization called the U.S.–China Peoples Friendship Association (USCPFA). I became a member of the board in 1977 and soon began working in cooperation with the Chinese Peoples Association for Friendship with Foreign Countries— known as Youxie—organizing tours to China. Youxie was in effect the travel agency for the Chinese government. In those days, before the normalization of relations, it was difficult for ordinary Americans to get into China, and USCPFA was the main American group that Youxie worked with.

I spoke with President Carter to encourage the process of normalization that Nixon had begun (and Gerald Ford had continued) and to offer USCPFA support for that effort. He told me that a number of people in Congress were fighting against extending full diplomatic relations to China, and he asked that our group try to generate support from other Americans. He asked me to find people who would send letters of support to their representatives in Congress and to him. I thanked the president and said I would see what I could do. That's when I came up with the idea of taking the first group to China. I would take Americans to China, and they would come back and talk to their congressional representatives.

My first group—a large delegation of women lawyers, writers, and church leaders, and other prominent women—traveled to China in the spring of 1978, five years after I had gone with Shirley MacLaine. I was truly amazed at the change in the attitudes of the Chinese toward Americans since my first trip. Mao had died in 1976, and the people were so much more open to us. In 1973, they had been polite but often distant, and they had expressed very little interest in our culture. The guides were always quoting statistics about China's progress and bragging about how fantastic China's way of life was. We got the feeling that some things were hidden then—that the Chinese officials were putting on a good face. But five years later they were letting all their humanity out and admitting a need for help, reaching out to bring the light of others into their country. I was touched by their honesty and openness. When we returned to the United States, we did our part to explain to Americans that the Chinese were not some way-out group but were human beings just like us, who needed to be recognized. The women wrote and spoke with their senators and representatives about normalization and talked individually to many others about China and the dignity of the Chinese people.

Two or three months later, someone from Youxie called me and said I needed to come to China again soon. I asked, "Why do I need to come to China? I was just there."

"Well, it's very important that we plan for American tourists," was the reply. "We need your help." So in December 1978, at the request of Youxie, I took another delegation—twenty-one USCPFA steering committee members, both men and women—on a mutual "fact-finding mission." We traveled for twenty-one days and were allowed to go into any area of China we wished, and the Chinese in turn got our opinions and suggestions for future tourism. We were guided through the country and briefed by some of China's highest-ranking officials and were treated like dignitaries. I spoke in several places about our hope that relations between our countries would soon be normalized.

Not long before we were to return home, we were in Beijing and I was scheduled to meet with Deng Xiaoping, who was then China's vice premier. Deng sent word that he would be unable to meet with me as planned, and Li Xiannian, the finance minister, talked with me instead. The *People's Daily* newspaper published a photograph of me with Li Xiannian. Deng's assistant pleaded with us to stay in Beijing for a few more days. She was quite insistent, and I sensed that something big was brewing. But I explained that we had to catch a plane out of Hong Kong and would be in a big mess if we missed that plane. I wanted to ask her what was happening, but she was acting so secretive that it didn't seem appropriate.

When we returned to Hong Kong for our flight home, one member of the steering committee knocked on my hotel door waving a telegram from Youxie saying that the United States and China had agreed to normalize relations. I can still feel the goose pimples. We all went into a room with a radio, turned it on, and heard the news announced over and over. We were hugging one another and shouting, "Normalization is here!" I was very proud of my country and of our president, Jimmy Carter. And I was hopeful about what this would mean for the Chinese—not the government but the people I'd met, the ones who only wanted a better life.

Although I had been unable to meet Vice Premier Deng Xiaoping in China as planned, less than a month later, in January 1979, I met him in Washington, when he came to the United States to sign the normalization papers. President Carter and Deng had signing ceremonies at the White House, and the U.S.–China Peoples Friendship Association hosted a banquet for Deng and his wife at the Washington Hilton following the ceremony. At that time I unveiled the new emblem of the friendship association, a painting showing the flags of the United States and the People's Republic of China crossed. I had originated the concept. Immediately souvenir companies began making and selling lapel pins with this image, and soon everyone going to China wore one of these pins. It's been the symbol of American-Chinese friendship ever since.

Six years later, in July 1985, I saw Li Xiannian again—at the White House—and I gave him one of our friendship pins. After I met him in 1978, Li became president of the People's Republic of China, and he was the first Chinese head of state to visit this country, at the invitation of President Ronald Reagan. (Deng Xiaoping was vice premier when he came.) President Reagan invited me to the White House for President Li's arrival and a state dinner honoring him. It was a thrill to see the United States and Chinese flags flying on the White House grounds for the welcoming ceremony on the South Lawn. I remember how pale and weak Reagan looked because he had just gotten out of the hospital after cancer surgery. Before the dinner that night, Reagan skipped the receiving line, but I had an opportunity to shake hands with President Li and to give him a friendship pin. Through his interpreter I reminded him of our meeting in China. He nodded and gave me a big smile.

Working with my Youxie friends Wang Ping-Nan, Li Shout Pao, and others in China, our China-American friendship group created a people-to-people exchange program to promote personal diplomacy between the two countries. For nearly twenty years I organized tours and cultural exchanges with China, and trade missions, and I entertained Chinese visitors in America. I'd put together an American group, make the arrangements on this side, and lead the delegation; the Chinese would make all the arrangements on the other end.

In the years just after normalization and into the 1980s, Youxie was working to develop the tourist industry in China and wanted Americans' insights and recommendations about services for tourists. So they arranged trips for my groups throughout the entire country. Occasionally I assisted Americans in making business connections in China. Ray Haley from Greenville had a company, Haley Marine Gears, that needed to buy parts from China, and I made the business transactions for him. My main interest, however, was developing friendship and understanding between the people of the two countries. After

I became involved in the National Conference of Black Mayors, I set up many tours for mayors to visit China. The American mayors would meet mayors in Chinese towns and cities, enabling their city leaders to exchange ideas on a very personal level with Americans in similar positions.

Some of my Chinese friends told me that I'd been to more places in China than they had. I visited the arid, mountainous western provinces and lush, tropical Hainan Island in the South China Sea. Hainan was the resort where heads of state went for negotiations and Mao had a summerhouse. Youxie had asked me to bring a group to look at possible tourist sites and advise the Chinese on what kinds of places Americans would like to see. In those early days, no tourists or even ordinary Chinese people had ever been to the government's compound on Hainan Island. We had that beautiful place all to ourselves. The beach was completely isolated. I walked out there and saw huge seashells—three or four feet long—lying on the edge of the ocean. Because I was the group leader, the Chinese put me up in the building where the heads of state stayed. Today Hainan Island is a popular international vacation spot. I like to think our group had something to do with that development.

Mao's summer place was quite different from Yenan, the birthplace of Chinese communism, where in 1948 Mao's Long March ended a twenty-year civil war to defeat the Nationalist Chinese. Yenan is an area of hills and caves where the Communist leaders lived during the war. I was surprised to see how familiar the land seemed—much like the bluffs around Vicksburg, Mississippi, forty miles from my house in Mayersville. From a distance, their flat sides look almost like stone, but they are really soft enough that people can—and do—carve their names into the surface. I called those hills in Vicksburg "writing hills." I later found out that the hills in Vicksburg and Yenan are fine clay, called loess, created over hundreds of thousands of years by blowing winds. And just like the Chinese, many people in Vicksburg had dug caves in the bluffs, where they lived during the Union bombardment of Vicksburg during our country's Civil War. There are even similar tales about running out of food and eating shoe leather. What goes around really does come around—around the entire world.

Once when my group of Americans arrived in Canton, our Youxie colleagues put us on an airplane, and I wasn't sure where they were taking us. All we knew was that it would be cold, because they had made sure we all had warm coats. There weren't but three or four Americans on this trip, including Margaret Whitman, the New York woman I'd met on Shirley's trip, and a doctor who was head of a California medical school. Accompanying us were Wang Ping-Nan, the director of Youxie, and Yao Jinrong, our interpreter. (Yao was the best interpreter I ever had. He was the only one who could translate my jokes so the Chinese would understand them.)

After a bit, I looked out the window. We were flying over the most spectacular sight I had ever seen. Yao said the mountains were the Himalayas and we were on our way to Tibet. We would be among the very few Americans to visit Tibet at that time. The doctor had badly wanted our group to visit there, and I asked the people at Youxie to put Tibet on our itinerary, but they made no promises. So this was a big surprise. The year was 1980, a time of relative goodwill between China and Tibet. After China had taken political control of Tibet in 1951 and tried to get rid of the influence of Buddhism, the highly religious Tibetans revolted. The Dalai Lama managed to get out of the country in 1959. During the 1960s, the Chinese government retaliated by burning or closing all Tibetan monasteries and banning all religious practice. In 1976 the ban was lifted and some monasteries reopened, and by 1980 Tibetans were able to show their beliefs openly.

The Himalayas, covered in ice, were so white there were blue stripes on them. There's no wonder Tibet is called the "Rooftop of the World." I learned later that the valley bottoms of Tibet are higher than the highest mountains anywhere else in the world. I was literally on top of the world. The Himalayas were so close below us it looked like our plane was going to hit one of the peaks. Then all of a sudden our plane dropped down on one of those mountains, and there we were in Tibet. I had never seen anything like it. I might as well have landed on the moon, because this place did not resemble any place I had ever seen. There were mountains with ice, but it looked like desert all around.

We had landed at the Gonggar airport in eastern Tibet. There we picked up an interpreter who spoke Tibetan and Chinese, since Yao spoke only English and Chinese, and we all piled into a little van. As we headed on a narrow mountain road to Lhasa, the capital of Tibet, we saw a couple of outhouses on the side of the road: They were public toilets. The driver stopped, and we got out to use the toilet. I saw two women walking down the road wearing long dresses, long colorful aprons, and head rags wrapped and tied in little points. When they saw us, they stopped. I was standing out in front of the toilet waiting to go in, and they spotted me and ran over. One woman held up her hands like she was praying and said some words I couldn't understand, and then she fell on her knees and stretched out flat, in front of me—went straight down and pulled straight out. It scared me so bad. I didn't know what in the world was going on or what to do.

Then some other Tibetan women up the road saw me, and they took off running and throwing up their hands and falling down before me. I was standing there trying to get to this little outhouse on the side of the road. By that time our interpreters were going back and forth to the women and to each other. Yao was trying to keep the women away, and he grabbed me and said, "Go to the toilet." And when I got inside, the Tibetan women came in, too, and they watched me squat, like they had never seen anybody like me in the toilet before. It was the biggest commotion I've ever seen in an outhouse!

When I came out, our group didn't know what to do with me because by now there was a drove of people who had all come to see me. The men were trying to keep them off me, but Tibetans were still stretching out on the ground in front of me. They didn't bother the white women or the men—just me. I didn't know who they thought I was supposed to be. It was scary to have all these women rushing up on you and falling down. I looked closely into their eyes, however, and I could see that they were not hostile toward me, but I didn't know what this was all about.

Finally we got back into the van. My friend Margaret was laughing so hard, she like to have died. A sense of humor will get people through a lot of stress. We moved on down the road, and I saw a great big carving of Buddha in the side of the mountain. I wanted to see it, so we all got out. I was standing there looking at Buddha, and somebody saw a bunch of women coming down the road, so they grabbed me up, put me back in the van, and off we went again. I asked Yao what was happening with all these women, and he said, "Oh, they haven't ever seen anybody that looks like you." I was used to my blackness being a novelty sometimes in other parts of China, but this was something else. We stayed in the bus the rest of the way to Lhasa.

As we entered the city, I looked out the window and saw a huge palace glittering in the sun. It was the Potala Palace, the winter home of the Dalai Lama, who had been in exile in India since 1959, and it was laden with gold. We went into Lhasa to a villa where we were to stay. We explored the city the next day. I bought a Tibetan outfit and a brightly colored apron and wore it around. I thought that all the commotion had ended.

Lhasa is the site of Jokhang Temple, which is to the Tibetan Buddhists what the Vatican is to Roman Catholics—the center of Tibetan Buddhism. It's actually a maze of small temples, and pilgrims from all over Tibet come to pray there. Of course, I wanted to see the place where the people went to pray. It was in the center of town, and we drove over. As soon as I stepped into one of the temples, which was lit with hundreds of candles, some Tibetan people saw me, and they hit their hands together above their heads in a clap. They spoke the same Tibetan words those other people had said, and they started stretching out flat before me. Oh, my God, I said to myself, here we go again. Yao saw what was happening and said, "Come on."

We started to leave, and people all around in the temple took off behind us. We were running to the van. When we got inside, they wouldn't let us fasten the door. Their heads were inside the door before we could get it closed, and we were trying to get their heads out of the door so nobody would get hurt. The interpreter who spoke Tibetan wasn't with us. Yao was speaking Chinese, we were speaking English, and they spoke Tibetan, and nobody knew what anybody was saying. And I was standing there figuring out what to do.

It was clear they considered me a very special person of some religious significance—a black goddess or a Buddha of some kind—and there was nothing I could do to convince them otherwise. If they believed so strongly that I could help them, I knew I needed to do something. So I asked Yao to tell the driver to open the door. He opened the back door of the van, and I went back there and stood there before all the Tibetan women. I started speaking, "Om, baba, do la, see mo, gabo goo," and stretched out my arms. I didn't know what I was saying, and of course neither did they. One by one the Tibetans came up to the door of the van. I spoke my "blessing" and extended my hands over them. The Tibetans then walked away with their hands up. I never even got out of the van. I finished up with that bunch and saw another crew of them coming. But Yao yelled "Go" in Chinese, and our driver took off.

"Well," Wang Ping-Nan said, "if we lose the Dalai Lama, we've got the Dalai *Mama*!"

We had a lot of fun with the Dalai Mama story, but I don't mean to belittle the women's behavior. I respect all people's religions as I respect the people themselves. In truth, I was awed by their behavior and felt a strange but deep sense of responsibility, though I didn't understand exactly why. When I returned home, I read that the black goddess is prominent in many Eastern religions and that the Tibetans recognize several deities who are dark. I learned that in Tibetan Buddhism all deities are forms of Buddha—"enlightened ones." In past lives the Buddhas were ordinary people, and they continually take human form again to help people on their paths to enlightenment— compassion, wisdom, and the lessening of negative emotions. When Tibetan Buddhists prostrate themselves and say prayers, or mantras, they are focusing their minds on their own goal of enlightenment. I hope I was of some help.

I am troubled today when I witness the lack of tolerance among some religious people for the religious views of others, and see how intolerance continues to play itself out in the politics of our country. I think of fanatical conservative Christians today branding those who do not hold their views as "un-American." And I remember the Ku Klux Klan spewing hatred and inciting violence in the name of Christianity. The religious principles I know from my upbringing, and from other religions as well, are about compassion and love—the Golden Rule—and acceptance. That's what the Tibetan Buddhist women I encountered were seeking. The democracy I struggled to become a part of ensures equal rights under the law for all people, regardless of a person's religion, or lack of one.

It's not just religious intolerance that worries me. It's our current administration's official intolerance of the beliefs and ways of other countries, which has bred an appalling arrogance that is actually simple-minded and provincial. Who are we to say what's right for civilizations that were already thousands of years old when our own nation came into being? How can we fully know? In this time of terrorists and nuclear power, we need all the trust and understanding and peace we can possibly get in the world. Yet our country violates international treaties and tramples on the human rights of others. It seems fitting here to quote the Dalai Lama: "In the practice of tolerance our enemy is the best teacher."

I don't claim to be an expert on foreign affairs or on religion, either, but I know firsthand the humiliation of having my human dignity trampled on and also the trust that comes from being accepted for who I am. And I've never found anybody anywhere in the whole wide world who feels any different.

21

You Need Roots *and* Wings

EVERY DAY OF MY LIFE has been an education. At the age of fifty I finally got a diploma to prove it. In 1982 the National Rural Fellows program awarded me a graduate fellowship to attend the University of Massachusetts at Amherst, to work toward a master's degree in regional planning. The National Rural Fellows was a nonprofit organization providing funds for disadvantaged adult students to continue their education.[1] My friend Starry Krueger was one of the NRF founding directors, and I knew about the program but never imagined I would qualify, because I didn't have an undergraduate college degree. With my eighth-grade education and a high school equivalency certificate, I landed on the U Mass campus in June 1982. Eleven others also received NRF fellowships that year.

The requirements for the regional planning degree were two summer semesters of course work on campus in Amherst and an internship in a government agency or in some other organization involved in planning. I was the mayor of Mayersville at this time, but the vice mayor, Robert T. Williams, filled in on a day-by-day basis when necessary. During my time in Amherst, I came back to Mayersville at least once a month to handle business personally. In between trips, I was

---

1. The National Rural Fellows program no longer exists, but its counterpart, the National Urban Fellows program, still operates.

talking on the telephone to Mr. Williams or someone in the mayor's office day and night. I interned in the Mississippi governor's office in Jackson, so during that period I was able to be in Mayersville fairly often.

The first day on the campus I was walking around in a daze, looking at the old ivy-covered buildings and the new tall ones, and right in the middle of the campus I discovered the library. It was twenty-eight stories high and named after W. E. B. Du Bois! I went inside, and I was struck dumb. I had never seen so many books in one place. In Mayersville, our library was a bookmobile that came every other week from Yazoo City. When I was growing up, I didn't have access to a public library. If there was a public library in West Helena, it was only for whites. Our school library was only a few shelves of tattered books. So, whenever I could, I escaped to the W. E. B. Du Bois Library.

Planning students were required to know calculus in order to draw designs for streets and parks and such. The professor who taught calculus was a long-legged, animated man from Lebanon. I didn't always understand everything he said, but I understood enough at the start to know I was way out of my element in calculus class. I told him right up front that I didn't understand mathematics, and that I didn't know whether I was going to be able to do it. He started flailing his arms and prancing around the room, shrieking in exasperation, "You are an African American woman and you have been in the civil rights movement and done all these other things and you don't know that your ancestors created mathematics?" I sat there looking blankly at him, but he kept on: "Well, you better ask your ancestors how you are going to learn this, because you *are* going to learn it." That's the way he was: tough but interested and dedicated to making sure we learned—a natural teacher.

Oh, Lord, I thought, what am I going to do? The Fellows program is paying for me to come up here to school, and I'm not going to be able to do the work. They'll send me back to Mississippi!

So I spoke to my calculus teacher after class, and he said he would arrange a tutor for me. I was assigned a kind, patient nineteen-year-old young woman who worked diligently and patiently with me day after day. She said, "You can do this, and I will make sure you can." In honesty, all I wanted to do was get the lowest passing grade; I figured I could do well enough in the other classes to make up for it. When I got my final grade in calculus, it was a B. I was so excited I didn't know what to do, because those people didn't give you anything unless you earned it. I'm glad I pushed myself to learn calculus, but I have never used it as a planner. When I needed plans drawn, I always found someone else to do it!

The other courses were fascinating. I was learning things that I could actually use in Mayersville—concepts and practical techniques, resources, and problem solving. Planning, I learned, is "systematic problem solving." The professors got a kick out of having a student who was the mayor of a small town in rural America. One of them would mention some program or agency that would help my town, and as soon as class was over, I'd head straight to the telephone to make sure Mayersville took advantage of it. It pleased me greatly when Professor John Mullin, who directed the regional planning department at U Mass, described my work as a student in *Planning* magazine: "It was quite remarkable; there was knowledge, synthesis, and action, all in a period of fifteen minutes."[2]

My favorite classes were the ones in which a group was given a hypothetical problem to solve. Each group member was assigned a specific role to play, and we acted out the situation. For example, we'd role-play hearings about community controversies: The city wants to use a piece of property, or it designs a plan requiring all the trees to be the same height, or some such, and many people are opposed. The point was to teach planners how to listen to all the people and let them discuss and argue, try to be helpful, and then figure out how to resolve the matter. As planners, we learned to develop plans around the people. The people are the power, because they are usually going to pay the bill. But the people don't always understand all the issues, and a planner has to help them, keep them involved and informed. Many projects take ten to fifteen years to get done; legislation and elections, new programs, new guidelines, a dozen other bureaucratic realities of

---

2. *Planning*, March 1994, p. 18. This article was published at the time the American Planning Association gave me a Distinguished Leadership Award for an Elected Official.

problem solving slow the process. I was already learning these things firsthand as a mayor. Voters often don't understand why things can't be accomplished overnight, and those who are opposed to an idea will try to wear you down. Everybody has to be important to a mayor. Among the good things about keeping the same mayor in office are that voters can hold that person accountable and the mayor can finish the plans she or he put in action. Role-playing games were an excellent way to learn how to be a planner or a mayor.

My internship in the Mississippi governor's office wasn't a game, but it sure was fun. Each student was responsible for finding the agency where he or she would intern. I approached Governor William Winter about my program, and he allowed me the fantastic opportunity to work with him and his staff as "assistant to the governor." Organizing and planning don't go anywhere without a strong passionate leader like William Winter to direct the charge. I will always be grateful for the opportunity to experience at close range an honest, open individual at the top working his heart out every day for the education of our people. Governor Winter took a chance on me, and I consider him and his wife, Elise, among the kindest, wisest, most honorable people I've ever known.

Governor Winter had made educational reform the top priority of his administration. His program, which was first put before the state legislature in January 1982, called for state-supported kindergartens (Mississippi was the only state that didn't have them); a lay state board of education that would appoint a professional superintendent of education (it had been an elected position); the extending and strengthening of compulsory school attendance laws; and many other measures to improve educational standards and practices. When the legislature failed to enact his Education Reform Act in its regular session, which ended the first of April, Governor Winter put together a massive statewide drive to develop grassroots support for his program. And that's when I came into the picture.

My office was on the twentieth floor, the top floor, of the state office building, down the hall from the three principal men planning the campaign—Dick Molpus, director of federal-state programs; Ray Mabus, legal counsel to the governor; and former congressmen Frank Smith. I was able to attend their strategy meetings, help plan strategy, and carry out some of the strategy we planned. It was just like planning and organizing a major political campaign or a voter registration drive. The governor called me his secret weapon.

My main assignment was to mobilize the community in the Delta behind the governor's bill. Votes from the Delta legislators were the hardest votes to get. Since almost all the public school students were black and almost all the legislators were white, the lawmakers weren't being pressed by their white constituents to pass the education bill, and not too many black people pressed white legislators for anything. I went from town to town and talked to principals and teachers and set up meetings and rallies with citizens. Sometimes I accompanied the governor, and his helicopter would land on the levee in Mayersville and pick me up. My job was to explain the program, get citizens' support, and encourage voters to talk with their state senators and representatives. I also tried to get a sense of their thinking on the subject, which would help us in planning strategy. I listened to their opinions and ideas and tried to impress upon them how much power an individual voter really has. "You hold the key to the election or defeat of your representatives and senators," I said. "And don't forget that next year [1983] is election year in Mississippi."

The governor's office worked from June to December to generate support. In December 1982, over the protest of many of the legislative leaders, the governor called a special session of the legislature to deal with education. Few people thought the education reform bill would pass—except the governor and those of us who had been a part of the grassroots campaign. The people were fired up and letting the legislators know it, but things didn't move well in the early days of the session. The bill remained tied up in committee, and the speaker of the house was not helping.

The time had come to have a chat with my own state representative, C. B. "Buddie" Newman, who happened also to be the speaker of the house and a strong force in opposition to the bill. Newman was a guardian of Mississippi's conservative old plantation mentality, and he and I didn't always see eye to eye on things. I'd get mad at him, but I could usually count on his help and generally supported him. He was always someone I could talk to, who would listen to what I had to say. I didn't harass him with every little thing I needed in Mayersville; I picked my battles carefully and waited until the time was right. Sometimes timing is everything; and when the time comes, you have to think fast and move fast. I knew the voices of the people around the state were getting louder and harder for Newman to ignore. The speaker was up for reelection in his district, too, and, more critically, for the speakership of the house.

I called and asked if I could come to his office to discuss the education bill. When I got there, he had two other people in his office— Representative H. L. "Sonny" Meredith, the head of the Ways and Means Committee, and Robert Clark, who had been the first black legislator elected since Reconstruction and was now chairman of the Education Committee. The three key people were right in one room. Clark was in favor of the bill, but he needed the speaker's help to get other members of the Education Committee to vote it out of committee. Meredith was a longtime ally of Newman's.

I wanted to get to the bottom of their thinking, and I put the crucial question to them quickly: "Why won't you all let the bill out of committee?"

The speaker said, "The people don't want it. Mississippi is not going to go along with that big a change to our system."

"Well, Mr. Speaker, folks sure are talking bad about you. They're saying *you* are the one holding it up. It looks bad on your part."

"There's no use putting it to a vote; it's going to lose."

"If y'all will let it out and let the members vote and they vote it down, then those opposing you will know it wasn't your fault," I said. "That way people won't be talking so bad about you."

"Well, Unita, you know how it is."

And that was the gist of our meeting—a direct, polite exchange of ideas but no resolution. But the next thing I knew the whole house was debating the bill, and a couple of days before Christmas, the Education Reform Act was enacted into law. The grassroots strategy had worked. Political columnist Bill Minor called it "the miracle of Christmas." I didn't see it that way. To me it was regional planning at its best. And the best regional planning has a lot in common with grassroots organizing: Go to the people.

The following year, I went back to Massachusetts for my final semester. In late summer of 1983, at the age of fifty, I put on a cap and gown for the first time in my life and received my diploma for a master's degree in regional planning.[3]

With my fancy new degree in hand, I couldn't wait to be back in Mayersville full-time to practice systematic problem solving. Most of Mayersville's five hundred citizens were the poorest of the poor. About three-quarters of our population lived below the poverty level, which in the 1980s was $5,572 a year for an individual and $11,203 for a family of four. A third of our residents were over sixty years old. Since decent housing was a major problem for these people and I had a background in housing, I was determined to get better housing for our people. In the 1980s, after Ronald Reagan came into office, the federal dollars available for housing and other projects became scarcer. I had to find other sources. From my longtime friend Mississippi activist Aaron Henry, who was chairman of the board of the National Caucus and Center on Black Aged, I learned that federal funds were available for the elderly and handicapped.

With the help of Aaron Henry and Sam Simmons at NCBA and the support of HUD's regional administrator, James Roland, Mayersville received approval in 1984 for twenty rental units to be built at a cost of $550,000. After construction began in 1985, Mayersville people came out every day to check on the progress. Parents brought their children to watch bulldozers and giant dump trucks and diggers. It was great entertainment for the whole community. The rental units were opened in 1987 and named Unita Blackwell Estates. I believe we were the smallest community to get housing for the elderly. This may seem a small achievement—twenty apartments—but it took years of trying to work through the system and then twisting all the arms we could. In a lengthy *Washington Post* feature about our new housing project, W. E. Holcomb, president of the Issaquena County board of supervisors, is quoted: "Five years ago, when I heard Unita talking

---

3. In 1995 the University of Massachusetts awarded me an honorary doctorate. I also have honorary doctorates from Tougaloo College, Wheelock College, and Franklin Pierce College.

about this project, it seemed like a pipe dream. I had to be shown it could be done."[4]

Pipe dreams are often necessary for problem solving. If you can't dream a solution, you'll never achieve one. And sometimes, even when you reach the goal, things don't work out. I received another large federal grant to finance a housing development, but by the time the money came, the cost of the land had risen above what the government had agreed to pay, and we had to decline the money. Well, most of it. We kept fifty thousand dollars to buy a fire truck, which was part of the original application. We already had gotten a police car.

A big source of help for me as mayor was the National Conference of Black Mayors, which had been organized in 1974 by a group of southern mayors who already had created the Southern Conference of Black Mayors. NCBM started as a way for black mayors to get together and talk about their common problems and share information about solving them. It grew quickly to provide the mayors with management training and assistance in developing services and programs within communities. This organization was especially helpful to me in developing a "programmatic approach" toward solving our problems. I tried to find out about every available organization with an established program that could come into our community—Head Start for young children, senior citizens programs providing means and activities for older people, groups that sent food and clothing, literacy courses for adults, after-school tutoring programs.

One really successful and helpful program made it possible for anyone in the community to get groceries at reduced prices. In Mayersville there was not a real grocery store, just one small shop, more of a convenience store. The nearest grocery story was in Rolling Fork, eleven miles away. So the town bought food in bulk—chickens, sausage, vegetables, and fruits—and once a month families came to town to purchase it for fourteen dollars a box. A large family could buy five or six boxes. In return for each box, the family had to give two hours of time to community service. They could visit with old people, babysit for young mothers, help give out food, or do some other helpful task.

---

4. *Washington Post,* March 21, 1988, pp. A1, A6.

We used the honor system. I had a list of all those who had bought food the month before, and I'd ask each one, "What did you do?" We'd usually have two or three hundred people at the city hall each month when the food was distributed.

Being mayor in a little town like Mayersville is not about trying to help people get what they *want*. It's about trying to fill their needs. Everybody *needs*. Mayersville has no doctors, dentists, or lawyers. To get these services, our people often have to go to Vicksburg or Greenville, some forty miles away, in opposite directions. Since many people—especially older ones—did not have cars and couldn't afford to pay for transportation, the town made a van available to take them. On certain days each week, the van was scheduled to go to these places, and people could sign up for a ride. Sometimes people just need somebody to talk to about their problems, and the mayor is often the only person they have. As mayor, I became marriage counselor, psychiatrist, doctor, lawyer, mother, and confidant.

My biggest concern has always been for our young people. Many of them wouldn't have opportunities unless somebody reached out. I wanted to help them succeed in school. I wanted them to develop self-esteem and a belief in themselves and a desire for a fulfilled life. I wanted to uplift them and make their lives more interesting. I wanted them to see what goes on outside their community. Besides basic services, I wanted to provide a way for people in our community to see other lives and other places. Most of our young people have never lived anywhere other than Issaquena County, nor have their parents and grandparents. I arranged for cars and people who would take children out of our county—not major trips, just day trips to nearby towns. We took them to the zoo and museums in Jackson, to Vicksburg and Greenville at Christmas to see the decorations. Mayersville children have roots and that is good, but I believed they needed wings, too.

I set up summer activities for our school-age young people, from elementary students all the way into high school. It was a program that evolved over the years. I had friends in other parts of the country who always knew of college-age young people who wanted to do something significant with their summer vacations. They would call and ask if I needed people to help out in the summer. So nearly every summer I had several students in town who would take children on nature walks and organize games or help them with reading or algebra. They'd gather in the back of the city hall or in a church or under a tree. I remember one of our first summer leaders; her name was Mollie. When she first began, only five or six children came, but by the end of the summer there were so many children they couldn't all fit in the city hall. It was wonderful to see our children being encouraged, having people say to them, "You can do it." And my heart is full now when one of them—all grown up, with a college degree and a good job—comes by to say, "Thank you, Miss Unita, for getting me started on the right track."

One of the personal highlights of those years was having dinner at Mrs. Shipp's house—the same Mrs. Shipp I'd confronted about Jeremiah's grandmother Miss Vashti's welfare check those many years earlier, before I even got into the movement. Mrs. Shipp called and said her daughter was visiting and wanted to meet me. Her daughter knew of my civil rights activities and my travels around the world. So Mrs. Shipp invited me to dinner at her house.

Now that was something in Mayersville. The day I went over to her house, folks all around town were saying, "Unita's at Mrs. Shipp's house eating dinner!"

Mrs. Shipp, her daughter and son-in-law, and I sat down at her dining room table and ate dinner. We had a nice meal, good conversation, and Mrs. Shipp talked about how she had learned over the years that I was a good person and I just wanted the best for everybody. She never brought up the incident of the welfare check and neither did I. I think both Mrs. Shipp and I realized that day that when you're on the road to freedom, you eventually have to free those who were opposed to you. By freeing others, you're freeing yourself, too.

While I was mayor, many visitors from around the country and world came to Mayersville to see what a tiny town was doing to resurrect itself and help its citizens. It was not uncommon to see Chinese or Egyptians or Africans in town. The whole community turned out to honor a group of Chinese dignitaries with a Mississippi catfish fry on our courthouse lawn. I wanted our own people to meet and interact with our foreign visitors from other places. That's one way we can expand our views and learn to trust other human beings. And we can begin to appreciate our own place more, too. The most gratifying thing about being mayor was that our people started to believe in our town. Residents in Mayersville were developing a real sense that our town was more than a speck on the map. Mayersville mattered. It was part of the larger world.

One of my Chinese friends said, "Unita, you are like a falcon that flies out across the world and then goes home to nest." No matter where I have gone, in this country or another, I'm drawn back home to Mayersville, Mississippi.

I've often been asked why I stayed in my little town when I could have gone to other larger or more exotic places to live and work. It's an easy question for me to answer. I stayed here because I love this place and the people who live here. I know and understand them, black and white—their needs, their difficulties, their goodness, and their craziness, too. I stayed because our needs are great. Our problems have faces and names and families. I believed that here in Mayersville I could put all I'd learned to best use and make the greatest contribution to helping others. There's a closeness in small towns like Mayersville that you don't find in cities. You can walk the streets, and you don't see fear in the eyes of those you meet. People don't feel trapped here. They like it here. If we can help these tiny towns develop and help the people solve their problems, we'll go a long way to making this country a better place.

I was blessed with opportunities as an adult to learn and to work. I was lucky to be given wings to see the world. But Mississippi is home. My values are deeply rooted here. I draw strength and inspiration from the land where l set my feet barefootin'. I need—we all need—roots *and* wings.

22

Do All You Can Then Step Aside

I'VE HAD POLITICS IN MY LIFE ever since Freedom Summer.
I'm inspired and frustrated and invigorated and disappointed by
politics, but it's always interesting. Politics is not just about voting
one day every four years. Politics is the air we breathe, the food we
eat, and the road we walk on.

When Terry Donavan, director of the fellows at the Institute of Politics at the John F. Kennedy School of Government, called to tell me
I'd been selected as a fellow, I was elated. As a fellow, I spent the fall
semester of 1991 at Harvard University. I had my own office at the
Kennedy School on the banks of the Charles River, overlooking a
courtyard. Terry Donavan found an apartment for me on Mount Auburn
Street, just off Harvard Square. Every morning I'd walk out my front
door, and it seemed the entire world was parading before me—students, professors, tourists, and ordinary citizens from this country
and every other one. It was like a visit to the United Nations.

Like the other fellows—there were seven of us—I led a study group
once a week for the twelve weeks of the program. I was a Harvard professor! This was a noncredit discussion group, open to undergradu-
ates, Harvard professors and staff, and community residents. My topic
was "Eyewitness to the Civil Rights Movement: 1964 to the Present."
Each week I invited a guest speaker to participate. Bob Moses and Julian
Bond were among those who spoke. Julian was a professor of African
American studies there, and I was a guest lecturer in his classes as

well. He told me that the only time he had ever gotten an "Amen" response from his students was when I spoke to them!

In addition, Terry arranged highly distinguished scholars and political leaders to speak to our group at lunch each week. I especially remember hearing Robert Coles, the Harvard psychiatrist, who has written about children and poverty and human rights. He had become interested in children and civil rights while serving in the military in Mississippi. What a sensitive and gentle genius. Our group had informal suppers a couple of times a week, where we met local politicians, students, and professors. There were also major forums at the Kennedy School with national political leaders. It was all very heady stuff, but I jumped in with both feet. Sometimes I even managed to convince myself that I looked like a Harvard professor!

I was fifty-seven years old when I was an Institute of Politics fellow. It's funny how some details stand out in your mind. I remember that Terry took me to the infirmary for a minor ailment and the doctor asked when I'd had my last physical examination. "I've never had one," I said. "When you're as old as I am and as black as I am, and you grew up in the Mississippi Delta, you didn't go to the doctor." And I explained that, except for the time after Jerry was born, I hadn't been sick enough to need a doctor. Well, that doctor said the time had come and he was going to see that I had a complete physical. He kept me in the infirmary for a couple of days, running tests and checking me everywhere. When he released me, he said that my physical condition was that of a person twenty years younger. I said, "I guess maybe working in the cotton fields was good for something, but it was probably all those turnip greens I ate."

I had decided not to run for reelection as mayor when my term ended in the summer of 1993. I had served sixteen years and just completed a two-year term as president of the National Conference of Black Mayors. It was time to assess my life and decide what I wanted to do next, or so I thought. But the opportunity to run for the U.S. Congress came along, and I barefooted right on into the race. When President Clinton appointed the U.S. representative from my district, Michael Espy, to be the secretary of agriculture, we had to have a special election to choose his successor. Since it was a special election, there would be only a couple of months to campaign. The governor set the election for March 30, 1993.

It was an open election, meaning that Republicans and Democrats ran on the same ticket. There were no party primaries. Eight candidates got into the race. I was the only woman. There were four black men and three white men. All were Democrats except Hayes Dent, a young white Republican, who was an aide to Republican governor Kirk Fordice. The Republican strategy was to run only one candidate and get most of the white votes, which would probably assure him a spot in the runoff. The seven Democrats would split the remaining votes. The Democrats had no strategy, or none that most of us knew about. The Second Congressional District is known as the Delta district, but it also includes much of Hinds County and Jackson, the state capital. The district has a slight black majority, so it was likely that one of the black candidates would win a runoff spot and face the Republican.

Three of us were at the top of the heap vying for that spot—Henry Espy, Mike's brother and mayor of Clarksdale; Bennie Thompson, Hinds County supervisor, from the Jackson area; and me, from the least populated part of the Delta. Henry Espy inherited the support of Mike's organization. The Democratic executive committee voted not to endorse a candidate, but the state Democratic chairman, Ed Cole, was running Bennie's campaign and pulled in many of the state party workers.

Henry and Bennie immediately made a lot of noise and headlines— Bennie anointing himself the grassroots candidate and charging Henry with elitism. I based my campaign on my proven ability to get things done as movement organizer and mayor. "They can say what they *will* do," I told a reporter, "but I say what I *have* done and what I am doing." I also campaigned on my training as a regional planner and a problem solver with national and international standing, and on my friendship and working relationship with President Bill Clinton. My base of support consisted of both blacks and whites. Many of them had lived through the civil rights movement and understood its hard-won benefits to our state. Bob Boyd from Greenville, longtime friend and Democratic worker and colleague, directed my campaign, and I had wonderful volunteers—Sarah Johnson, Thelma Barnes, Betty Jo Boyd,

L. C. Dorsey, Lillie Ayers, Liz Workman, and many others. Delta Design Group in Greenville created print and media ads. One of my favorite pieces was a special section for Delta newspapers. The front page had a photograph of President Clinton leaning toward me as I whispered into his ear; the headline read: "When Unita Blackwell talks, the President listens."

Early in the campaign I met James Earl Jones—the celebrated actor with the most majestic voice—at the University of Mississippi, where we were both receiving awards, and we talked about the Delta. He was born and spent his first six years on a plantation in the community of Arkabutla about thirty miles from Lula. As I recall, this was only the second time he'd been back to Mississippi since he and his mother moved to Michigan. I told him about my congressional campaign and asked if he'd be willing to endorse my campaign. I learned long ago never to be afraid to ask for help, starting at the top. He agreed immediately and said he'd be happy to record radio and TV spots for me. When I gave Bob Boyd Jones's telephone number and instructions to get in touch with him, I think Bob was skeptical. But he made the call and Jones responded, and we arranged a time when both of us were in New York to tape the spots. I can hear his deep voice resounding over the airways:

> This is James Earl Jones. Unita and I were both born and raised in the Mississippi Delta. The rich heritage of this land has shaped her values and given her the vision and courage of a true leader. . . . Some people talk change. Unita Blackwell delivers.

Friends from around the country helped with fund-raising, hosting fund-raising events in New York and Washington, as well as in Mississippi. Emily's List, the organization that helps progressive women candidates, supported my candidacy and raised tens of thousands of dollars. But that didn't compare with the huge sums flowing in to Espy from agricultural PACs and to Thompson from labor unions and Jackson businesspeople.

"Unita Blackwell, the pioneer civil rights figure with sparkling national credentials, is the most fascinating entry in the race and . . .

could be a key player in the Tuesday primary." That's what Mississippi political columnist Bill Minor wrote in his syndicated newspaper column three days before the election. When the votes were counted, however, Bennie Thompson and Hayes Dent captured the runoff seats; Henry Espy was third, and I came in fourth. I was disappointed, of course, but philosophical—everybody in politics has to be philosophical: I did my best and it wasn't meant to be. I immediately and enthusiastically endorsed Bennie Thompson and worked to get him elected. He was a Democrat and he was my friend. Bennie Thompson has been a fine congressman and continues to serve our district well. He calls on me for advice, and I ask his help from time to time.

Today I take a historical view of the race. Although we used radio and television advertising and had the support of national fundraising, much of my campaign was an old-fashioned grassroots campaign, run with volunteers and friends and neighbors. I found that Mississippi politics wasn't grassroots anymore; it was big business—big money, paid strategists, and political operatives. Mississippi had entered mainstream American politics.

When you're barefootin' through life and run into an ant bed, you have to stick your feet in a pool of cool water and then get right back out on the road. Later that year when the Mayersville board of aldermen had an unexpected vacancy, a group of people petitioned to get me to run for the seat, and I did. I felt that not doing so would go against my deep conviction that public service is a privilege and that anyone the people want, who can serve, should serve. At the end of one term as an alderman, I was asked to run again for mayor, and I did and won, serving until 2001.

The 1990s were the Clinton presidential years. Bill Clinton was the first Democratic president since President Carter. I didn't have an official role in his administration as I'd had in Carter's, but I visited the Clintons at the White House on several occasions. Oh, how I've loved the Clintons, both of them, ever since my brother-in-law, Reverend Perkins, introduced Bill Clinton to me years ago when he was governor. I had worked with Hillary on issues relating to children and families. Over the years I saw Bill Clinton at many political functions and meetings. When I was president of the National Conference of Black Mayors, I introduced him when he spoke to our national convention in Kansas City, Missouri. The photograph of Clinton and me used in my campaign material was taken there. I also remember being at a Jefferson-Jackson dinner in Mississippi, where Bill Clinton was speaking. In the middle of his talk, he was handed a note, which he read aloud: "A Cadillac with a license plate reading U-N-I-T-A 1 is blocking the hotel driveway. Will the owner please move the car immediately?" When I stood up to leave the room, the future president laughed and said, "Well, this is a first for me; we'll just wait until the mayor gets back."

In the early 1990s I thought we finally had a chance to create significant jobs for Mayersville people. The Mississippi legislature legalized gambling casinos on the Gulf Coast and navigable waterways, as long as the local people approved it. Since Mayersville is on the Mississippi River, I and several others began trying to get a casino; Issaquena County gave its approval. Nearby Vicksburg was the first choice for a casino in our vicinity, but the town was divided on the issue, and so the developers turned their attention our way. Everybody here was excited. But Vicksburg changed course and approved the casinos, and Mayersville lost the Isle of Capri and the opportunity for developing into a gaming resort.

In my last term as mayor, I was able to get freedom schools established again in Mayersville for three summers. Marian Edelman came through for me, as she always did. She and the Children's Defense Fund trained the teachers. Winifred Green and Oleta Fitzgerald helped raise the fifty thousand dollars needed to operate the program each year. Oleta was also instrumental in helping me get funding from the U.S. Department of Agriculture to build a multipurpose center for our community, which would provide space for freedom schools and other town activities.

After much thought I agreed to run for reelection in 2001. My opponent was Linda Carol Short, a young woman who'd grown up in Mayersville and participated in our early summer programs. When the votes were counted, I was the one who came up short, by a handful of votes. Some of my supporters wanted me to ask for a recount, but I didn't even consider it. As one who has seen politicians and movement leaders hang on too long, hesitant to step aside for another generation, I know it's important to let in new light. The people of Mayersville had decided it was time for the younger generation to take over, and I willingly accepted their judgment.

People sometimes don't understand why I wasn't devastated by losing the mayor's race and the congressional race a few years before. I won't say I wasn't disappointed. I knew I would have gotten a lot done as a congresswoman, and there was unfinished work in Mayersville. But when you've gone through the pain and struggles that I have— when you've sat in the lion's mouth pulling teeth and come out alive— losing an election is no more than a little cat scratch. When you've barefooted the political highways and byways of the world, you know that you're a servant of the people, hired and fired by the voters. You understand and appreciate that from the top of your head to the soles of your feet. You accept defeat as well as victory because the people have spoken—and because politics is more than winning elections. It's ordinary citizens standing up every day and speaking out and doing whatever they can to help people and keep this country free. Losing an election means it's time to step back and reflect on where you've been and start thinking about where your feet can take you next. Barefootin' is about moving on.

23

Just a Little Step Will Do

T'S SO QUIET IN MAYERSVILLE these days you can hear a
gnat walking on cotton. In my seventies heading into old age, I'm
at that stage of looking back over my life. Some days I feel like I've
grown younger over the years, because I dared to have hope and hope
keeps you youthful. Then other days I feel like I'm a million years old
because the world is rushing by. But my experiences have given me
the wisdom of understanding. There's a satisfaction inside me that I
have been a part of a struggle and a creative process. I participated,
instead of being a person who sits on the sidelines. I was helping
others and helping myself—doing for myself instead of having others
do for me.

My life is a miracle over and over again. When I think about it, I'm
amazed and I can't really explain how or why. I didn't have any of the
qualifications a person is supposed to have to do the things I've done.
Sometimes it seems like I was snatched up and put in those situations.
I'd be sitting with some group feeling inadequate, and someone would
ask me what I thought. I'd tell them, and they'd say, "Oh, that's good."

Such was the case in June 1992, when an official from the John D.
and Catherine T. MacArthur Foundation phoned to tell me they were
giving me a $350,000 fellowship. The caller explained that the founda-
tion wanted to free "exceptionally gifted individuals" from economic
restraints, and that I could use the money however I wished—no

strings attached. *U. Z. Brown, the little fast girl from Lula, Missis-sippi, got a "genius grant"!*

At the time, my salary as mayor was six thousand dollars a year. My first thought was, I'll never have to worry about money again. I soon found out I wouldn't get it all at once, but in monthly installments over a five-year period. Income and Social Security taxes were taken out, of course, and for the first time in my life, I experienced the painful satis-faction of giving the government nearly half my money. Of course, my friends, family, and a lot of mere acquaintances got the idea that "Unita is rich" and that I had money to hand out to everybody. Some of them still think so, but that money is long gone.

Jerry's son, Germaine, who was thirteen at the time, had recently come to live with me. It's common in the southern black community for grandmothers to help raise their grandchildren. Big Mama had helped raise my sister, Augusta, and me. Since I believed strongly in the value of a good education, the first thing I did with the MacArthur money was to send Germaine to Piney Woods, a boarding school in Mississippi, and when he finished, I sent him to the Savannah College of Art and Design. I also made some repairs and improvements on my house and paid off the mortgage. Then I bought a new car. My brother-in-law said, "Unita, you need a Cadillac." I said, "Me? Drive a Cadil-lac? I can't do that." I was thinking that riding around in a Cadillac, I'd feel like I was putting on airs—or acting "saditty," as some black folks might express it. But he said that a Cadillac is a safe, well-built car that would last me a long time, and he convinced me that's what I needed for the traveling I did. So I bought myself a 1994 Cadillac Fleetwood Brougham.

Maybe if I had it to do all over again, I might spend the MacArthur money differently. Maybe I'd invest it more wisely. But probably not. I'd never before had any money in my whole life. So I used the money to buy those things we valued most when I was growing up because we didn't have them—a good education for our children coming up, a dependable car, and a comfortable house to live in forever. Today I'm enjoying my house more than ever, my Cadillac still gets me where I want to go, and Germaine is working in Savannah and doing well. My son, Jerry, recently retired from the Navy and lives on the Gulf Coast with his wife, Carla, my second grandson, Naji, and my step-grandson, Donovan. I look forward to their visits several times a year.

I buried my dear mother Birt on a blazing hot day in July of 2005, She lived a block from me in Unita Blackwell Estates, our housing development for the elderly, until about a year before her death, when she had to move to a nursing home in Rolling Fork. During her last year, I drove over to see her a couple of times a week and took her to church on Sunday. She was a joy to me right up to the end. Her funeral was a wonderful old-fashioned "homegoing" celebration at Rose Hill M.B. Church in Mayersville, with family and friends coming forward to sing and to speak of her sweet spirit. I cut branches from the crepe myrtle trees in my front yard, which she loved, and laid them across her casket. As the pallbearers carried her body out and the women ushers in white followed, the congregation sang joyful verses of "When the Saints Go Marching In." We buried her in a small cemetery near Highway 1, and then everybody gathered at the Mayersville Community Center and enjoyed the good cooking of neighbors and friends. Birt's spirit was very much with us, and she would have loved it all.

Since leaving office I've slowed down some, but I haven't stopped. I'm still traveling a little and giving talks, and I serve on some local and national boards. Every day when I wake up I look out my window at my old shotgun shack—Miss Vashti's house, the one we call the freedom house. Some people think an old, rundown house is an eyesore. But when I look at it, I see history. I haven't torn it down because I never want to forget where I came from, who I am, or the struggle of our people.

I think about how far we've come as a nation from where we were, and how far we still must go to get the "liberty and justice for all" that we pledge our allegiance to. The civil rights movement transformed my life and changed our country for the better. But there is still racial prejudice and intolerance and mistreatment of people who have a different race or national origin or lifestyle. It's just quieter and laying low these days. So we can't sit down and rest. People are still enslaved by poverty and debt—those who don't have a job at all and the working poor, holding down two and three jobs to try to support their families and live in a decent house and send their children to college and pay their doctor bills. We—as a nation and as individuals—have got to stay concerned about the problems of all our people, the poor and the powerless, the ordinary citizens, because in America we promise liberty and justice for *all*. And our government must never again allow Americans to suffer as they did after Hurricane Katrina slammed the Gulf Coast in the summer of 2005.

I'm not lonely in Mayersville. Plenty of folks come by to see me, many of them young people in their teens and twenties. They come from across the state and from across the country to this little town way out from nowhere. Some of those who worked with me in the movement bring their children. Teachers and college professors come with groups of students. Some of the young and the not-so-young come on their own—writers, photographers, journalists, historians, interested citizens. They've read the books and watched the movies and television programs about the civil rights movement; they've been to museums and seen the posters and pictures and relics of those days. They want to meet someone who was in the movement. They want to hear the stories, and they want to see where things happened. They want to know the truth.

I show them where the burning crosses stood and where we'd hide at night. We walk over to the courthouse, and they stand where I stood when I tried to register and the men with guns surrounded me. I take them to the freedom house. Inside, they're drawn to the wall where the movement names and telephone numbers are written on the bare wood. Sometimes I see them run their fingers over the faded writing, as if by touching the words they can *feel* the truth.

I know when the visit has meant something to them. I can see it on their faces. And they talk. They're concerned about the way our country is headed—about unnecessary wars, about the destruction of the environment, about paying for their college education, about making a living, about democracy slipping away, about our government abandoning its people. They want to believe that their vote matters and that they matter to the people running our government. They want to know that life is more than making a living, that they can make a difference. They tell me, "We want to be a part of something important, something that matters. We want to be in a movement."

I hear the same questions again and again. "What can I do? Can we really change our country, change the way our government works? Can people change? How does a movement work?"

At this stage of my own journey, I believe my work is to give hope to young people and to those of any age who're searching for more out of life. Like the SNCC workers who pointed the way for me, I want to start folks barefootin' on the road to freedom. I try to help them understand our political process and how to participate in it, to see the power of votes and how movements change our country. I want to help them believe in themselves.

We start with voting. Too many people aren't voting. I hear it all the time: "It's no use in me voting; the politicians won't listen to what I say; they're looking out for themselves and their buddies that gave them a bunch of money." When we first started trying to register to vote, we knew we might fail, but that didn't keep us from taking the step. We could've said, "It's no use trying to register, because they're not going to let us vote anyway." If we had, blacks probably still wouldn't be able to vote. But we didn't. People died for the right to vote. They were thrown out of houses, hunted down, beaten, and jailed for the right to vote. My seven-year-old son saw his mother dragged into the street and thrown in a garbage truck to be hauled off to a cattle barn at the state fairgrounds. And now Mississippi has nine hundred black elected officials in the state and enough black voters registered to determine the outcome of elections throughout the state. We can elect people who will help us, but only if we vote.

Here's just one example of what's happening because people don't vote. Millions of people work at minimum wage jobs, if they can find a job at all, and millions of them do not vote. Yet it is elected members of Congress who establish and control the federal minimum wage. In 2005 the federal minimum wage was $5.15 an hour, and it hadn't changed since 1997. For a minimum wage worker to earn what his congressman made in one year ($162,100), that person would have to work forty hours a week, every single week—all fifty-two of them—for more than fifteen years. I say this about that: *If the voting-age people who work for minimum wages would actually vote, they could elect representatives and senators in nearly every state who would increase the minimum wage to a humane level.* Votes matter. And they've never mattered more than right now.

The truth is that we're letting someone else control our livelihood. The privileged ones entrusted with the power to make the laws and lead this nation are keeping the poor and the working poor in financial slavery, the slavery of poverty and debt. And not just by setting the minimum wage. Our government cuts taxes for the rich instead of helping families working three jobs to be able see a doctor and pay for the medicine that they need. Untold numbers of hardworking, God-fearing family people can't pay their light bills or buy gas to drive to work, yet our government protects huge profits at the energy companies so they can pay ungodly salaries to their executives. Our government limits the amount of money courts can cause corporations and doctors to pay people they have injured or whose family members have been killed. The president of the United States wants to *spend* trillions of dollars to *reduce* Social Security benefits, which are a nice thing for the rich but essential for the rest of us.

I think about the poor people in Forest Heights in Gulfport whose houses were wrecked by Hurricane Katrina. I remember the compassion and imagination and commitment that our federal government put into helping those people have homes of their own. Yet, so far, I've seen little from our government that suggests anything close to that compassion, imagination, or commitment to help them and others rebuild their homes and lives. Only after U.S. Rep. Gene Taylor pitched a tent in the House of Representatives to summon compassion for Katrina victims did Congress begin to pay attention (reminding me of our CDGM "romper room lobby"). Then Mississippi Senator Thad Cochran, chairman of the Senate Appropriations Committee, had to attach Katrina relief to an appropriation for the Iraq war ($453 billion) in order to get $29 billion for the poor people on the Mississippi Gulf Coast and New Orleans. Four months had passed since the hurricane.

We live in a country where our leaders daily abuse their power at the expense of the rights of the people—by not telling the truth, by smothering criticism, by helping the greedy, by hiring cronies and hacks, by endorsing intolerance—all under the banner of patriotism. And in December 2005 we learned that in the name of fighting terrorism President George W. Bush had secretly ordered eavesdropping on American citizens, ignoring existing laws requiring court approval as well as the Fourth Amendment to the U.S. Constitution. As one who lived for years under the constant watch of the Mississippi Sovereignty Commission, which claimed to be ridding our state of Communists and other un-American elements, I find this deeply troubling.

The greed and arrogance of people running this country in 2005 is unbelievable and, to my mind, immoral. The United States of America is the richest country in the world; yet we're the worst at taking care of poor people. We say this is a moral country. Where is the morality of our leaders? A moral country takes care of its people. It's time to put morality, compassion, courage, and creativity back into our government. We, the people, can do it by voting. And by speaking the truth.

Change depends on people knowing the truth. Change depends on people speaking that truth out loud. That's what movements do. Movements educate people to the truth. They pass along information and ideas that many others do not know, and they cause them to ask questions, to challenge their own long-held beliefs. Movements inspire people to rise to their best. Movements are the way ordinary people get more freedom and justice. Movements are how we keep a check on power and those who abuse it.

Movements are not radical. Movements are the American way. A small group of abolitionists writing and speaking eventually led to the end of slavery. A few stirred-up women brought about women's voting. The Populist movement, the Progressive movement, the anti–Vietnam War movement, the women's movement—the examples go on and on of "little people" getting together and telling the truth about their lives. They made our government act. *It's not the president or Congress that makes change happen. It's the people. Us. We are the movers. The president and Congress follow us.*

I've come to find out that most people think and act the way they do because they don't know any better. Most people will change when they see the facts presented to them that show a need. There's always a hard-core group who'll never change, no matter what, and you can't help them, but it's a small group and you can overcome them. I can't count the number of white Mississippi folks who've told me: "I treated black people the way I did because that's the way I grew up. Prejudice was so deep in my mind that I never even thought about how unfair and wrong it was. But once the facts were presented to me, I was shocked at my own ignorance, and I never felt the same again." Black people, too, had to learn the truth. We had to face ourselves and our fear—of the known and the unknown—and believe that we could have a better life.

We have to take responsibility for our own lives. All our problems can't be solved by government. It pains me to see young black people today who choose ignorance and futility over education and opportunities that brave men and women risked their lives to secure for them, *because they don't believe in themselves.* Too many of our people still allow their lives to be determined by the action or inaction of others, because they don't believe in themselves. As individuals and as a society, we must change these self-destructive ways.

The first step to bringing about change, to starting a movement and making a movement work, to moving yourself toward a more productive and meaningful life is to set out barefootin'. Step out wobbly as a child, and start walking down the road. When you're barefootin', you don't have to have a plan worked out in advance. Barefootin' means being open to the possibilities and being available to act when one possibility comes along. It means starting right where you are and learning as you go. Barefootin' means believing in yourself and having faith.

You can't sit around and wait for somebody else to carry you. Get on the road and use your own two feet. Explore the side roads and back roads, and don't be afraid of going down the wrong roads. Get mud between your toes. Do more for others than for yourself. Reach out and catch your neighbor's hand. You be the one who starts a movement. Start barefootin'.

Your first step doesn't have to be a big one. *Just a little step will do.* You don't need to change the world all at once. You don't have to shoot for the moon. Just do something small that will make a difference in your everyday life. *Big changes are the result of lots of little steps.* Emmett Till's mother didn't know that the sight of her son's poor battered face would kindle the civil rights movement. She wanted that coffin opened up to show the people the truth. When Fannie Lou Hamer cried out, "I question America. Is this the land of the free and the home of the brave?" she had no idea she would touch an entire country and provoke fear and action from the president of the United States. Mrs. Hamer just knew she was "sick and tired of being sick and tired." And she had to step out.

When you were a child and went barefooted, you were free. You may not even have had any shoes, but your toes didn't get pinched. You had to be barefooted to climb a tree and scale it to the top and look out and find yourself in brand-new territory.

Barefootin' means hope. Because of your hunger to satisfy your soul, you start walking. Sometimes you skip and jump and run. Sometimes you trip and fall. It takes courage to go barefooted. You don't know what you might step on, what pain might come, but you keep on walking, and it makes you tough.

When you're barefootin' the road to freedom, you have to watch and fight and pray. Watch the road so when you run up on a roadblock, you can cut a new path and go around. Watch the other fellow on the road and yourself as well. Fight for the right of way. Fight for the right to stay on the road. Fight to keep yourself open to understanding. Pray for the strength to finish what you started. And don't let nobody turn you around.

You can do it. Your spirit is in your feet, and your feet can run free.

Acknowledgments

For years people have asked me to write a book about my life. When I ended my term as mayor of Mayersville in 2001, I knew the time had come to do it. I also knew I needed help. Meanwhile, JoAnne Prichard Morris, retired executive editor of the University Press of Mississippi and the recent widow of writer Willie Morris, was picking up the pieces of her life and looking for a fresh start. Although JoAnne and I had both spent most of our lives in Mississippi, we had never met.

For the good fortune of our association, we're indebted to my friend Terry Donovan, former director of the Institute of Politics at Harvard. Terry knew of JoAnne through mutual friends in Mississippi, former governor William Winter and Peyton Prospere, who had suggested she might be just the person to work with me. "I've talked with JoAnne, and she knows all about you," Terry said. "Why don't you give her a call?" I did, and a few days later I drove to Jackson to check her out in person. We talked for hours that day. She was open and honest, and my spirit picked up right away that I could trust her. Both of us intuitively knew we could work well together; we agreed that day to get started. And that's how two women—one black and one white, who had grown up in the Mississippi Delta (JoAnne a decade or so behind me), but, because of the color of our skin, had lived worlds apart—barefooted into writing this book.

Without JoAnne's persistence, patience, and enthusiasm, this book would not exist. She conducted dozens of interviews with me, talked with my family, friends, and colleagues, dug through my disorganized papers and memorabilia. She probed and prodded me at all hours of the day and night, always pressing for more, until she pulled my story out of one. I think she knows more about me now than I know about myself! The result of our collaboration is more than a book; it's an enduring friendship.

We're indebted to several people at Crown who believed in this book from the beginning: former Crown executives Chip Gibson and Teresa Nicholas; Crown's publisher, Steve Ross; and senior editor, Christopher Jackson. Chris is the finest of editors: He personally cared about every idea and every word of this book, and his insights enhanced and improved the quality of our work. Special thanks go also to production editor Susan Westendorf and copyeditor Patricia Herbst for making the words right; to assistant editor Genoveva Llosa for keeping us all on track; to Laura Duffy and Lenny Henderson for the striking jacket and book designs; and to Philip Patrick and Tina Constable, who went the last mile to make this book achieve its potential.

We're grateful to Carol Cox, Winifred Green, Betty Jo and Bob Boyd, Ruth Williams, and Ginger Tucker, who helped JoAnne get the manuscript into its final form. My special thanks go to attorney Isaac Byrd, Dr. Melessa Phillips, Mary Jenkins, and Gloria Sturdevant for their invaluable guidance and support. We also appreciate the assistance of Juanita Dabney, who transcribed hours of our taped conversations.

And finally, I want to thank those people, too numerous to list here, who taught me the lifetime of lessons that form the basis of this book. Many of them are named in the text, but at least as many unnamed others are responsible for helping me become the person I am today. Writing this book made me realize all over again how very fortunate I am to have had such splendid teachers and friends. I thank them all from the bottom of my heart.

About the Author

Unita Blackwell, who did not finish high school, and worked in Mississippi Delta cotton fields until she was thirty years old, is a fellow of the Institute of Politics at the John F. Kennedy School of Government, Harvard University, and she holds a master's degree from the University of Massachusetts. In 1992 the MacArthur Foundation named her a fellow and recipient of its so-called Genius Grant. Blackwell was elected mayor of Mayersville, Mississippi, in 1976. The first black woman mayor in the state, she served for twenty years. From 1990 to 1992 she was president of the National Conference of Black Mayors. She was project director for the Student Nonviolent Coordinating Committee in the 1960s and a member of the Mississippi Freedom Democratic Party delegation that crashed the 1964 Democratic National Convention. She holds four honorary doctorates and has received numerous other awards for her contributions to human rights.

JoAnne Prichard Morris is an editor, writer, and publisher. As editor she has acquired and developed more than two hundred books, including the bestselling Sweet Potato Queen books. She worked closely with her late husband Willie Morris on many of his books, including *My Dog Skip* and *My Cat Spit McGee*, and she completed and edited his novel *Taps* for posthumous publication.